'Till the Trumpet Sounds!
1 Corinthians 15: 52.

Willie Greel.

SURVIVAL?

SURVIVAL?

God's Fabulous Future

by
William Freel, B.D.

PREFACE
by
DR. F. A. TATFORD

Published by
The Berrico Group of Companies, London, W3 6AU, England

BERRICO PRODUCTIONS LIMITED
57/59 CHURCHFIELD ROAD
ACTON, LONDON, W3 6AU

Copyright © Berrico Productions Ltd 1976

ISBN 0 905518 00 4

*The Bible references in this publication are taken from the
Revised Standard Version of the Bible, copyrighted 1946, 1952,
© 1971, 1973 by the Division of Christian Education,
National Council of the Churches of Christ in the USA,
and used by permission.*

DEDICATION

I dedicate this book to my wife Betty, who has been my devoted
partner in all of my Christian service and constantly encouraged me
to publish these studies on the Apocalypse. It is appropriate that I
should mention my daughters Ann and Lorraine in the dedication,
as they could belong to the generation that will see the fulfilment of
the prophecies disclosed in Revelation.

Origination, design and artwork by
Berrico Advertising & Marketing Ltd.
Printed by Berrico Publicity Co. Ltd.
London, W3 6AU, England

WILLIAM FREEL, B.D.

WILLIAM FREEL

Born in Motherwell, Scotland, William Freel trained as an engineer and thereafter studied at the Bible Training Institute in Glasgow where he gained the College Diploma with distinction, and Dip.Th. from London University. After this training, he was a Bible Teacher and Evangelist with the Christian Brethren, but later, returned to studying for two years at the Baptist Theological College, Glasgow during which time he earned the B.D. from London University.

William Freel has preached in Europe, Africa, Israel, and the U.S.A. He has had two pastorates in Scotland – Rattray Street Baptist Church, Dundee, and Viewfield Baptist Church, Dunfermline. In October 1974 he became Pastor of Duke Street Baptist Church, Richmond, Surrey. He is married and has twin daughters.

PREFACE

In a world which has rejected the basic concept of law and order, the problems due to indiscipline, lack of restraint and universal tension — added to those arising from a burgeoning population, sexual permissiveness, racial hatred, scientific and technological developments, ecological conditions, etc. — have created a widespread sense of instability and insecurity. The gloomy prognostications of scientists and philosophers, and the pessimistic pictures of economists and sociologists, contrasting with the optimistic predictions of politicians, have completely bewildered the average individual and, confused by the medley of voices, he asks in which direction he can turn to discover what really awaits him.

Fortunately, man is not left to his own imagination regarding the future. The God, who brought the world into being, has revealed His plan and purpose for it. It is with this that this book is concerned. The last chapter of the Bible affirms that a revelation of the future has been made and that there is a special blessing for those who show an interest in the revelation (Rev. 22:6,9).

There are countless commentaries on the Apocalypse, but this one is different. Mr. Freel weaves his exposition around unusual and well executed illustrations, which facilitate an understanding of the Divine message. To a greater extent than other expositors, he also lays considerable tribute on the rest of the inspired Word in the interpretation of this last Book of the Bible and, in addition, ensures throughout a practical application of the teaching of the Book rather than treating the Revelation as merely an interesting eschatological document.

Mr. Freel's exposition is sound and Scriptural, and this commentary deserves the widest possible circulation.

FREDK. A. TATFORD

ACKNOWLEDGEMENTS

One of the most precious words in the New Testament is *koinonia*, meaning fellowship and partnership. This book is an example of Christian *koinonia*, reminding us of the co-operation enshrined in the word.

In my former pastorate, Viewfield Baptist Church, Dunfermline, I received help and inspiration from twenty-six oil paintings, painted by Adam Russell, a deacon of the church, and an accomplished artist. Ronald Wilkie, another deacon of the church and a professional sign-writer painted the map.

When I became pastor of Duke Street Baptist Church, Richmond, Surrey, I was encouraged by the deacons to repeat the series of studies on Revelation at the Sunday services. During this second series of expositions, I widened my research and I have appended a bibliography of the books to which I am indebted and acknowledge the quotations taken from these writings.

Robert and Judith Berry, members of Duke Street Baptist Church, have made it possible for me to publish this book and to reproduce the paintings in full colour, and I appreciate their inspired enthusiasm. Knar Altounian and Julia Wykes have made a herculean effort in the typing of the manuscript and copy-editing; they have carried out their task with expertise. Many people have helped in different ways and none more than Joan Larwood who controlled the administration involved in the pre-publication sales. I am also indebted to the staff of The Berrico Group of Companies who have been most helpful.

Dr. F. A. Tatford, one of the most respected teachers of prophecy in Britain, kindly agreed to write the Preface and I appreciate his help and suggestions.

AUTHOR'S INTRODUCTION

The Revelation is, as the title suggests, an unveiling. In this book there is a firm promise that Christ can be seen clearly. Our Lord is not incidental to this prophecy. He is fundamental to its understanding. What we are about to consider is one of the most important Christological documents in the New Testament.

Dr. Merril C. Tenney makes this point in his book when he suggests the following outline:

	Christ communicating	Rev 1:1-8
Vision 1	– Christ in the Church	Rev 1:9 - 3:22
Vision 2	– Christ in the cosmos	Rev 4:1 - 16:21
Vision 3	– Christ in conquest	Rev 17:1 - 21:8
Vision 4	– Christ in consummation	Rev 21:9 - 22:5
Epilogue	– Christ challenging	Rev 22:6 - 21

No one should deny that Revelation is a picture book. In an old issue of *Famous Artists' Magazine* there is an extract from the biography of Norman Rockwell, who said, 'I have always wanted everybody to like my work, so I have painted pictures that didn't disturb anybody; that I knew everyone would understand and like.' In contrast to this painter, the Holy Spirit, through the Revelation, presents pictures that afflict the comfortable and comfort the afflicted. The philosophy of Divine disturbance is a major ministry of the great Apocalypse. These pictures shatter our complacency, baffle our thinking, and question our destiny, but many of us fail to see that Christ is active and authoritative.

The twenty-six full colour paintings in this book have a two-fold purpose – they are illustrative and interpretative. Their general presentation helps us to see what John saw, but their particular presentation helps us to understand what John knew to be the unfolding of the Divine purpose. My expositions make use of the paintings in these two ways. It is a unique presentation, combining the works of preacher and painter, which, as most of us think pictorially, should help us to understand the Revelation.

A Scottish preacher from the last century, W.M. Clow, presented a word visual of Revelation in this way:

A Scottish mid-summer day often dawns calm, entrancingly clear and sweet, with mountain and moorland and loch lying in mystic and enchanting light. Before the sun is far above the horizon the sky has become overcast, the mists have crept down and begin to drift up the glens. The storm breaks, and the tempest is out among the hills. Towards evening, the winds are hushed, the clouds are gathered away, and the sun sets in azure light, fretting a few bars of mist with gold, and lifting one's thoughts to the throne of God. This is something like the recollection that rises into the memory in the reading of this book of Revelation. It opens with a song. It has its morning of clear and dazzling light. The eye looks out on a scene of heavenly beauty. Soon the darkness gathers; the mist of sin falls over the landscape. Then there is heard the noise of battle and the cry of pain, as storm after storm passes over the world. As the book closes, the storm ceases, the clouds drift away, and the light falls upon a scene of splendour and we find ourselves looking in through the gates of the city of God.

It is my prayer that we may find ourselves looking through the gates of the city of God.

Many Christians have lost the promised blessing associated with Revelation through neglect. A minister who described the Apocalypse as a 'Monty Python's Flying Circus' was advertising to all that he was an ignoramus! Other Christians misread and misinterpret the Revelation. The book is a great favourite with them. They have amongst their ranks highly intelligent people and while generally sincere, they dwell on the lunatic fringe of religion following fanciful interpretations and making the book the happy hunting ground of every form of extravagance. Another group of well-meaning Christians have established the interpretation of prophecy as the basis for church fellowship. This violates the fact that the doctrine and person of Christ is the foundation of our fellowship.

Before embarking upon the study of the Apocalypse, we ought to memorise Revelation 1:1-3

The revelation of Jesus Christ, which God gave him to show to his servants what must soon take place; and he made it known by sending his angel to his servant John, who bore witness to the word of God and to the testimony of Jesus Christ, even to all that he saw. Blessed is he who reads aloud the words of the prophecy, and blessed are those who hear, and who keep what is written therein; for the time is near.

ARTIST'S INTRODUCTION

In this book are the reproductions of a series of paintings which have become one of the highlights of my life. Commencing from a small request for a chart to help illustrate a sermon, it developed into a major challenge carried out under great pressure and at full speed involving much study and reference. It was always my intention to carefully repaint each picture, but I decided to leave them untouched, lest I should lose some of the feeling and my original reaction to the subject.

Christianity and painting are two things I have been interested in and involved with for most of my life. In many ways I find them so complementary and my reactions to them so similar. Both are durable; they are concerned with the inner man and are not confined to the ordinary everyday business and secular life. They form a real background to my life; they influence my thinking, inspire me at various times and are a taskmaster, but yet, in spite of their intense challenge to me and my constant reference to them, they can give peace, reassurance, uplift to the soul, and are a relaxation from daily stress.

When the Reverend William Freel, who at the time was Minister of Viewfield Baptist Church, Dunfermline, invited or challenged me to illustrate each week the chapter on which his sermon would be based, he and I were off on a 'pilgrim's progress' journey together such as I certainly had never envisaged.

The book of Revelation has always had a special significance for me, perhaps because my father who was a local lay preacher had a great interest in prophecy. I recall so vividly how the family gathered round the fireside in the evening when I was a young boy and my father related his wonderful interpretations of the warnings and promises contained in the Apocalypse and of the great things that would take place before Christ's Second Coming.

I trust that my humble efforts will inspire some of the readers of this book to look again at the Book of Revelation and see for themselves some of the transcendentally glorious visions shown to John concerning God's Fabulous Future.

Adam Russell

TABLE OF CONTENTS

INDEX TO PLATES

SURVIVAL?

The Apocalypse

Chapter I

The introductory verses of Revelation highlight three concepts that continue throughout the book: revelation, communication and edification.

Verse 1 deals straight away with revelation:

The revelation of Jesus Christ which God gave him to show to his servants what must soon take place.

From the Greek word *apokalupsis* we have the meaning of uncovering or unveiling. That is why the transliterated title *'Apocalypse'* is given to the last book of the New Testament. Throughout this book we are enjoined to see Christ and know His power and purpose. The aim of this climactic book then, is not to obscure Christ, but to make Him known.

The second important feature occurs in verse 2:

Who bore witness to the word of God and to the testimony of Jesus Christ, even to all that he saw.

Here is the service of communication. Paul, in his letter to the Corinthians, explains that only the initiated can understand the disclosures of Revelation.

Now we have received not the spirit of the world, but the Spirit which is from God, that we might understand the gifts bestowed on us by God. And we impart this in words not taught by human wisdom but taught by the Spirit interpreting spiritual truths to those who possess the Spirit.

1 Corinthians 2:12-13

The calculating, cynical, critical mind of the secular world cannot cope with the conquering force of the communication of Revelation. This crown of New Testament literature is a senseless document to the unbeliever. The earth-chained mind does not accept the opportunity to move in the realm of the supernatural world. Its receptivity to spiritual communication is non-existent because the satanic agency jams the divine broadcast, making it unintelligible. This is explained in 2 Corinthians 4:4:

... the god of this world [Satan] has blinded the minds of the unbelievers, to keep them from seeing the light of the gospel of the glory of Christ, who is the likeness of God.

Only God's hand can lift the massive material curtain out of the way and give the natural man the reality of spiritual communication. The Apocalypse is not a sealed and forbidden shrine, but a place of unfettered access; it is not a castle in the air but a communicative document about a new city where Christ is supreme and where righteousness reigns.

Edification is promised to the reader in verse 3

Blessed is he who reads aloud the words of the prophecy, and blessed are those who hear, and who keep what is written therein; for the time is near.

This is the first of seven beatitudes found in the Revelation. The others are found in chapters 14:13; 16:15; ·19:9; 20:6; 22:7,14. These passages are worth committing to memory. We can be built-up spiritually and improved morally through the reading of, and listening to, the Book of the Revelation.

The expression - 'for the time is near' suggests 'not soonness, but rapidity of execution once something starts'.

God's programme disclosed in Revelation directs us to the realm of the supernatural and the eternal, and assists us to grasp the meaningfulness of immortality. In Lord Tennyson's biography, a story is told of Napoleon. A friend was urging on him how much glorious the artist's immortality is than the soldier's. He asked how long the best painted and best preserved picture would last. 'About 800 years,' he was told. 'Bah!' Napoleon exclaimed with contempt – 'telle immortalité!' Such a poor immortality!' Revelation presents the best immortality. It teaches us that we can live not for eight hundred years, not eighty times eight hundred, but for ever and ever. That is edification indeed!

Verses 4 and 5 inform us about 'seven churches that are in Asia', 'seven spirits who are before his throne', and 'Jesus Christ the faithful witness, the first born of the dead, and the ruler of the kings on earth'. Some questions arise from the study of this verse – Why seven churches? Why seven spirits? And why are these three titles used to describe the Lord?

The typologist notes that the number seven occurs over fifty times in the Revelation. There are seven candlesticks, seven stars, seven lamps, seven seals, seven horns and seven eyes, seven thunders, seven angels and seven bowls. Seven has a two-fold symbolism representing perfection and fulness.

Three reasons may be given for choosing seven churches. The dispensationalist sees in the churches a movement in the history of Christendom. To him it is no accident that we commence with Ephesus and conclude with Laodicea. Dispensationalism claims that the seven churches embrace the whole church period, that is, they give a panoramic view of the experience of the Church in seven dramatic phases.

Ephesus covers about thirty-five years from Pentecost to AD 70. Within those years the Church that knew all the wonder and power of Pentecost had left its first love and was experiencing a slow deterioration.

Smyrna embraces the persecution of the Church from AD 70 - 312. As the Church did not repent, so God sent chastisement, many were martyred, but despite the opposition, the Church made reasonable progress.

Pergamum marks the introduction of evil doctrines that were introduced between AD 312 and AD 606. These included idolatry, confessions, penance and purgatory. The doctrine of the Nicolaitans indicates the domination of the clergy over the people.

Thyatira represents what has been described as the 'illicit marriage' between the Church and State. This period, AD 606 - 1520, was known as the Dark Ages.

Sardis highlights the dead phase of AD 1520 - 1750. Formalism and ritualism had taken the place of the Gospel. Many of the great doctrines had been lost. There were only a few individuals that were faithful. During this time, Martin Luther raised his voice and protested against the false doctrines of the Roman Church. He preached justification by faith, and with the help of God, became the instigator of the Reformation.

Philadelphia indicates the time of great spiritual revival between AD 1750 - 1900. The Gospel was preached with liberty and power. During this period the Church enjoyed the blessings of the great preachers such as Wesley, Whitfield, Finney, Spurgeon, Moody and many others. Prayerful and practical emphases brought about the inauguration of the missionary societies during the nineteenth century.

Laodicea provides the analysis of the present-day Church — AD 1900 to the coming of Christ for His Church. We are living in a period of indifference. We are not cold in our denial but we are not hot in our testimony.

The geographer on his examination of Ephesus, Smyrna, Pergamum, Thyatira, Sardis, Philadelphia and Laodicea discovers that they lay on the trade route that encircled the province of Asia.

Dispensationalist, typologist and geographer may suggest their reasons for the inclusion of the seven churches, but we must not forget that John, the Seer, was inspired by the Holy Spirit to include the seven churches as the risen Lord had a special message for each of them at that particular time in the history of the Church.

When we study the significance of the seven spirits, we are instructed by the same principle of interpretation used in our understanding of the seven churches. The Holy Spirit has a perfect and full ministry.

The Person of Christ

Our Lord's three titles give a masterly introduction to His person. He is the faithful witness which reminds us of the earthly ministry of Jesus as a witness to God the Father. On earth He gave a loyal and accurate witness to the character and purpose of the Father. Christ is the only reliable contact between the present and the future.

The Firstborn of the Dead suggests that He is the first to have a complete victory over death. This is stated with authority in Romans 6:9

Christ being raised from the dead will never die again; death no longer has dominion over him;

His resurrection is more than the resuscitation of mortal flesh, it is an essential change of body which to us is a mystery and a marvel.

Ruler of the Kings of the Earth is a magnificent title. It is a prophetic statement regarding the coming kingdom when He shall be the supreme ruler of the universe.

Having considered verse 5, which reminds of what Christ is, we are led into the great spiritual truth of what Christ does:

To him who loves us and has freed us from our sins by his blood and made us a kingdom, priests to his God and Father, to him be glory and dominion for ever and ever. Amen.   Revelation 1:5b-6

There is no doubt that the Apocalypse is full of fascinating landscape. In fact, sky, sea and land are brilliant with a million refracted rays of glory. Although it is a challenge to paint the scenery, we must not forget that the Revelation of Jesus Christ ought to have an impact in our lives. His grace works within us and the evidence of that operation makes our eyes homes of peace because we have a spiritual serenity based on that special work of Christ within us. The words before us constitute a Christian song. There is a lovely spontaneity about them and they are not dealing with the abstractions of a frigid theological system. Christianity is personal, involving a deep relationship with Jesus Christ, and this relationship is demonstrated in four ways.

Personal Value
First of all Christ has given to us a new sense of personal value – 'to him who loves us'. John, like ourselves, lived in a day when the individual did not count. The ordinary individual was demeaned. Modern society tends to dwarf the individual. Take, for example, the ideas and analysis of the existentialist, Martin Heidegger. He claims that man experiences 'thrownness', that is to say, man is thrown into a world to exist there in his situation as a finite entity; thrown into a world where he must project his possibilities not disclosed to him by theosophical reasoning, but rather in his affective states or moods, of which the basic one is anxiety. Then man experiences 'fallenness'. He flees from the disclosure of anxiety to lose himself in absorption with his instrumental world, or to bury himself in the anonymous impersonal existence of the mass, where no one is responsible. When this happens man has fallen away from his authentic possibility into an unauthentic existence of irresponsibility and illusory security. In the mode of unauthenticity, existence is scattered and fragmentary. Let us remember that in our Lord we have a new sense of personal value.

Not only is man dwarfed by society, but he is in constant danger of being dwarfed by the material, by the very bigness of the visible. Scientific advance and space travel make the individual feel insignificant. A certain psalmist felt that same sense of insignificance in the presence of the greatness of the universe of which he was part.

When I look at thy heavens, the work of thy fingers, the moon and the stars which thou hast established; what is man that thou art mindful of him, and the son of man that thou dost care for him?   Psalm 8:3-4

Yet the psalmist encouraged himself with the indisputable fact that God cared for him in a personal way.

Then, sometimes we are dwarfed by the formidable fact of the population explosion. We are so many! What does one single individual count among the millions who walk the earth today? Yet, John remembered that the Master does not look simply at the flock, but at the individual sheep. He remembered that when the shepherd missed one, he went out into the wilds and searched until he found it. The Good Shepherd never loses the individual in the crowd, 'He calls his own sheep by name' (John 10:3).

Perhaps John also felt insignificant by a sense of his own inadequacy. But when John was feeling his own worthlessness to a painful degree, he recovered somewhat by reminding himself of the personal love of Christ. We need this sense of personal value today. 'For everyone who fails by thinking too grandly of himself, it is certain that many fail by thinking too meanly of themselves'. Consider your personal value in the sight of God. Live enthusiastically, demonstrating the fact that He loves us! (verse 5). The present tense of the verb speaks of a constant attitude that remains the same now as it always was; a love that is as intense for His present disciples as it was for the Twelve of whom it was said that 'having loved His own that were in the world, He loved them to the uttermost'.

Personal Victory
Verse 5 tells us that He has freed us from our sins by His blood. This liberty is the key to personal victory. Christ has freed us, or loosed us from our sins. Revelation deals with redemption of the cosmos, but it begins with the salvation of the individual. The work of Christ is not only the judgment of the world, but it is primarily the cleansing and liberating of each single believer. The book can appeal only to those who have experienced the deliverance that forgiveness in Christ's blood can bring, and who are thereby prepared for the hope of His coming.·

Our personal victory cannot be separated from the freedom which Christ's forgiveness imparts. Our Lord said, '. . . everyone who commits sin is a slave to sin' (John 8:34). The writer of the Proverbs declares, '. . . he is caught in the toils of his sin' (Proverbs 5:22). Bunyan pictured his pilgrim as struggling under the bondage of a heavy burden until he comes within sight of the Cross, where his burden rolls away.

Christ has freed us from high-handed disobedience, the struggle and the failing of desolate days and useless years. The emancipating Lord imparts His own renewing and victorious life into our impotence, and in Him we conquer the pitiless tyrants. God promises us that because of His Son's blood, the despotism of sin is overthrown and Satan's iron sceptre has been wrenched from his grasp.

Personal Virtue

Christ has given to us a new sense of personal virtue. Jesus has made us citizens of the Kingdom of God. He found us a classless people. We were refugees, displaced persons, faceless individuals. But our Lord conferred on us citizenship. To be a Roman citizen in Biblical times was a privilege; one that John doubtless did not possess. But he had been made a citizen of the Kingdom. He had been brought into a right relationship with his Lord. He had found a master and he was no longer a non-person.

When we consider the responsibility that we have as citizens of the Kingdom of God, it is salutary to read in 2 Peter 3:10, where the apostle is outlining the prophetic events,

But the day of the Lord will come like a thief, and then the heavens will pass away with a loud noise, and the elements will be dissolved with fire, and the earth and the works that are upon it will be burned up.

In verse 11 he gives us the application:

Since all these things are thus to be dissolved, what sort of persons ought you to be in lives of holiness and godliness, waiting for and hastening the coming of the day of God . . .

Therefore, beloved, since you wait for these, be zealous to be found by him without spot or blemish, and at peace.

2 Peter 3:11,14

The study of prophecy must produce a holy life before God and men – it ought to provide irrefragable proof that we are citizens of God's Kingdom.

The citizenship had brought John into a new fellowship not only with his Lord, but with his fellow Christians. He had become a part of a great whole, a citizen of a great commonwealth. He was a member of that group who were no longer, as Paul put it: 'strangers and sojourners, but . . . fellow-citizens with the saints and members of the household of God' (Ephesians 2:9).

With this new citizenship had come also a new sense of belonging. John was a Jew, and had been imprisoned by the tyrannical power of Rome. The Emperor was arbitrary, unreasoning, despotic and cruel; he seemed to have absolute power over John's death-threatened body, but the Seer's affections, enthusiasms and dedication were governed by God and that awareness of citizenship made him indifferent to the anger and hostility of an earthly kingdom. John refused to be one of the melancholics, vexed by crowding anxieties. As a citizen of the true kingdom he possessed, 'the lowly heart which leans on Him – happy anywhere'.

Personal Vocation

Christ has given to us a new sense of personal vocation. 'Priests to his God and Father' (verse 6). In other words, John is saying, 'He has given me a position of highest usefulness. He has given me the privilege of working at a task that is infinitely worthwhile. He has made me a priest.' All Christians have been called to the priesthood. Every Christian is a priest unto God.

What are some of the privileges of priesthood? Under the Old Testament system, only the priest had the right of access to God. When the Jew entered the Temple, he could pass through the Court of the Gentiles, the Court of the Women, the Court of the Israelites – but there he must stop; into the Court of Priests he could not go; no nearer the Holy of Holies could he come. Now it is to be noted that in the vision of the great days to come, Isaiah 61:6 says:

You shall be named the Priests of the Lord.

In that day every one of the people would be a priest and every one would have access to God.

Christ has given to us an open door into God's presence. We can go to Him personally. We can enjoy His fellowship. He gives us the right of approach to Himself, but through this approach He gives us the the privilege of being a channel through which His amazing love and mercy may flow to others. We can make others aware of the presence of God. This is the supreme vocation, functioning in the true priesthood.

THE THEME

The great hope of the Christian church is presented in Revelation 1:7

Behold, He is coming with the clouds, and every eye will see Him; every one who has pierced Him and all tribes of the earth will wail on account of Him. Even so. Amen.

This text has been called the motto, or the theme of the Book of the Revelation. The motto is a mosaic of quotations. 'He is coming with the clouds,' alludes to Daniel 7:13: 'There came with the clouds of heaven one like unto a son of man', who received the Kingdom from God. 'Every eye shall see Him and they that pierced Him' recalls Zechariah 12:10

. . . they shall look unto me whom they have pierced; and they shall mourn for him

The intention of Revelation is to concentrate in its visions the heart of the prophetic teaching of the Old Testament and to bring it to its climax in Christ.

Here is the public manifestation of the Second Advent; it is universal in its appeal because it shall be witnessed by all men without regard to time or space. 'Every eye' transcends geographical limitations. It is almost a fantasy to state that an instrument on the moon can transmit pictures to every part of our planet, but it happens. Television and radio leap over geographical barriers, and so does the Second Advent. 'Every one who pierced Him' carries back in time to the crucifixion: 'all the tribes of the earth', means that no race of people is excluded. The one great universal event that will focus all places, times, races and expectation is the return of the Lord. 'That one far-off divine event toward which the whole creation moves'. The first part of verse 7, 'He is coming with the clouds' means that He will come with glory.

There are two important words used in the New Testament regarding the Second Coming of Christ. There is *parousia* —meaning presence, and *epiphaneia* – meaning public manifestation, or, as the expositor Rotherham says, 'the forthshining of his arrival'. It is the latter which is presented in our text.

How important is the Second Coming of Christ to us? One scholar accuses Christians of lowering the standard of redemption by substituting thanatology for eschatology. What did he mean? He suggests that we fix our anticipations upon our departure through the gates of death, instead of lifting them to Christ's return through the gates of glory. If we make death our hope, let us not be surprised if others learn to make him their hero.

Why is it that so many Christians make death their executor leaving thousands and millions to be dispensed by his bony fingers? Because they are exitists, rather than adventists; their going and not Christ's coming being the goal towards which they calculate. These are the two ideals which confront us – and our Lord put it in these memorable words – 'Do not lay up for yourselves treasures on earth . . . but lay up for yourselves treasures in heaven.' (Matthew 6:19)

Previous to the Reformation there were desperate corruptions associated with the so-called visible Church. Some believers, having abandoned all hope from prelates and councils took the name of Expectants and simply waited for the intervention of God. We, too, are characterised by expectation, but we must not only look forward to the deliverance of the Coming One, but sometimes take our seat with Him in His throne and share His attitude and anticipation as He sits there, 'expecting till His foes be made His footstool'. Or, to take this same principle from another angle — 'Your eyes will see the king in his beauty; they will behold a land that stretches afar' (Isaiah 33:17). Happy are the Christians who are so long-sighted as to catch glimpses of that better country, amid the turmoil and crushing anxiety of the present experience, but they are intensely happy if they can look down upon this country through the far reaching vistas of that, viewing the present life from the exalted standpoint of our Redeemer's throne.

Now this leads to one of the fashionable new words current today. It is lifestyle and refers to the manner in which a person lives his life. It is inclusive of the person's clothes, words, actions — in short, it is almost equivalent to the Greek word which is translated 'conversation' in the Authorised Version and 'manner of life' in the Revised Standard Version. Or to follow the modern trend, 'life-manner' which is synonymous with 'life-style'. The Second Coming of Christ ought to have a tremendous impact upon our 'lifestyle' or 'life-manner'.

Let your lifestyle be without covetousness.

Hebrews 13:5

Let your lifestyle be honest among the Gentiles.

1 Peter 2:12

Let him show out of his lifestyle his works with meekness and wisdom.

James 3:13

The Holy Spirit has guarded this great hope of the Church by the delicate accuracy of definition.

This Jesus, who was taken up from you into heaven, will come in the same way as you saw him go into heaven.

Acts 1:11

Consider the words of Isaiah 25;9,

Lo, this is our God; we have waited for him, that he might save us. This is the Lord; we have waited for him; let us be glad and rejoice in his salvation.

Let us make the Advent scene real by the use of a historical incident. When those who upheld the banner of truth had almost lost heart, and Protestantism seemed failing, John Knox accepted the invitation from the true-hearted ones, and left Geneva for Scotland. When he landed, quick as lightning the news spread abroad. The cry arose everywhere, 'John Knox has come!' Edinburgh came rushing into the streets; the old and the young, the rich and the poor were mingled together in delighted expectation. All business, all common pursuits were forsaken. The priests and friars abandoned their altars and masses and looked out alarmed, or were seen standing by themselves, shunned like lepers. Studious men were roused from their books, mothers set down their infants and ran to inquire what had come to pass. Travellers suddenly mounted and sped into the country with the tidings, 'John Knox has come'. Ships leaving harbour contacted others at sea to tell the news. Shepherds heard the tidings as they watched their flocks upon the hills. The wardens in the castle challenged sound of quick feet approaching and the challenge was answered, 'John Knox has come!' The whole land was moved; the whole country was stirred with a new inspiration, and the hearts of enemies withered.

Now, if that was the effect of the sudden presence of a man like ourselves, a man whom we will rejoice to meet in the Kingdom, but only a man, what will the land feel, what will the earth feel, when the news comes, 'Behold, He is coming!'?

Those who decline the Christian hope must have their substitutes. Some of the replacements are attractive but superficial. An unhealthy optimism has taken the place of abject despair. Pessimism has driven many people to drink, drugs and sex. Many people are attempting to escape from harsh realities and so fashions in clothes suggest a backward look; the revival of the old sentimental songs indicate what Alvin Toffler calls 'the psychological lust for the simpler, less turbulent past'. Some people are placing their faith in the system of astrology, hoping that this will work. Ben Adam called astrology 'the ancient conspiracy'. The problem with astrology is that it contains an appreciable substratum of truth, that is to say, some of the predictions 'come to pass' in the Bible expression. That is why some folk take astrology seriously. Those who reject the hope of Christ's coming, can be attracted to the horoscope, fortune tellers and other methods of telling the future. 'Your future in the stars' is preferred to 'the Bright and Morning Star'. While some are taken up with star-gazing, others are involved in a mad pursuit for pleasure. The trip of self-indulgence is not new, it just expresses itself in different ways; in a hypnotic trance before the television or an abandonment to sex, drink and drugs. Politically motivated people have been amongst those who have jettisoned religion as a means of hope. We are told that faith is a myth, man is a useless passion, hell is other people; what we really need is the totalitarian state, the classless society; in other words, a system in which the individual does not matter. There is no acceptable substitute hope that can replace the hope of the Christian Church. Christ is coming again.

The Readers Digest affirms that to be happy, we must have someone to love, something to do, and something to hope for. Christ provides all these for the believer.

'While we live this life', said the Apostle Paul, 'We hope and wait for the glorious denouement of the great God and of Jesus Christ our Saviour'.

Our text closes with the two exclamations – 'Yes' and 'Amen'. In the Greek the two words are *nai* and *amen*. The point is that *nai* is the Greek and *amen* is the Hebrew, for a solemn affirmation – 'Yes, indeed', 'So let it be'.

THE ALPHABET AND THE ALMIGHTY

Revelation 1:8 introduces us to this amazing statement:

'I am the Alpha and the Omega', says the Lord God, who is and who was and who is to come, the Almighty.

Here is a strange juxtaposition. On the one side the God of heaven is saying 'I am the Alphabet' and on the other side He is saying 'I am the Almighty'. The alphabet is something we use in speaking, the Almighty is someone to whom we speak. The alphabet has to do with words; the Almighty with works and wonders. From the alphabet we can have inscribed poetry; from the Almighty we can have inspired power. Here is a great revelation in which our Lord is called the Alphabet and the Almighty – the A to the Z, the Alpha to the Omega, the beginning and the ending, the first and the last, and He is the Almighty.

Three times in Revelation we find the title Alpha and Omega – Chapter 1:8; 21:6; 22:13 – and the astonishing fact is that the first two of these unmistakably describes God, and the last one unmistakably describes Jesus Christ. A title which is the title of God is given unhesitatingly and without qualification to Jesus Christ. Here the Bible exclaims 'Jesus is Lord!' and 'Jesus is God!

Let us begin with the fact that Alpha and Omega, the Beginning and the End, is characteristically a title of God. It is so in Hebrew thought. Isaiah hears God say,

I, the Lord, the first, and with the last; I am He.

Isaiah 41:4

I am the first and I am the last; besides me there is no god.

Isaiah 44:6

I am He, I am the first, and I am the last.

Isaiah 48:12

Josephus the Jewish historian calls God 'the beginning and the end of all things'. The Jewish rabbis loved curious methods of exegesis. The Hebrew word for truth is *emeth.* Hebrew originally had no vowels, and the word *emeth* is made up of three consonants —*aleph, mem* and *tau.* The rabbis declared that *emeth* is the symbol and the name of God, because they said *aleph* is the first letter of the alphabet; *mem* is the middle letter, and *tau* the last letter. They argued that the word *emeth* stands for the beginning, the middle and the end, and therefore for God.

Even the Greeks believed that we needed some power at the beginning, at the end and in between. Ancient Greek commentators explained that God was the beginning because He is the creative cause of all things; He is the end, because He is the goal to which all things go; and He is the middle because He is equally present in all things.

When Jesus is called the Alphabet, the analogy denotes His completeness and comprehensiveness. In the use of this title we see that Jesus Christ is being interpreted in nothing less than terms of God.

Christ is God's alphabet. God communicates through His Son. It is significant that 'The Word became flesh and dwelt among us', the result being, 'we have beheld his glory (John 1:14). God communicates and Christ is the means of communication. He is the Word. When the alphabet is used properly it clarifies. As Christians, let us use language, or the alphabet, to give clarification and make clear 'what we believe, why we believe, and in a more definite way, in Whom we believe'. Our Lord is the alphabet of God, but on occasions our faith is put to the test. Dark experiences buffet our trust, and moments of agony bring statements to our lips which question the providence of God. In the divine method, Jesus comes with grace, strength and courage. He clarifies the dilemma, He leads us out of the labyrinth, and gives us the assuring words of 1 Peter 5:7

Cast all your anxieties on Him, for He cares about you.

As you grasp the meaning of the alphabet of God, He will clarify some of your experiences.

The alphabet also conserves. There is no doubt that the alphabet has maintained thought and preserved important ideas. Consider the history of the Bible, the contents of the Old and New Testaments, which prove that language has kept in circulation the principles of Divine Revelation — *aleph - tau; alpha - omega;* A-Z. This is an amazing fact. Visit any museum or record vault and you will discover that the alphabet is one of our greatest conservationists.

What a wonderful analogy — Jesus Christ is a Conservationist! He is the cohesive principle of the universe, or in the words of Scripture, 'He upholds all things by the word of His power.' The universe holds no ultimate terrors for the believer who trusts in Christ. In fact, the believer is held securely in Christ's hand, and no one can pluck him out of His hand.

He who suffered shipwreck, spent a night and a day in the deep, knew perils in the city and in the wilderness, endured cold and nakedness, could write, 'I am persuaded that neither death, nor life, nor angels, nor principalities, nor powers, nor things present, nor things to come, nor height, nor depth, nor any other creation shall be able to separate us from the love of God, which is in Christ Jesus our Lord' (Romans 8:38).

God the Almighty — what a wonderful title! It reminds us that God is in control, that he can provide for us. It seems almost ludicrous in these days to quote the psalmist, 'Thou openest thy hand, thou satisfiest the desire of every living thing' (Psalm 145:16). But man's main problem is not in the skill of production but in the skill of distribution. When man destroys good food, he has no authority for questioning the providence of God.

When we consider the amazing exuberance of life which confronts us everywhere in the world we are further reminded that God is Almighty. Look, for instance, at a stagnant pool through a microscope. It is anything but stagnant — it is alive with life. Or take a walk in the woods in autumn and look at the ground strewn with thousands of seeds and nuts capable of reproducing the plant or the tree from which it fell. This life is evidenced in human reproduction. The universe abounds with life and in this wonderful life we observe the consistency of God.

Then there is also the astounding variety of form and colour displayed in the universe around us. In plant life, in animal life, in human life, and even in inanimate things. What delightful variations of shape and shade surround us on all hands! There is no monotony in the Almighty. Consider further the immensity of the universe. Scientists tell us that in relation to the myriads of other orbs that are in space, the wayside planet we inhabit is like a tiny speck of dust in Euston Station in relation to all the other specks of dust around it, or like a single grain of sand among all the other grains of sand on all the seashores of the world. They further say that if the earth were to fall out of its orbit and spin away into space, it would create no more disturbance in the surroundings than dropping a very small pebble in the Atlantic Ocean. And yet God, the Almighty, has a perfect plan for this planet and we are caught up in His wonderful purpose. The Apocalypse presents the final drama of God's plans. Here is history's culmination and prophecy's fulfilment.

John: The Writer
John now introduces himself.

I, John, your brother, who share with you in Jesus the tribulation and the kingdom and the patient endurance, was on the island called Patmos on account of the word of God and the testimony of Jesus. I was in the Spirit on the Lord's day. . .
                                                                    Revelation 1:9-10

He tells us the facts that he considers fundamental. He tells us that he is a Christian, that he belongs to the brotherhood, and that he has come to share in the patience of Jesus. Patience here is a rich word. It looks in different directions. It means power to endure, power to suffer. Sharing the victory of Jesus in his own personal life, John has also entered into the fellowship of His suffering. Not only does he share in the sufferings of the Lord, but he also shares in the sufferings of his fellow Christians.

John's personal allegiance to Jesus Christ had precipitated him into trouble. Here is the description of his trouble

I was on the island

But here is the statement explaining his victory

I was in the Spirit.

John's sentences might be translated, 'I came to the island' and 'I came to the Spirit', or 'I found myself in the isle' and at the same time 'I found myself, to my great satisfaction and joy, in the Spirit.' In both phrases he avoids the word for continuous and absolute being, and he chooses a word which describes a particular episode and a distinct experience in the chequered story of his life.

On the Island

God's hand as well as Domitian's, had sent him to Patmos, the uninviting rock out in the Aegean Sea, a kind of concentration camp. Here John was ostracised from all those outward aspects of church fellowship. He was deprived of the fellowship of Christian friends. He was cut off from the privileges of worship with fellow Christians. He could not fulfil his ministry as a preacher, and now in old age, he was compelled to work with other exiled men in the marble quarries. As Patmos was an island, surrounded by the cold Aegean waters, so John was an island of faith engulfed by cold, positive antagonism.

Naturally there is that about this experience of John in Patmos that is unique. But there is also that which is not unique. Life is constantly bringing us into some kind of Patmos. This rocky island, not quite thirty miles round, was not the home John would have preferred for himself.

Patmos was a place of pain. There are people who have pain as a constant companion. They did not choose such a companion, but the companion chose them. We are afraid of pain; we do not welcome it and, if possible, we try to avoid it. The tyranny of pain is a despicable despotism, but we must not forget that there are the Patmoses of the mind. Translated from the bustle and variety and exhilaration of Ephesus to this rock in the Aegean, John might suppose himself deprived of intellectual stimulus and left to a dull stagnant existence. This has happened often in our day. Sometimes we hear the euphemism 'brainwashed' which really means, 'we have bludgeoned his thinking'.

John understood God's resources and did not entertain the melancholy delusion, but many of us are not so happy. We feel as if we were excluded from rich regions of thought, of imagination, of learning, of truth, which are open to our more fortunate neighbours. It never will be ours to tread the streets of the populous city of speculations and ideas, never ours to look around over the far-reaching landscape of art and letters and science and research, never ours to climb the splendid mountains of philosophy and religion. We have come to the narrow and insignificant isle, and in the isle with its scanty access and inexorable boundaries we seem destined to stay. Is our Patmos pain? Is it some restriction of circumstances? Is it a slavish attitude of the mind? We all have our Patmos.

How do we react to our Patmos? John refused to capitulate. We ought to follow his example. There are varied ways in which we allow ourselves to be defeated by our circumstances. Sometimes we give way to self-pity. John might have told himself, 'I have tried to live right. I have tried to do my duty the best I could. I have stood for my Lord when it cost me popularity, when it cost me my freedom. But though I have not let Christ down, it seems that He has let me down. Why should this happen to me?' But he did not!

If it happens that our Patmos is one that has affluence for its architect, then we may suffer a situation that is equally tragic. Instead of giving way to self-pity, we may give way to self-conceit.

On some occasions a subtle Patmos can bring us a soft prosperity that leads us to a bland optimism, but on other occasions, a harsh Patmos leads us to a harshness and bitterness that destroys our spiritual lives.

John might have surrendered to this trying situation through disillusionment. Rome seemed invincible, whereas the Church looked like a weakling. This attitude is very prevalent in these days. With the whole world in chaotic flux, how futile seems the effort of any one individual to bring some semblance of order.

John refused to be mastered by circumstances. It is true that he was 'on the island'; it is equally true that he was 'in the spirit'. He did not simply endure his hard situation; he utilised it. It was out of this prison experience that the Apocalypse was born.

John was in the Spirit on the Lord's Day. This phrase is not incidental. The Apocalypse contains a large number of repeated phrases, some of which are significant as marks of progressive thought. 'In the Spirit' occurs four times in the Apocalypse.

I was in the Spirit on the Lord's day.

Revelation 1:10

At once I was in the Spirit.

Revelation 4:2

And he carried me away in the Spirit into the wilderness.

Revelation 17:3

And in the Spirit he carried me away to a great, high mountain.

Revelation 21:10

Comparison with the context makes it clear that 'in the spirit' is not identical with Paul's declaration in Romans 8:9, 'But you are not in the flesh, you are in the Spirit, if the Spirit of God really dwells in you', since Paul is contrasting two moral or spiritual states rather than the normal state of consciousness and the state in which the vision appears. The Seer of Revelation, under the power of the Holy Spirit, was transported in consciousness to a new scene of action where spiritual realities and future events were disclosed to him, and where he received revelations that were not given under ordinary circumstances.

Each occurrence of this phrase locates the Seer in a different place. In the first one he was on the island, in a concentration camp; in the second one he was standing before the throne of God and sees the majesty of God; in the third one he was taken into a wilderness and he looks out and sees the apostate church, after the Bride of Christ, the true Church has been taken away; and in the fourth, he was carried away to a high mountain and 'saw the holy city, Jerusalem, coming down out of heaven from God'. Two of these incidents have to do with antagonism and two with adoration.

Thirty years before John was imprisoned on Patmos, Seneca, the famous Roman philosopher was banished to the island of Corsica. And what did he say about it? He said, 'This is a living death. There is nothing here but exile and an exile's grave.' Seneca had come to the isle, but he had not come to the Spirit. And what about you and me? In the glorious light of the presence of God let us face our Patmos. What is it? Face it earnestly — circumstances, limitations, troubles, loneliness — we can all share the triumph of the psalmist:

The Lord is my light and my salvation; whom shall I fear? The Lord is the strong-hold of my life; of whom shall I be afraid?

Psalm 27:1

The question that Jesus Christ posed to His disciples is relevant today; namely, 'Who do you say that I am?' Peter's answer came with a leap of inspired insight; 'You are the Christ, the Son of the living God.' (Matthew 16:15-16). This answer was not devised by human analysis. It was not produced by the subjective thinking of the human mind; it was given as an objective divine revelation. Flesh and blood did not disclose it; this truth is a sovereign disclosure from God.

John, on Patmos, receives an initiatory revelation. It is not that his subjectivity has gone berserk, but that divine objectivity has become operative. In fact, in the Apocalypse there is a remarkable balance between objectivity and subjectivity.

DAZZLING PORTRAIT

In Revelation 1:12-20 we have a description of a dazzling portrait.

Then I turned to see the voice that was speaking to me, and on turning I saw seven golden lampstands, and in the midst of the lampstands one like a son of man, clothed with a long robe and with a golden girdle round his breast; his head and his hair were white as white wool, white as snow; his eyes were like a flame of fire, his feet were like burnished bronze, refined as in a furnace, and his voice was like the sound of many waters; in his right hand he held seven stars, from his mouth issued a sharp two-edged sword, and his face was like the sun shining in full strength.

When I saw him, I fell at his feet as though dead. But he laid his right hand upon me, saying, 'Fear not, I am the first and the last, and the living one; I died, and behold I am alive for evermore, and I have the keys of Death and Hades. Now write what you see, what is and what is to take place hereafter. As for the mystery of the seven stars which you saw in my right hand, and the seven golden lampstands, the seven stars are the angels of the seven churches and the seven lampstands are the seven churches.

There is a vast difference between a photograph and a portrait. The instantaneous photograph catches its subject in a single pose, which may or may not be typical; the portrait is the artist's attempt to give the permanent impression of the person. An artist composes a portrait, putting together details which may never have been found at the same moment in actual life, and omitting others which blur or confuse the dominant impression. These verses in the opening chapter of the Apocalypse present a portrait, not a snapshot. Each detail is carefully chosen, the symbolism abounds with spiritual lessons. We must examine the portrait with reverence.

Jack Chambers, one of Canada's highest paid artists, calls his painting style Perceptual Realism, that is, he tries to transcend photography so that a viewer cannot only see what attracted the artist, but can feel it through other senses. It seems that the Apocalypse anticipated perceptual realism. The visions and 'motion pictures' of the Apocalypse demand our total involvement spiritually, intellectually, emotionally and physically.

John's immediate reaction to the vision of the glorified Lord is instructive. 'When I saw Him.' exclaims John, 'I fell at his feet as though dead'. The artist's painting of the vision has reproduced the overpowering effect of the encounter between the Lord and John.

Observe, first of all, that there is the general impression. There is the composite title Son of Man - the long robe and the golden girdle. But this general impression demands detailed analysis. Of course, the Son of Man was the veiled title appropriated by our Lord to present Himself as Ruler of the Universe.

The word which describes the robe is *poderes* which means reaching down to the feet. A robe is the symbol of character. The significance of *poderes* is three-fold. This is the word which the Greek Old Testament uses to describe the robe of the high priest. (Exodus

28:4; 29:5; Leviticus 16:4). A priest, as presented in biblical teaching, is a man who himself has access to God and who opens the way for others to come to God. Even in the heavenly places, Jesus, the great High Priest, is still carrying on His priestly work, and opening the way for us and for all men to the presence of God.

But other people besides priests wore the long robe reaching to the feet, and the high girdle. Such a robe was the dress of great ones, such as princes and kings. *Poderes* is the description of the Robe of Jonathan, of Saul and of the princes of the sea (Ezekiel 26:16). The robe that the risen Christ was wearing was the robe of royalty. He was dressed gloriously and majestically like a king. Here is One with the authority of God.

There is another important part of this picture. In the vision of Daniel, the divine figure who came to tell Daniel the truth of God was clothed in fine linen – the Greek Old Testament calls his garment *poderes* – and girt with fine gold. This, then, is the dress of the messenger of God. Now the great messenger of God is the prophet. So this general portrait presents Jesus Christ as the divine and supreme messenger of God. He brings us assurance from God. When our confidence in God wavers, then our Prophet brings us a reassurance from God.

Now we come to particular details regarding the portrait of Christ. Every descriptive word is used in a symbolic sense. Here is a passage which introduces us to the thrilling wonder of symbolic art, or 'perceptual realism'.

The hair white as wool and snow symbolises age and purity. Eternity and sinless and stainless purity combine. Christ is the apex of the pinnacle of humanity – manhood as God intended it to be.

His eyes of flaming fire symbolise his infinite power to see and his perfect understanding. Dr Talmage once said, 'The eyes of Archibald Alexander and Charles S. Finney were the mightiest part of their sermons. The fire of spiritually passionate souls burned in them'. George Whitefield enthralled great crowds with his eyes, though they were crippled with strabismus. The Holy Spirit lit them. Martin Luther turned his great eye upon an assassin who came to take his life, and the villain fled. Under the glance of the human, the tiger, five times a man's strength, snarls back into the jungle.

Jesus' eyes were flaming fire. Perhaps we have discovered the reason why Christ's tormentors blind-folded Him. There was something overpowering about His eyes. We learn from a person's eyes. It has

Plate No. 1

been known for one man to say of another, 'He looked through me'. The X-ray eyes of science fiction may not be a fantasy after all!

Now consider: His feet were like beaten brass, as it had been refined by fire in a furnace. No one really knows what the metal is. The Greek word has been translated as beaten brass. Dr William Barclay suggests it was the compound called electrum, which the ancients believed to be an alloy of gold and silver, and more precious than either. The symbolism notes that the Christ is irresistible in His ongoing. The human foot is one of the most important parts of the body — structurally beautiful and extremely efficient — with the mystery of muscle contraction, cushion system, automatic oiling system, and powers to move up and down, with heel movement and tiptoe movement, whether in running or walking. Our portrait painter underlines the importance of the feet.

His voice was the sound of many waters. This is the description of the voice of God in Ezekiel 43:2. But there is also the suggestion that we catch here an echo of the little island of Patmos. 'The roar of the Aegean was in the ears of the Seer'. H. B. Swete has a lovely thought here. The voice of God is not confined to one note. Here it is like the terrifying surge and thunder of the sea. But the same voice of God can be like a still small voice — 1 Kings 19:12 — or, as the Greek version of the Old Testament has it, like a gentle breeze.

He had seven stars in his right hand. The seven stars are the messengers to the churches.

From His mouth issued a sharp two-edged sword. This appears grotesque in the narrative and in the painting, but this is the symbol of His authoritative teaching.

His face was like the sun shining in full strength. The portrait of Christ here seems to have little in common with the winsome, radiant and approachable Christ we meet on the pages of the Gospels. He seems vastly different even from the risen Christ who walked and talked in such intimate fashion with those two friends who were making their sad way back to Emmaus on the first Easter Sunday. The whole portrait in this passage presents Christ as the One who is majestic, aweful, eternal-conqueror and King.

Now we observe the description of a posture. 'John fell at His feet'. In the New Testament there are many examples of people approaching the Lord — 'kneeling before Him', 'falling before Him', 'leaning on His bosom', and here in the Apocalypse John falls at His feet.

Modern Christianity has become very sophisticated. We no longer fall at Christ's feet. Our polished approach to our faith prevents us from taking the humble place. We pay a terrible price because of our sophistication. If we do not fall at His feet, then we shall not feel His right hand upon us. This is a highly significant revelation. It is the hand that gives expression to our visions and dreams. It is through the hand that we must translate our visions and dreams into reality. It is said that when a famous man returned one day from viewing the statue of Venus, he burst into tears, saying, 'she has no hands!'. That is, she is beautiful, but impotent.

John's posture gives us his reaction to the glorious vision. Jesus' hand translates the vision into reality. When Christ's hand is upon us, we are nerved and fortified.

THE INSPIRATION OF A PROCLAMATION

I am the living one; I died and behold I am alive for evermore, and I have the keys of Death and Hades.

Revelation 1:17

Our Lord wanted John to live in the good of the Resurrection. 'This was the driving message behind the revolutionary force of the Christian message; theme of every sermon; master motive of every act of evangelism. Not an epilogue to the Gospel, not a providential after-thought; not an appendix to the faith' (Dr J. S. Stewart). The Apocalypse is one of the strongest evidences for the resurrection of Christ. He is alive for evermore. This means that the future is secure in His hands. We need not tremble for the future. The Living One has secured it.

He respects our humility, but He asks us to 'fear not'. He reminds John, and us, that He possesses the keys. These keys symbolise authority, and that over Death and Hell — or as the Greek would suggest — Hades. Christ has defeated death. We need not fear. Death is not the 'final absurdity of existence'. Our Lord has withdrawn the sting from this monstrous foe. In the words of 2 Timothy 1:10,

He has abolished death and He has brought life and immortality to light through His glorious gospel.

Chapter II

According to Revelation 1:13 our Lord is in the midst of the churches. Christ is characterised with a majestic mobility and an overpowering presence. Some, with a sense of their own omnicompetence, imagine that they have immobilised Christ having anchored Him at a convenient distance. They do not want the Lord to disturb them, but in spite of their actions, our Lord walks in the midst of the churches, making an accurate analysis of their spiritual condition.

Each church has an angel. No clear statement is given as to whether he is a guardian angel, that is, a supernatural being with the responsibility for supervising the individual churches, or whether the word *angelos* is to be taken in the non-technical sense of 'messenger' as it is used outside the New Testament. The context suggests that each angel is the leader of the church and so might well be equated with its minister or pastor.

The Lord indicates that the churches are under His control and in the time of peril, He will preserve them and will not let them go. Rigid inspection, powerful protection and loving evaluation must precede the judgment of the churches.

Before examining in detail the messages of the Lord to the seven congregations, it will help us in our understanding when we consider the painting (Plate 2) that gives a representation of the seven churches. Our Lord taught that He was the vine and His followers were the branches, conveying the principle of a union based on life (John 15). In the painting the vine and the branches are represented as one — Christ is in the midst of the churches. The churches are described as 'the seven lampstands' in Revelation 1:20, suggesting the idea of union as seen in the Jewish seven-branched candelabra. Beneath the stained-glass window effect of the seven churches there is the gold foundation reminding us that the seven churches are the golden lampstand.

EPHESUS – THE STRENUOUS CHURCH Revelation 2:1-7

Ephesus was at that time a prosperous city. The temple of Diana, one of the seven wonders of the ancient world, was located here. The Greeks dedicated the city to her and derived a lot of money from the tourists who bought the images of the goddess. Diana was the apotheosis of sensuality, the goddess of fertility, life, sex and reproduction which was represented in the images by giving her a multiplicity of breasts. Eunuchs and priestesses who were associated with the temple, committed shameless acts and encouraged the worship of the symbols of sexuality. Here paganism was strong, sensual and overmastering.

Acts 19 highlights the story of the planting of the church. Ephesus had known the ministry of the eloquent Apollos; a three-year teaching ministry of the apostle Paul which established a strong church; Timothy's pastoral ministry and the apostle John's fatherly care helped to make the church stronger. Now the Lord speaks with frankness to the congregation, reminding them that He is the one 'who holds the seven stars in his right hand, who walks among the seven golden lampstands' (verse 1).

The spiritual analysis is introduced by the uncomfortable disclosure, 'I know'. These two words have an explosive effect upon the cosy complacency of.the Christian fellowship. Some Christians make excuses about their inconsistency, lack of responsibility and spiritual lethargy, but these excuses are so flimsy, weak and unpersuasive that they are tantamount to lies. The risen Christ, with the eyes of fire, looks into our spiritual condition and says, 'I know'. Some Christians think that they are too clever for God; with a supercilious attitude they think that it is easy to hoodwink God, but 'He knows'! There is no escaping His incisive analytical gaze; His accurate analysis of the church is balanced.

First of all He knows about the aggressiveness in their loyalty.

I know your works, your toil and your patient endurance, and how you cannot bear evil men but have tested those who call themselves apostles but are not, and found them to be false; I know you are enduring patiently and bearing up for my name's sake, and you have not grown weary.

Revelation 2:2-3

44

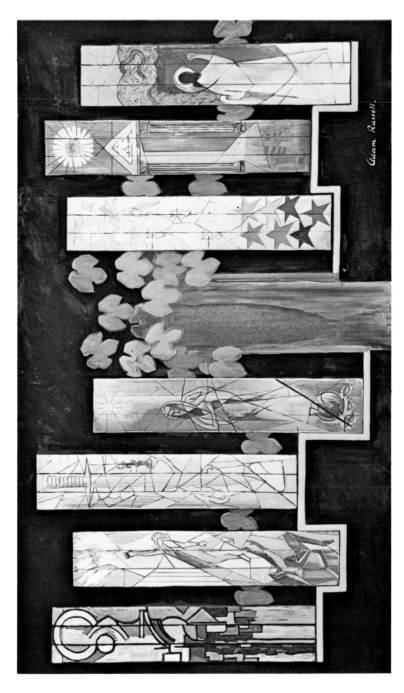

Adam Russell.

Plate No. 2

45

The church was not a comfortable club for the conserving of the life of a few Christians. It was an active congregation comprised of people who were not afraid of hard work, and so the Lord says, 'I know your works'. Their witness had made a difference to the city. Lives had been transformed, pagan homes had become the annexes of heaven, Diana had been dethroned in the hearts of the pagans and an outstanding witness had been established in the city.

Appreciation is recorded when the Lord informs the church 'I know your toil'. This word toil which in the Greek is *kopos,* is characteristic of the New Testament. Romans 16:12 reminds us that Tryphena, Tryphosa and Persis 'labour' in the Lord. In 1 Corinthians 15:10 Paul claims that he has 'laboured' more than them all. The special quality of *kopos* is that it describes 'labour to the point of sweat', or to the point of exhaustion. Strenuous, sacrificial effort lay behind the effort of the Christians in Ephesus. Laziness is dishonouring to the service of Christ and drones and idlers are not well placed in the Kingdom of God.

Their 'patient endurance' impressed the Lord. He recognised their courageous gallantry. All their efforts seemed to glow with the radiance of the risen Christ; their patience was not grim but glorious.

The Lord recognises their balanced orthodoxy and zeal for the truth; 'You cannot bear evil men and have tested those who call themselves apostles'. These Ephesian Christians knew whom they believed and what they believed. Itinerant preachers were put through a doctrinal test, if they failed the examination, their fellowship was refused by the church. These Christians who held to the true doctrine had a genuine zeal for integrity, they did not indulge in a distorted meekness which accepted moral mediocrity. Belief and behaviour were inseparable for the Ephesian Christians.

Secondly, the Lord knew about the abandonment of their love. He cautioned them by saying

But I have this against you, that you have abandoned the love you had at first.
Revelation 2:4

This statement could be written over many marriages. When love is abandoned in marriage, the relationship becomes dull and commonplace. First love ought to make progress and deepen with the years and when this happens, the couple have a permanency and trust in their marriage that money cannot buy.

Love for Christ, like the marriage relationship, ought to grow and glow. We ought to love the Saviour more today than we did at our conversion. The Ephesian church highly commended for its strenuousness, had left the joyous radiance of the first love. When glowing love turns cold in the church, then everything becomes formal. Love is the essential characteristic that makes the church attractive; where there is the lack of love, there cannot be winsomeness. Here is the age-long problem of the church activity without love; an atmosphere that reminds us of a deep-freeze situation rather than the warmth of the risen Saviour.

Thirdly, the Lord gives the church an admonition. It is profitable for all Christians to face His admonitions.

Remember then from what you have fallen, repent and do the works you did at first. If not, I will come to you and remove your lampstand from its place.

Revelation 2:5

This admonition contains two imperatives — 'remember' and 'repent'. The first commands a process or a practise. Let the Ephesian Christians keep on remembering the past; this is not an exhortation to live in the past, but to learn from the past, so we can accept the admonition as salutary; to keep on learning from the past is an evidence of our spiritual maturity. What does our spiritual graph tell us? The Ephesians were informed that their spiritual zeal had fallen, their love had abated, the spiritual experience of the church was at its nadir.

The second imperative is 'repent'. 'The tense contains the crack of a whip' (Dr. William Barclay). In other words, it is the opposite of 'remember'. There is no opportunity for pondering, the command is instantaneous and repentance should take place immediately. If there is the lack of remembrance and repentance, then the Lord threatens that there will be a 'removal' — 'I will come to you and remove your lampstand from its place'. Did this happen? Yes. In AD262 the city of Ephesus was destroyed, including the temple of Diana. Today, Ephesus is a heap of ruins among the hills and there is no Christian witness in that particular area. If remembering does not lead to repentance, then the Lord makes a removal; He withdraws the power and effectiveness from our witness. The painting that highlights the church in Ephesus majors on the importance of the candlestick symbolising the acitivity and power of the Holy Spirit.

When the admonition is obeyed, there is the victorious experience of access to the tree of life which is in the paradise of God. This tree is the symbol of eternal and spiritual vitality which is developed in all its fulness in Revelation 22.

SMYRNA – THE SUFFERING CHURCH Revelation 2:8-11

About forty miles north of Ephesus there stood the city of Smyrna. Jews were drawn to Smyrna because of the attraction and challenge of its commercial prosperity and as a result, they formed the major part the city's population. The Jews believed in *detente* with the Roman authorities but not with the small band of Christians in Smyrna. The city was rich, proud, beautiful, fanatically loyal to Rome, and no easy place in which to witness for Christ.

Smyrna is known today as Izmir and has a population of 300,000 and possesses an outstanding harbour. Izmir is a Turkish corruption of the word Smyrna which was derived from one of the main exports - myrrh.

This perfumed material was used copiously in the embalming of the dead. Typologists teach that myrrh represents the fragrance of Christ to God in His sacrificial death. Christ's death went up to God as a sweet smelling savour, which became a blessing to man. Myrrh is the result of the crushing of fruit and bark, that is, the perfume is the result of suffering. It is no accident that the church that suffers for Christ's sake is located in Smyrna.

The Lord presents Himself to the Smyrnean believers in Chapter 2:8 as 'the words of the first and last, who died and came to life'. We have noticed before that the title 'first and last' describes Christ's deity, but now He mentions His death and resurrection to those who are threatened with martyrdom. As He has passed through death, so His followers need not fear the experience of the confrontation with the final enemy.

In the middle of His message to the church, the Lord gives the fellowship, by way of a parenthesis, a great compliment. In Chapter 2:9 He says of the church – 'You are rich'. What is our idea of a rich church? Do we see a luxurious furnished building with a priceless organ, an educated and polished ministry and a well-to-do congregation with a millionaires' row? The church in Smyrna was not rich in material possessions, yet this is the only church in the New Testament that the Lord describes as being rich. The Laodicean church thought it was rich because it had great material possessions, but the Lord said of that church, 'You are wretched, pitiable, poor, blind and naked' (Rev 3:17). The Lord is not arguing against money, but He is reminding the church that material possessions can give us a sense of false security. True riches are spiritual and this enrichment is based upon our personal relationship with Jesus Christ through His gracious Holy Spirit. When our Lord said that the church was rich, He was giving the fellowship His highest commendation.

As the Lord continues with His message to the church in Smyrna, He recognises the painful persecution that they have been called upon to endure. He says to them

I know your tribulation and your poverty . . . and the slander of those who say that they are Jews and are not, and are a synagogue of Satan.

Revelation 2:9

Smyrna was a slandered church; it knew the agony of character assassination. The church's reputation was in shreds.

From church history, we learn that there were six main slanders levelled against the early church. The story was circulated that the Christians were cannibals! This accusation was based on the information that at certain meals they ate a body and drank blood; of course this was the communion service, misunderstood by the pagan mind. Another meal that the Christians had was called the *agape*, that is, a love feast. The coarse pagan understanding interpreted the love feast as occasions for orgies of lust and immorality.

Sometimes a happy family was torn asunder because some of the members had become Christians; this situation evoked the criticism that Christians tampered with family relationships. One of the strangest accusations levelled against the Christians was atheism; as the heathen could not see any idols or images, they concluded that Christians were unbelievers! The church was described as being comprised of politically disloyal citizens who would not acknowledge the lordship of Caesar. It is apparent how Christians were considered potential revolutionaries. The Christians were accused of being destructive because they predicted the end of the world as a blazing disintegration.

These six slanders encouraged people to persecute the church and in Chapter 2:10 the Lord prepares them for the onslaught.

Do not fear what you are about to suffer. Behold the devil is about to throw some of you into prison, that you may be tested and for ten days you will have tribulation. Be faithful unto death, and I will give you the crown of life.

This impoverished church was about to be attacked. Dr. William Barclay highlights the significance of the two words in Greek for poverty. *Penia* describes the poor man who has nothing superfluous; *ptocheian* describes the state of the man who has nothing at all. The Smyrnean Christians experienced the latter, but the worse had yet to be. Imprisonment and martyrdom lay ahead, but they had to be unafraid.

They are informed that they shall have tribulation 'ten days'. Some have seen in the ten days the ten persecutions of the church in secular history, but the expression seems to be used to signify a limited period, that is, a short period that was soon to come to an end.

The Lord promises the crown of life to those who show themselves loyal to death. The painting that represents the church in Smyrna conveys the idea of the fire of martyrdom. One Christian is depicted in prison with the flame-effect upon him, the other Christian is seen reaching to the golden splendour of heaven where there is the reward of the crown of life. The one who conquers death shall not be hurt by the second death, that is, eternal separation from God.

PERGAMUM – THE SHREWD CHURCH   Revelation 2:12-17

Some modern churches seek to express a Christian truth in their architectural forms. For example one church moves inward to the pulpit which is the focal point. Windows and walls converge on it and the outbuildings are like two outstretched arms inviting the world to come. Another church shifts the emphasis. It has a glass wall at the east end of the sanctuary and outside the wall, standing naked and stark in the paved forecourt, with houses, factories and busy streets beyond, stands the cross. The cross is in the world.

These two modern church buildings typify the debate which is engaging the church today. Bring the world to the church; take the cross to the world. This is the tension in the church. To hold the balance, we need the spirit of wisdom. Only a spiritually shrewd church can maintain the equipoise between these two emphases. The church in Pergamum was a shrewd church. Christian witness was in the centre of Satan's capital. By the grace of God the Christian fellowship invited the world to come to them, but it also took the cross to the world. In facing this tension, the Christians established a strong church, but they were not without faults; the shrewd church succumbed to the temptation of compromise.

Pergamum was a religious centre. Temples had been built in honour of Zeus, Aphrodite and Aesculapius, the god of medicine who was recognised as the patron god of the city. Pergamum was a heathen pantheon and had a weakness similar to that found in the city of Athens – it was too religious! Pergamum was a cultural centre. The library was famous and the shelves housed more than two hundred thousand books.

Our Lord presents Himself to the church as the One who has the sharp two-edged sword, (verse 12). Two words are used in New Testament Greek for sword. *Machaira* is the short sword or dagger and is referred to in Hebrews 4:12. *Rhomphaia* denotes a Thracian weapon of large size and occurs in Revelation 1:16; 2:12,16; 6:8; 19:15 and 21. Five of these contexts refer to the Lord's judicial utterances. The symbolism of the large Thracian sword is used in the painting that represents the church in Pergamum. We are reminded that the sword is two-edged; the Greek word *distomos* literally means 'two-mouthed', suggesting that our Lord speaks with double authority.

Commendations are given to the church in verse 13

I know where you dwell, where Satan's throne is; you hold fast my name and you did not deny my faith even in the days of Antipas my witness, my faithful one, who was killed among you where Satan dwells.

They held fast the name of Jesus Christ, their personal loyalty to Him was firm and dependable. They did not waver in the face of the fiercest opposition. Further, they did not deny His faith. There are two applications of this statement. It could mean that they had held tenaciously to Christ's faith in spite of intense persecution, but it could also mean that they had not denied our Lord's personal faith. Remember He is described as 'the pioneer and perfecter of our faith' in Hebrews 12:2. The Lord, when on earth, was known as a man of faith and when He was suffering on the Cross it was His enemies who testified, 'He trusted in God'. Both aspects of faith operated effectively in the church in Pergamum; the Christian witness survived in Satan's capital because men and women lived by faith. The Satanic influence is shown in the painting by the serpent which was the symbol of Aesculapius, the serpent god. In Smyrna, Satan seemed to operate through the Jewish synagogue, but Satan's throne is in Pergamum and the evil one is engaged in open conflict with the Church of Christ. Satan is the sworn antagonist of the Christian witness which is strong and effective, but he is not too interested in the complacent church which has lost its spiritual unction.

An enthusiastic conquering church always meets opposition and Pergamum was no exception. One of the members of the Christian fellowship had already given his life in the service of Jesus Christ. It is difficult to believe that Antipas was this martyr's true name. The name derives from two Greek words - *anti* meaning against, and *pas* meaning all. Antipas was a nickname suggesting that he stood against everybody and everything. He epitomises the strength of the testimony of the local church in Satan's capital.

The Lord's commendation is followed by condemnation,

But I have a few things against you: you have some there who hold the teaching of Balaam, who taught Balak to put a stumbling block before the sons of Israel, that they might eat food sacrificed to idols and practise immorality. So you also have some who hold the teaching of the Nicolaitans.

Revelation 2:14-15

What is the teaching of Balaam and what is the teaching of the Nicolaitans? Balaam is a Hebrew name and Nicolaus is a Greek name. Balaam comes from two Hebrew words *bela* which means to conquer, and *ha'am* which means the people. The name Nicolaus (the founder of the Nicolaitans) derives from two Greek words, *nikan* which means to conquer and *laos* meaning the people. The two names are synonymous, as we have the same meaning expressed in its Hebrew and Greek form. These two sects had a similar aim, namely, to subjugate the people. Some scholars see in this heresy incipient sacerdotalism and priestcraft.

Numbers 22-25 splashes on the canvas of ancient history the story of the prophet Balaam. He has been called the 'angelic devil'. This may seem lurid and sensational but it attempts to describe concisely one of the most complex characters in the Old Testament. The doctrine of Balaam as we find it in the book of Numbers is that Balaam encouraged Balak, the King of Moab to instigate the inter-marriage of the Moabite women with the men of Israel, resulting in obscenities and abominations that brought a plague which killed 24,000 Israelites. The teaching of Balaam and the Nicolaitans attempts to brainwash the people into believing that God's promises are unconditional and that they hold good whether we face our responsibility or not. This doctrine compromises with the world and leads to the sin of presumption. A sharp warning is given by the Lord in verse 16.

Repent then, If not, I will come to you soon and war against them with the sword of my mouth.

The challenge of Christ's teaching is obvious; no Christian can experience the peace of God when he resists the teaching of God!

In verse 17 the Lord promises certain rewards

To him who conquers I will give some of the hidden manna and I will give him a white stone, with a new name written on the stone which no one knows except him who receives it.

The hidden manna takes us back to the Old Testament. When the children of Israel lacked food in the wilderness, God provided them with manna. This special food helped the Israelites through their time of crisis. When the trial passed, they were instructed to take a pot of manna and put it into the Holy of Holies in the Tabernacle. This pot of manna eventually found its place in the Temple built by Solomon. In 586 BC the Temple was destroyed, but a legend was circulated that before the Temple was desecrated, Jeremiah acquired the pot of manna and hid it on Mount Sinai and that when the Messiah came, Jeremiah would accompany Him and produce the hidden pot of manna. Those who accepted the legend believed that when a Jew ate the hidden manna he was enjoying the blessings of the Messianic age. Christians believed that Christ was the true Messiah. He was the bread of heaven that came down to earth. To know Christ is to participate in the hidden manna, and to have Him as Saviour and friend means that we enter into the blessedness of the new world.

To the overcomer, there is promised a white stone. Attractive explanations have been offered regarding the significance of the white stone. When a man was justly acquitted at his trial, he was given a white stone. It was his evidence that he had been declared not guilty. Because of this secular background, some students of the Scripture see in this analogy the truth of justification. Sometimes the white stone was given to a man who had been successful in battle; the stone was the symbol of his victories. Again, the white stone is seen to have the spiritual significance of being 'more than conquerors through him who loved us' (Romans 8:37). The stone is the symbol of spiritual triumph. In New Testament times when a man received the freedom of a city, he was not given a key, but he received a white stone, so it is suggested that when the Christian receives the white stone from God, he is presented with the freedom of the New Jerusalem. But there is another spiritual application associated with the white stone under the heading of 'The Tessara Hospitalis'. This name was given to the white stone which contained the names of two friends. The white stone was divided in two and each friend carried his half of the stone which contained not his own name but that of his friend. The two parts of the stone could be passed on to posterity, but the day could arrive when two people would meet, each having his part of the white stone and their friendship was established immediately upon the basis of that friendship created long ago. The white stone stands for a perennial friendship. What an outstanding fourfold blessing – justification, triumph, freedom of the New Jerusalem and an everlasting friendship. Remember He has written our new name on the white stone!.

THYATIRA – THE SENTIMENTAL CHURCH   Revelation 2:18-29

The message given to the church in Thyatira is longer than the messages addressed to the other six churches. Thyatira was reputed for its famous purple cloth which was sold throughout the known world. Lydia, whom we meet in Acts 16 was a commercial traveller from Thyatira and according to the New Testament record, she was the first convert in Europe, although she herself was an Asian. Lydia may have founded the church in Thyatira, but there is no positive evidence to support this claim.

Christians were faced with a religious and commercial challenge in the city. Apollo was worshipped under the symbol of the sun god, but the patron god was usually represented on horseback as a conquering hero having a two-edged battle-axe across his shoulder. The tradeguilds in Thyatira presented an acute problematical situation to the Christians engaged in commerce. All the trade meetings began with a sacrifice offered in the deity's name. Formal homage was given to the patron deity throughout the proceedings and the Christians had to stand against the excess and open corruption of a pagan society. From the Lord's-message to the church in Thyatira we learn what the Christians were doing and some of the characteristics of this Christian fellowship are 'writ large' in this epistle.

The epistle begins with a striking salutation

The words of the Son of God, who has eyes like a flame of fire, and whose feet are like burnished bronze.

Revelation 2:18

Jesus comes to the church with all the authority of God. His penetrating eyes are like flames of fire and they expose the church and the individual. His strong bronze-like feet suggest that He is irresistible. Christ is greater than Apollo the brilliant guardian of Thyatira. He outshines the pagan deity. There is none comparable to Jesus Christ.

Sound psychology is utilised by our Lord. Before He announces His criticisms of the church, He gives them encouragement. He points out that they have some spiritual qualities in their possession. He reminds them in verse 19, 'I know your love'. Jesus still had first place in their hearts and their devotion to Him kept their spiritual experience vigorous. He also reminds them that He knows their faith (verse 19). No one can become a Christian without faith, but their faith was not just a saving faith; it was also a sustaining faith; they lived by faith and displayed a constant trust in the Saviour.

The Lord reminds the church that He knows their service (verse 19). Their lives were equipped to fulfil the sublime call to Christian work. Their ministry was persevering, definite and at times invincible. Service to them was not lethargic and perfunctory motivated by a cold sense of duty; no — their service was prompted by a warm enthusiastic aggressive love.

'Patient endurance' characterised their witness (verse 19). Patience has been defined as 'the spirit of peace under pressure'. It is that quality of loveliness which survives vicissitude and change; it is the attitude that knows sanctification to be protracted and progressive; it believes that trust is deepened by peril and that courage is developed before the threat of the enemy. God is not hurried and hasty. In nature, He makes us wait through the spring and the summer for the growing of our food. In redemption, He puts many years between the fall of man and the coming of Christ. The Lord loves to see patience in His people!

The climax of the Lord's commendation of the church is breath-taking — 'Your latter works exceed the first' (verse 19). They are greater because they have a deeper motive behind them and a developed maturity to actuate them. The experience of many Christians is a reversal of this statement, namely, their first works exceed their latter. Their interest has vanished, enthusiasm evaporates, disillusionment comes with middle age and they lose heart.

In Thyatira then, there was a 'five-star' church; love, faith, service, patient endurance and abounding work earned the highest praise, but the church had many problems. These problems, strangely enough, came from the teaching of a woman called Jezebel. She is represented in the painting as a seductive woman; in fact, Jezebel is the most hated woman in the Bible and she has been called the Lady Macbeth of the Old Testament. This leader in the church of Thyatira was, according to James Moffat, 'a Jezebel of a woman'.

From the Old Testament we learn that Jezebel was a pagan who introduced false religion to Israel through her marriage to King Ahab. Elijah, the prophet of fire reminds us of Jezebel's influence.

... the people of Israel have forsaken thy covenant, thrown down thy altars, and slain thy prophets with the sword; and I, even I, only, am left; and they seek my life to take it away.

1 Kings 19:10

Things were not as desperate as he thought, but there is no doubt that Queen Jezebel had apostasised the nation of Israel.

The Old Testament Jezebel helps us to understand the New Testament Jezebel. She was a woman who taught false doctrine and associated with that doctrine there was undermining of the Christians' moral standards. Jezebel had great prestige and from her place of authority she could influence many people. Further, she had an outstanding ability in leadership and with her dashing and daring she spread her evil doctrine.

Christians in the church at Thyatira had become sentimental in their outlook. They had allowed a woman to draw them away from the true doctrine. Jezebel presented to them what she called 'the deep things of Satan'. This teaching appealed to the conceit of many in the church. The shallow and superficial considered themselves to be peers, but the so-called deep doctrine led to self-will which made sin attractive and harmless, 'teaching and beguiling my servants to practise immorality and to eat food sacrificed to idols' (verse 20). The Lord's statement is most startling. He asserts

. . . and I will strike her children dead. And all the churches shall know that I am he who searches mind and heart, and I will give to each of you as your works deserve.   Revelation 2:23

The Lord will not tolerate spiritual and moral disaster. Our Lord's intervention works in two ways. One day Ezekiel saw the cloud of God's glory forsaking the Temple. It left the mercy-seat, to linger on the threshold of the house. Then it rested on one of the gates. Then it moved to the hill on the east of the city, and from Olivet, it returned to its native heaven. That is one method of discipline. He withdraws His glory, or as we noticed in the church in Ephesus, He removes the lampstand. But the other method is most drastic and very dramatic – people are disciplined by death which is administered by the risen Lord. Those who dabble in 'the deep things of Satan' are endangered with the threat of death. We must not condone any teaching that anaesthetises the conscience and weakens our sensitiveness to sin!

In verse 26 the Lord promises a reward to the overcomer

He who conquers and who keeps my works until the end, I will give him power over the nations, and he shall rule them with a rod of iron . . . and I will give him the morning star.

This promise is twofold, embracing the use of authority and the possession of the morning star. These are represented in the painting (Plate 2). Authority is symbolised in the breaking of the potter's vessel by the iron rod and the scintillating star reminds us of the bright and morning star.

The promise of authority derives from Psalm 2:8-9

Ask of me, and I will make the nations your heritage, and the ends of the earth your possession. You shall break them with a rod of iron, and dash them in pieces like a potter's vessel.

Paul, the apostle, expresses a similar truth in 1 Corinthians 6:2

Do you not know that the saints will judge the world? And if the world is to be judged by you, are you incompetent to try trivial cases?

The Christian church should be characterised by the authority of the sovereign Lord. In the spiritual kingdom, there is no room for doubt, no excuse for indifference, no possibility of neutrality. Christ's authority is our authority and there are occasions when we ought to apply it.

The promise of the morning star leads us into an interesting study. Four suggestions have been made regarding the application of this teaching. In the experience of the patriarch Job we learn that as God informs him of His creative grandeur, there is the unusual disclosure that the 'morning stars sang together'! It has been suggested that this was the song of the principalities and powers in the heavenly sphere as they worked in the spaces of new creation. The Lord is the Prince of Creation and is the cohesive principle of the whole universe. Associated with this approach, there is the teaching of Isaiah 14:12 concerning Lucifer, the angelic being who rebelled against God. Lucifer means light-bringer and Lucifer is the name of the morning star. If we can accept that interpretation, then the Lord, the Prince of Creation in offering Christians the morning star, is offering victory over principalities and powers in overcoming Lucifer, the devil

The morning star is also referred to in Daniel 12:3

And those who are wise shall shine like the brightness of the firmament; and those who turn many to righteousness, like the stars for ever and ever.

This interpretation suggests that the morning star is the reward that comes to those who have a right relationship with God and who assisted others to share in a similar relationship.

Further, it has been suggested that the morning star is the promise of the first resurrection. 'As the morning star rises after the night', so the Christian will rise after the night of death'.

Finally, and perhaps the most appropriate interpretation is that our Lord in the Apocalypse calls Himself 'the bright morning star' (Revelation 22:16). So what He is doing is exciting and thrilling; He is promising Himself to those who maintain their loyalty to Him in the face of persecution. Christ promises the bright morning star to all who have an unbending and rigorous antagonism to false doctrine and share with Him His righteous antipathies.

Chapter III

SARDIS – THE SHAMMING CHURCH

Sardis was a wealthy city, commercially active and secure. It was built on an elevation that was protected on three sides by sheer cliffs. On the fourth side there was an isthmus that could be defended by a small group of men against an attacking army. Although it was considered impregnable, it had been captured because of the complacency and over-confidence of the defenders.

The city of Sardis had a reputation for impregnability but it had been captured; the church in Sardis had the reputation for being alive, but it was dead! Apart from the few in Sardis who remained loyal, the members of the church are condemned by the Lord. He introduces Himself as

The words of him who has the seven spirits of God and the seven stars
Revelation 3:1

The seven stars are featured in the painting (Plate 2). We have already noticed that the seven stars represent the churches and the pastors, but the painting emphasises what the Scripture is teaching, as the reputation of the church is symbolised in the seven golden stars, so the actual condition of the church is seen in the darkened, dead stars.

Some churches fail to see things as they are, but the Lord is authoritative and analytical and sees things as they ought to be seen. Christ demands the healthy exercise of self-analysis.

I know your works; you have the name of being alive and you are dead. Awake, and strengthen what remains and is on the point of death, for I have not found your works perfect in the sight of my God.
Revelation 3:1-2

The church was well known and it was favourably known. Everybody thought it was a live church, but its reputation was a sham. It has been said, 'Life is beautiful; life can laugh and love and sing, but death is the supreme ugliness'. The Lord having held a spiritual autopsy declares that the church is dead. Apart from the few members who had not soiled their garments the church is dead. The church has reached the depths of supreme ugliness, but it is unaware of its terrible condition. Christians are urged to remember what they have received and to repent because of their condition.

How can we recognise a live church? First of all it is an integrated church. When a person becomes a corpse, he begins to disintegrate. Life contains the principle of integration. A church that is filled with factions is a dead church. It has disintegrated.

Secondly, empathy is an evidence of a live church. It does not just get alongside of the people; it is prepared to get inside people and know their struggles, conflicts and feelings. Such a church brings to men and women the invincible love of the Lord Jesus Christ.

Thirdly, a live church is emotional. By the grace of God it modulates the notes of tears and laughter within the human experience. Intellectual sophistication has a deadening effect upon the spiritual well-being of the church. 'The church that lives, thrills with emotion, is full of laughter, and full of tears, perpetually breaks into song, and is silent again in the silence of pain'.

Fourthly, a live church is a growing church. Each member grows in grace and the knowledge of the Lord Jesus; yes, and the church proclaims the propagative message of the gospel. A living church sees men and women transformed by being born again and then added to the church fellowship. A church grows, not by importing Christians from other fellowships, but through a high spiritual productivity that is inspired by the out-flowing power of the Holy Spirit.

In verse 5 the Lord reminds them of the rewards

He who conquers shall be clad thus in white garments, and I will not blot his name out of the book of life; I will confess his name before my Father and before his angels.

There are three rewards here: first the purity of the white garment, then the security of the Christian's name being inscribed and retained in the Book of Life, and finally the assurance of being in the Father's presence.

'The Book of Life' is worthy of deep consideration. To understand its significance we must examine the secular background and the spiritual concept of the Book of Life. Practically every city of New Testament times kept a roll or register of its citizens. The name of every child born in the city was recorded. If one of the citizens lapsed and was guilty of disloyalty to the city's standards, discipline was exercised by the erasing of his name from the register. But if one of the citizens accomplished some great work which deserved special distinction, he was honoured by having his name written in golden letters in the citizens' roll. If we accept the secular background to our understanding of the Book of Life then we have to acknowledge that everybody who is born into this world has their name inscribed in the Book of Life, but those who reject Jesus Christ as Saviour and spurn the mercy of God have their names expunged from the Book of Life.

Does the teaching of the Bible agree with the secular practise? Moses said

'But now, if thou wilt forgive their sin — and if not, blot me, I pray thee out of thy book which thou hast written'.

Exodus 32:32-3

It may be argued that Moses' name was not erased from the book, but we must not avoid the obvious fact that Moses believed that names could be removed from the book.

'Let the wicked be blotted out of the book of the living', said the Psalmist, 'let them not be enrolled among the righteous'. (Psalm 69: 28). The Book of Life, according to this statement, contains the names of the righteous and the wicked, but the latter are blotted out at death if they have no faith in the Lord, whereas the former are retained in 'The Book of Life'.

Daniel, in his prophecy, states

And there shall be a time of trouble, such as never has been since there was a nation till that time; but at that time your people shall be delivered, everyone whose name shall be found written in the book.

Daniel 12:1

This conveys the idea of security. Many Christians are convinced about eternal security. There are Scriptures to support such a belief. Our Lord said

I give them eternal life, and they shall never perish, and no one shall snatch them out of my hand.

John 10:28

Romans 8 introduces us to the wonderful statement,

There is therefore now no condemnation for those who are in Christ Jesus

This same chapter concludes with the words

. . . nor anything else in all creation, will be able to separate us from the love of God in Christ Jesus our Lord.

Romans 8:39

We must hold to this teaching regarding the believer's eternal security, but from the Scriptures we find it is possible for a person to have his name deleted from the Book of Life. Is this an inconsistency? We think not. We are attempting to reverse the popular belief that when a man is born again, his name, at that moment is written in the Book of Life. This cannot be supported from Scripture. But in Scripture, there is the harmonious principle that all names, at birth, are written in the Book of Life, but those who have rejected Christ as Saviour and Lord have their names removed by the authority of God, and so Revelation 20:15 states

. . . and if anyone's name was not found written in the book of life, he was thrown into the lake of fire.

There were a few people in the church in Sardis who were real Christians, and they are depicted in the painting, crowned and dressed in white. As for the rest, they are nominal Christians having no real personal relationship with Christ. If they do not repent and trust Him, then their names will be removed from the Book of Life at their death.

PHILADELPHIA – THE STEADFAST CHURCH   Revelation 3:7-13

Philadelphia has the 'new-town' reputation about it, as it was the youngest of all the seven cities. It was founded with the obvious purpose that it might propagate the beauty and importance of Greek culture and language to Lydia and Phrygia. The city fulfilled this purpose and before AD 19 the people of Lydia had given up their own culture and were totally committed to the Greek outlook on life.

The church in Philadelphia is one of the most attractive in the New Testament. There is no word of condemnation against it, and the Lord intrôduces Himself to the church by making four definite assertions about Himself

The words of the holy one, the true one, who has the key of David, who opens and no one shall shut, who shuts and no one opens.

Revelation 3:7

Christ is the Holy One. This reminds us that the Lord is very high. Alps may be tunnelled by man's engineering genius; electricity may be harnessed for a thousand uses; man may travel to the moon, but man cannot reach to God's holiness. God states

I am the Lord, your Holy One, the creator of Israel, your King.

Isaiah 43:15

Christ uses the title of God because He is God and His holiness reminds us of our limitations.

Our Lord is also the True One. This reminds us that the Lord is very near. His character is beyond us but His conduct brings Him near. He is the one who is above us in holiness, but He is near us in truth. His character is wide apart from ours, lofty, imperishable and unattainable, but His conduct brings Him near to us, revealing His eyes of pity and His heart of unsearchable grace.

The 'key of David' belongs to Christ. This key symbolises kingly authority and Christ's declaration to His disciples

All authority in heaven and on earth has been given to me

Matthew 28:18

makes it clear that He has the absolute power to exercise kingship over the individual, over the church and over the world. Jesus is the Christ, the true messianic King.

Following on from the King's authority, we have the King's activity – 'who opens and no one shall shut, who shuts and no one opens (verse 7). Christ's executive position means that He is executing His work. Sometimes we find this difficult to accept. Our storms of mental doubt are sore, storms of temptation appear cruel and storms of bereavement are keen, but we must not allow our timidity and lack of trust to rob us of the ability of the Lord to open and shut the doors of our personal and general circumstances.

Now the Lord presents a challenging opportunity

I know your works, behold, I have set before you an open door, which no one is able to shut.

Revelation 3:8

It would seem that the open door is not a reward for fidelity, but the opportunity in which this church has proved its faithfulness. The painting that represents the church in Philadelphia emphasises the importance of the open door. Some Christians can become pessimists due to their inability to see that a door of opportunity has been opened. They imagine that the world is only a wilderness, that it is a misfortune to be here at all. Youth is a blunder, manhood is a struggle, old age is a regret. It is winter the whole year round. But they do not understand the possibilities of the Christian life. 'There are two good men', says the uncompromising Chinese proverb, 'and one of them is dead, and the other is not yet born'. But there is a third. It is he who has entered the opened door, having been 'born again' through faith in Christ. Conversion is tantamount to entering through the Lord Jesus who is the open door, Himself. Having gone through that 'door', we find that other doors are opened for us. We are not hopelessly entangled in a meaningless destiny and an irrevocable doom but we are related to the Lord personally and intimately and He offers the glorious promise of an open door that no adversary can shut.

The spiritual success of the Philadelphian Christians is described by the Lord.

Behold, I will make those of the synagogue of Satan who say that they are Jews and are not, but lie — behold, I will make them come and bow down before your feet, and learn that I have loved you. Because you have kept my word of patient endurance, I will keep you from the hour of trial which is coming on the whole world, to try those who dwell upon the earth. I am coming soon; hold fast what you have, so that no one may seize your crown.   Revelation 3:9-11

These Christians, though having little power, had kept His word and had not denied His name. They were loyal to His word. They held fast to the pattern of health-giving teaching. They defended the doctrine with soldierly courage and did not tolerate the dubious teaching of those who were out of harmony with the will of God. Isaiah speaking for God says, 'Therefore my people go into exile for want of knowledge' (Isaiah 5:13). Many Christians are in captivity because they do not have a working knowledge of the Bible. Satan conceals his dark purposes under fair pretences, as the Greek assassins sometimes hid their swords in the foliage of myrtle branches. Only the Word of God can assist us to understand the tactics of the devil. There are perils in ignorance!

These early Christians were not guilty of denying Christ's name. Loyalty to the Scriptures and the Saviour are conjoined. Despite their lack of human ability, they had an invincibility in the Lord that deepened and increased their faith. With their limited resources they did not demean the Lord's name. They followed the example of the disciples in Jerusalem, 'rejoicing that they were counted worthy to suffer dishonour for the name' (Acts 5:41). They knew His name and had put their trust in that name.

In verse 9 we have a statement that conveys the idea of compulsory obedience

I will make them come and bow down before your feet, and learn that I have loved you.

We cannot escape the fact that the antagonists of the gospel of Christ will be humbled, but another principle is revealed here; the enemies of Christ shall come and bow before the Christian's feet. This could be considered as a display of divine hatred, but the reason for compulsory obedience is given — it is to teach men and women the supreme lesson, namely that the Lord has loved the Christian. Sometimes Christians are neglected, despised, underrated and can be looked upon as 'non-persons', but their despisers will be taught a divine lesson. The foolish dreams of atheistic materialism will be dissipated and brought to the place of deep humility.

The Lord recommends the Christians of Philadelphia for keeping His 'word of patient endurance', and because they have kept His commandment, He promises to keep them. Dr William Barclay reminds us that in the Greek the phrase 'my word of patient endurance' is highly concentrated. It suggests that we have practised the same kind of endurance that Jesus practised and displayed in His earthly life.

A caution is given to the church: 'hold fast what you have, so that no one may seize your crown' (verse 11). The painting positions the crown above the door, emphasising the relationship between grasping the opportunity of the open door and holding to the crown of responsibility. It is not that someone is attempting to steal our crown, but that due to our failure to bear the responsibility we are disqualified, consequently the responsibility is given to someone else. This principle can be traced throughout the Bible. Esau, who under-estimated the value of his birthright, lost his place to Jacob (Genesis 25:29-34). Reuben, who literally fulfilled a prophecy — 'unstable as water', was replaced by Judah (Genesis 49:3-4, 10-12). Saul, who became melancholic, morbid and envious eventually lost his crown to David (1 Samuel 16:1-13). Shebna, who was hurled away violently from his stewardship, was replaced by Eliakim, a man fastened like a peg in a sure place (Isaiah 22:15-25). Joab and Abiathar, the military and religious leaders lost their places of authority to Benaiah and Zadok (1 Kings 22). The New Testament reminds us that Judas was put out of the apostolic band (Acts 1), and that the Jews lost their place to the Gentiles. Watch your crown of responsibility. None is indispensable!

Verse 12, 'He who conquers, I will make him a pillar in the temple of God', prompts Dr Clovis G Chappell to make the observation that God intends us to be pillars and not pillows in the church. A pillar is supportive. It helps to hold the church up. There are two classes of people in the church; those who lift and those who lean. The person who is a pillar in the church is steadfast and constant; his stability remains in the rough places of providence, it holds the arduous requirements of life, even when the soul is being shaped into nobleness on the anvil of grief; the dependability is masterful. The pillar is a thing of strength, but the artist reminds us that it is a thing of beauty also. There is such a quality as the beauty of holiness. Genuine goodness is characterised by charm and winsomeness. God's name is written upon the believer; that indicates character. The name of the New Jerusalem is also written upon the believer and that has to do with citizenship. Christians have a life-style that enjoys the spiritual and the supernatural in the now.

LAODICEA – THE SELF-SATISFIED CHURCH   Revelation 3:14-22

Laodicea was the Geneva of New Testament times. She was a leading banking centre and was rich in industries. Although the city was devastated by an earthquake in AD 61, the people rebuilt it from their own resources and declined help from the Roman authorities. Laodicea was famous for its medical school. The powder, collyrium, was manufactured in the city and was used to cure ophthalmic diseases. It seems that the powder, which possibly came from the mud of the thermal springs, was mixed with oil and applied to the eyes as an ointment. Textiles were also produced in Laodicea. Its most famous cloth was woven from an expensive glossy black wool and was made into carpets and clothing.

It is of great significance that the Lord said to the church in Laodicea 'you are . . . poor, blind, and naked' (verse 17). In other words, material wealth, medicines and expensive clothing and carpeting are no substitute for spiritual reality.

Little is known of the church at Laodicea. Paul knew of the church and may have visited it. Colossae and Laodicea were related to each other commercially and it is possible that the church in Colossae was related to the church in Laodicea spiritually as mother to daughter. There are a few references to the church at Laodicea in the Colossian epistle (Colossians 2:1-3; 4:13-16).

Our Lord uses descriptive words in His approach to the church at Laodicea.

The words of the Amen, the faithful and true witness, the beginning of God's creation.

Revelation 3:14

To abject failure Christ addresses Himself as the One incapable of failure.

First of all, there is the positive statement. Christ is the 'Amen' (verse 14). The root meaning of this word is that of a nursing mother, developing the concept of being built up. The derived meaning of today's usage is something that is certain, irrefragable and positive. Christ is the Amen, the absolute, cohesive power that holds the universe together, just as a nursing mother holds, nourishes and controls her baby.

Secondly, Christ is 'the faithful and true witness' (verse 14). His dialectic is triumphant and His logic irrefutable. He is faithful, so we can depend upon Him; and as His witness is true, it is obvious that we can trust Him for unthinkable years of the past and through innumerable ages of the future.

Thirdly, 'Christ is the beginning of God's creation' (verse 14). This is not suggesting that Christ is a created being. The text is speaking about rank. The Lord is incomparable and it is through Him that all things have been created (Colossians 1:15-18).

The Lord's condemnation of the church is forthright. It contains a spiritual shock therapy that must have challenged the Laodicean church. Consider these weighty words

I know your works: you are neither cold nor hot. Would that you were cold or hot! So, because you are lukewarm, and neither cold nor hot, I will spew you out of my mouth. For you say, I am rich, I have prospered, and I need nothing; not knowing that you are wretched, pitiable, poor, blind, and naked. Therefore I counsel you to buy from me gold refined by fire, that you may be rich, and white garments to clothe you and to keep the shame of your nakedness from being seen, and salve to anoint your eyes, that you may see. Those whom I love, I reprove and chasten; so be zealous and repent.

Revelation 3:15-19

Laodicean Christians had become lukewarm, He reminds them forcefully that their insipidity makes Him sick! When Christians become half-hearted and lack enthusiasm they evoke from the Lord a scathing rebuke. Christ despises listlessness and a half-heartedness that is based upon self-centred indifference. He demands commitment, and reminds us that neutrality is impossible.

Half-hearted people are hard to convince. They do not approve of the teaching of Christ and they are not against it. They have drifted into the church and continue to daydream through challenge after challenge. The lukewarm persons are disqualified from the full development of their spiritual gifts. Their achievement rating falls far below their ability. Sheer carelessness characterises their attitude to Christian service. Insipidity robs us of our winsomeness. Enthusiasts are attractive people, but the flabby repel. It is impossible for an insipid person to give leadership to normal people. Ordinary men and women, despite themselves, always follow an enthusiast.

The indispensable quality of the Christian life is a warm-hearted enthusiasm. Zeal burned within the heart of Jesus Christ. Young men were captivated by the fire in His soul. We can understand why people thought that this unwritten saying of Jesus could be true, 'He who is near me is near the fire.'

Laodicean Christians were self-sufficient. In their prosperity, they thought they needed nothing. The Lord commanded them to 'be zealous and repent'. To be zealous is to reach boiling point, the white-heat of true dedication. The 'wretched, pitiable, poor, blind and naked' have to recognise that they need everything that Christ offers them. High and holy zeal comes from the One who knocks at the door of the church. The painting depicts Christ knocking at the door. He has gold, refined by fire, the white garments and the eye-salve. Satan is represented by the serpent, the evil power finds it a comparatively easy task to take over the half-hearted church.

As the Lord knocks at the door of the church, He is the Suppliant asking for permission to enter. He waits and pleads and despite repeated refusals, He is not easily driven away. But the church must be impressed by her own responsibilities and dangers. The door must be opened from the inside and if it remains closed and barred, then the church is culpable of a terrible crime. The Lord does not force an entry; He awaits the church undoing the locks of indifference and self-righteousness, so that He may enter the church and enjoy fellowship.

Consider, then, the plea of verse 20

Behold I stand at the door and knock; if any one hears my voice and opens the door, I will come in to him and eat with him, and he with me.

But do not forget the promise of verse 21

He who conquers, I will grant him to sit with me on my throne, as I myself conquered and sat down with my Father on his throne.

Antagonist and adversary are conquered by the enthusiast for Christ. Disasters that seemed irretrievable, calamities that appeared as overwhelming as an avalanche are left behind by the victorious enthusiasm of the dedicated Christian.

He who has an ear, let him hear what the Spirit says to the churches.

Revelation 3:22

The Throne Of God

Chapter IV

Not many people see visions nowadays, and often those who do are not very greatly esteemed. They are regarded as lacking in practical value. They are demeaned in comparison with the men of prestige who let no blade of grass grow under their strenuous feet, and who are too keen and too energetic to miss a single golden chance of getting on. We must not underestimate these men of affairs. The world would lose its way and disintegrate without them. But it would be a prosaic and commonplace and sadly impoverished world if the others, the seers, the visionaries, were to disappear from it altogether.

Ezekiel the prophet, puts forward the claim, 'I saw visons of God'. John, in the Apocalypse claims, 'After this I looked, and lo, in heaven an open door!' (verse 1); 'And I saw in the right hand of him who was seated on the throne' (5:1); 'Now I saw when the Lamb opened one of the seven seals . . . ' (6:1); 'After this I saw four angels standing at the four corners of the earth' (7:1); 'Then I saw the seven angels who stand before God' (8:2); 'I saw a star fallen from heaven to earth' (9:1). Almost every chapter in the Apocalypse commences with 'I saw', 'I looked', etc.

Two things must be remembered when we speak about vision.

Firstly, it is necessary that the visions are high, holy, loving and beneficient. Ezekiel and John were exiles. Their visions of God inspired their hope and assured them that the Lord God continues to rule. When hatred attacks, it is a great consolation to have a vision of God's love and goodness.

Again, it is essential that obedience must succeed comtemplation, and activity must complete vision. So then, we must accept these two provisos – that our visions emanate from God and are approved by Him, and that we seek to translate them into act and fact.

THE VISION

John saw. He had a vision. W. Hendriksen points out, 'When a person has a vision, he may still be sensible to his surroundings'. Thus, for example, Stephen is fully aware of the presence of those evil men who are stoning him. In fact, he is addressing them while he has a vision of the heavens opened and the Son of man standing at the right hand of God. Similarly, the apostle John now has a vision. With wide-eyed wonder he beholds a door standing open in heaven. While he is looking, the same voice that spoke to him before in Revelation 1:10 addresses him. It is the voice of Christ, bidding him 'Come up here'. The seer's spirit receives the invitation to ascend to the throne above.

Access

Observe the spectacular teaching in these verses. First of all there is the open door, conveying the idea of access. This idea in the New Testament describes not our act but Christ's; not our coming, but his bringing us. This word was used of the introduction of an individual into the presence of a king.

Some people exist in a sealed compartment. God is cut off from them. They have no awareness of Him. There is no open door. No pleasure of access, no reality of divine power, no recognition of God. There is a tradition that Michelangelo, by his prolonged and unremitting toil upon the frescoed domes on which he worked, developed such a continual upturn of the head that, as he walked the streets, strangers observing his bearing considered him to be eccentric. We believe that in the beginning, God made man upright, both physically and morally. Some tell us that the derivation of *anthropos* - man - makes the word signify an 'uplooker'. Certainly, this originally constituted his marked distinction from the animals, that while they looked downwards towards the earth, he looked upward toward the heaven for which he was predestined. After sin came into the world, God asks the question, 'Why has your countenance fallen'? (Genesis 4:6).

Let us then look up, remembering that despite our circumstances, there is an open door, the door of access into the presence of the living God. God sets before every Christian his own door of opportunity.

Authority

Secondly, the throne conveys the idea of authority. We must never forget God's throne. Christians sing, 'God is still on the throne', and so He is! It was when John was in the Spirit that he saw the throne standing in heaven. Some Christians have lost sight of the reign of God because they are not in the spirit. The Revelation is essentially a book of the throne. The word *thronos* occurs in Revelation forty-five times, and only sixteen times in the rest of the New Testament. Instead of spending time on the 'locusts' or '666' let us think much of the throne. Chapter 4 is the throne chapter. All things are governed by the Lord of the throne. Remember - all things!

The throne is occupied - 'with one seated on the throne'. At that time, when Domitian was emperor, circumstances were so outwardly bad for the church that the harassed believer might have been excused if he had wondered whether the throne was occupied or not. There are times when God is silent, and faith is put to hard tests; but the answer to the doubt is just this - there was 'One sitting on the throne'. He has never vacated it. He still remains sovereign even when He is silent.

Let us remember the words of Psalm 2:1-4

Why do the nations conspire, and the peoples plot in vain? The kings of the earth set themselves, and the rulers take counsel together, against the Lord and against His anointed, saying, Let us burst their bonds asunder, and cast their cords from us. He who sits in the heavens laughs . . . '

Atmosphere

Thirdly, the stones and the colours convey the idea of atmosphere. John saw the One who occupied the throne, but John does not attempt to describe God in human shapes and forms. The Bible enjoins us to see God in the terms of light. Psalm 104:2 informs us that God covers Himself with light as a garment; and 1 Timothy 6:16 that God 'dwells in unapproachable light'. We are informed 'God is light'. What kind of light? John describes God in terms of brilliant colours of gemstones. There are three stones mentioned: jasper, carnelian and emerald. Each of these is represented in the chart conveying the multi-coloured symbolism of God's glory.

We know jasper as a dull opaque stone, but in the ancient world it seems to have been a translucent rock crystal. There are some who think that the stone mentioned here is the brilliant diamond, suggesting the transparent and flawless character of God, conjoined to a durability that symbolises everlastingness.

Carnelian was a blood-red stone. It speaks of a righteous wrath, a glowing red holiness that circumscribes God's unique person.

There was a rainbow round the throne, like unto an emerald. Strangely enough, it was a one-colour rainbow - not on this occasion of violet, blue, green, yellow, orange or red, but just one colour - green - an emerald halo. The ancients used expensive sunshades made of thin sheets of emerald, relieving the eyes from the effects of the strong eastern and tropical sunlight. Green is restful to the eyes: there is healing in the green of the trees and the fields. That is why some surgeons wear green gowns instead of white ones in the operating theatre, to relieve the glare. God's throne is rainbowed with green: once God's throne is seen in its true light, it is restful, reassuring, satisfying, comforting. The glare of God's righteousness is softened, for the throne is established in grace as well as truth. Majesty is tempered with mercy. None can gaze upon the naked glory of God. We can only see God through the rainbow of mercy.

These stones also take us back to the Old Testament and particularly to Exodus 28:17-20. It is significant that the carnelian is the first of the twelve stones, having the name of Reuben which means 'behold a son' and the last stone is jasper, having the name of Benjamin, 'the son of the right hand'. Combine the two meanings of the jewels associated with the throne - 'Behold a Son, the Son of my right hand' says God. This is even more fascinating when we realise that the emerald represents Judah, meaning praise! Where we have the mercy of God, we always have the praise of God's people.

We ought to be possessed with that faith which sees the sparkling colours of the God of Majesty. As we have seen His glory, there will be rainbows in our eyes, and these will cover every black cloud with gorgeous hues. No matter what the circumstance may be, we shall be enlightened by the colour associated with the throne of God and the being of God.

Plate No. 3

Administration

Fourthly, the elders convey the idea of administration.

Round the throne were twenty-four thrones, and seated on the thrones were twenty-four elders, clad in white garments, with golden crowns upon their heads.

Revelation 4:4

These twenty-four elders are represented on the chart by white rectangles. Scholars have suggested a number of ideas in an attempt to identify these twenty-four elders. We know that they are symbolic of something in the future.

Dr. William Hendriksen thinks that the twenty-four elders represent God's people of the old and new dispensation. We have, as it were, the twelve patriarchs of the Old Testament and the twelve apostles of the New Testament. In the Holy City, the New Jerusalem, the names of the twelve patriarchs are on the twelve gates and the names of the twelve apostles are on the foundation stones of the walls. The patriarchs and the apostles are the joint superstructure built upon the foundation of Jesus Christ, the Messiah and Saviour.

Dr William Barclay suggests that the most likely explanation of all is that the twenty-four elders are the symbolic representatives of the faithful people of God. This is similar to the former explanation; the difference between the two explanations is in definition. Hendriksen defines the twenty-four, Barclay takes them in a general way, embracing all the people of God.

The white robes are promised to the faithful (3:4). The crowns are those which are promised to those who are faithful unto death (2:10). The thrones are those which Jesus promised to those who forsook all and followed Him (Matthew 19:27-29).

Why twenty-four elders? Dr Ironside writes: 'When the twenty-four elders met in the temple precincts in Jerusalem, the whole priestly house was represented. The elders in heaven represent the whole heavenly priesthood. In vision they were seen not as an innumerable host of saved worshippers, but just twenty-four elders, symbolising the entire company.' In other words, the twenty-four elders represent the Church of Christ. The *parousia* has taken place, the Church is in heaven and will escape the Great Tribulation which commences in the seals of Revelation 6.

Action

Fifthly, the flashes of lightning, voices and peals of thunder convey the idea of action (verse 6). Throughout the Apocalypse are scattered a number of phrases which are related to each other, but which have no definite connection with concrete persons or objects. They are formulae which by their repetition show a sequence of thought and which mark out epochs in the unfolding drama of the book.

In Revelation 4:5 we have a general statement. It does not refer to any particular moment, but describes the awesome phenomena attending the manifestations of God. There are three other occasions, however, where flashes of lightning and peals of thunder relate to specific happenings.

From Revelation 8:5 we see that

the angel took the censer and filled it with fire from the altar and threw it on the earth; and there were peals of thunder, loud noises, flashes of lightning, and an earthquake.

This takes place at the end of the seventh seal.

Again, at the end of the seventh trumpet, Revelation 11:19 informs us

Then God's temple in heaven was opened, and the ark of his covenant was seen within his temple; and there were flashes of lightning, loud noises, peals of thunder, an earthquake and heavy hail.

At the end of the seventh bowl

And there were flashes of lightning, loud noises, peals of thunder, and a great earthquake such as had never been since men were on the earth, so great was that earthquake.

Revelation 16:18

Flashes of lightning are seen in the chart emerging from the throne of God. The Lord is never inactive, but is constantly involved in the fulfilment of His great purpose.

At the note of praise the twenty-four elders prostrated themselves in lowly adoration before the throne, again declaring God's timeless existence. Casting their crowns before the throne in token of homage and allegiance to Him, they acknowledged the matchless worth of their Lord and God, and ascribed glory, honour and power to Him.

The unreserved allegiance and whole-hearted tribute of the creatures were laid at the feet of the Almighty. J.N. Darby says, 'The living creatures only celebrate and declare; the elders worship with understanding. All through the Revelation, the elders give their reason for worshipping. There is spiritual intelligence in them.'

In verse 5b we are informed that 'before the throne burn seven torches of fire which are the seven spirits of God'. Here we have the

Godhead's burning flame. 'Our God is a consuming fire' is the challenging statement of Hebrews 12:29. The Lord states with authority 'I came to cast fire upon the earth' (Luke 12:49), and in Acts 2:3 when the Holy Spirit descended 'there appeared to them tongues as of fire'. The Godhead's fire of holiness is before the throne. Heaven's flame guarantees beautiful, stainless lives, without spot or wrinkle or any such thing. There is a celestial gleam before God's throne.

And there 'before the throne there is as it were a sea of glass, like crystal' (verse 6a), God's throne is peace. Its sea is transparent, still, never a storm to agitate its waters. The smooth translucent crystal reminds us that before God's throne the storms are ended, the battles have been fought. When we grasp the fact of the deep, unruffled peace of God's sea, then we realise that God is in control of every situation.

The Four Living Creatures
Now we consider verse 6b

And round the throne, on each side of the throne are four living creatures, full of eyes in front and behind.

In the Apocalypse two words are translated beast. One of them, *therion* means wild beast, and the other, *zoon* means living creature. The beings of Chapter 4 are personal creatures and servants of God, the highest of His creatures, the most honoured of His servants. *Theria* are evil individuals, systems or kingdoms. In each case the designation 'beast' is symbolical. Their four-fold appearance is described in much the same way as the cherubim in Ezekiel 1.

The suggestion that the creatures are full of eyes conveys the idea of perception. The multiplicity of eyes emphasises the extreme perfection of their insight. Associated with the concept of perception there is the associate idea of vigilance. The throne of God is secure. Around it there is a vigilance and a perception which is *par excellence*. We are baffled and perplexed because we lack the inspired insights of God's throne.

These four creatures are consistently represented in Scripture as associated with the judicial authority of God's throne. The number 4 is also commonly regarded as the number of material creation and particularly of the earth. Each of the creatures portrays one aspect of the character of God's judicial activity.

The Jewish rabbis believed and taught in the Talmud that there are four primary forms of life in God's creation. Man was considered the head of all creation; the ox was deemed the most important animal in domestic life; amongst the wild animal life the lion was considered supreme; finally, the eagle was considered supreme among the birds of heaven. Jewish teachers, explaining Numbers 2 believed that when the twelve tribes of Israel marched, they used the formation of four groups, each having three tribes. Each of the four sections had its own standard. Judah's standard was a lion; Reuben's standard was a man; Dan's standard was a flying eagle and Ephraim's standard was an ox.

In the New Testament we have four beautiful portraits of Jesus Christ which are usually called the four Gospels. Matthew presents Jesus as the King and the first gospel is usually represented by a lion. In Mark, Jesus is seen as the energetic and faithful servant of the Lord, symbolised by the ox. In Luke, we have enshrined the portrait of the human Jesus, the perfect man. John reveals the glory of Christ as the Son of God and the fourth gospel is usually represented by the eagle. Observe how the four living creatures around God's throne relate to the Old and New Testaments. The first resembled a lion which is the king of the beasts, symbolising the majesty and royal dignity of the Sovereign. The second was like an ox, representing the type of unwearying strength and patient endurance. The third had the face of a man, suggesting a sympathetic comprehension and intelligence. The fourth was a flying eagle, reminding us of keen vision and rapidity of action.

The chart represents these four creatures and Plate 4 emphasises the ox, indicating the relationship between the creatures of Revelation 4 and Ezekiel 1 by associating the animal with the wheel within a wheel, containing a multiplicity of eyes.

These marvellous beings declare unceasingly the holiness of the eternal God. God's holiness, His power, and His eternity are extolled in their song:

Holy, holy, holy, is the Lord God Almighty, who was and is and is to come!
Revelation 4:8

Never forget the three aspects of God's character which are emphasised in this song.

God's holiness reminds us that He is different from us. Dr William Barclay states, 'If God were like us, if He were simply an outsize and glorified human person, we could not praise . . . The very mystery of God, the very difference of God, moves us to awed admiration of His presence, and to amazed love that that greatness should stoop so low for us men and for our salvation.'

God's omnipotence teaches that He is greater than scientific power; nuclear explosions cannot make His throne tremble. Political

Plate No. 4

philosophers never afflict the Lord with agitated concern. His power is beyond dispute, it brooks no rival.

God's everlastingness is the recurring theme of the Bible: 'Kingdoms may rise, Kingdoms may fall, but the Word of the Lord endures for evermore'. Men might try to obliterate faith in God, but they can never obliterate God! God lasts!

THE WORSHIP OF THE UNIVERSE

And whenever the living creatures give glory and honour and thanks to Him who is seated on the throne, who lives for ever and ever, the twenty-four elders fall down before Him who is seated on the throne and worship Him who lives for ever and ever; they cast their crowns before the throne, singing, 'Worthy art thou, our Lord and God, to receive glory and honour and power, for thou didst create all things, and by thy will they existed and were created.

These verses give an amazing scene of an adoring universe ascribing its worship to Almighty God.

The chart relates to the adoring myriads by representing angelic beings in the circle of golden dots and the rest of the universe in the outer white circle.

The seer's earth is crammed with heaven. God's throne has become accessible to him. What John has been permitted to see takes him into the future and what he observes occurs at a crisis and a climax. The crisis will take place on earth as we shall see as we study the Apocalypse. The climax deals with the Church, now in heaven around God's throne. In every crisis and at every climax God acts. God is on the move. There is nothing static about the divine person. God moves in a mysterious way His wonders to perform. In Genesis 1, the Spirit moves upon the face of the deep. In 2 Peter, holy men of God spoke as they were moved by God. The mobility of God is an indisputable teaching of the Bible. As we anticipate the adoration of a wondering universe, we are mindful of a glorious past, thankful in the brightened present and hopeful for the disclosed future.

The Lion and the Lamb

Chapter V

John, the great visionary, bursts out with a radiant certainty, for he has heard the burst of praise and now sees the occupant of the throne. The throne itself would be of little consequence unless we know the One who occupies it. John knows that God is on the throne, so despite the fact that he is in a concentration camp he can say with the psalmist, 'This I know, that God is for me' (Psalm 56:9). He knows that God is. He had seen evidences of God in the silence of the templed hills, in the shimmering song of the brook, in the silver light of the stars. But external evidences did not satisfy. This man has a personal experience of God.

John knew that God cares. He came to realise through his own personal experience that God loved him individually. Life can never be the same to one who knows in his heart and realises in the inner deeps of his soul that God loves and cares, not simply for the world, but for him personally.

John discovered, not only that God cares, but that He is working on his behalf. He is seeking in every way within His power to bring him to his finest self and to his highest possibilities. This is not a promise of a road always made soft by a carpet of flowers. He did not protect him from every rude wind. On the contrary, his road was at times heartbreaking, rough and rugged. He knew what it was to pass sleepless nights. But he was convinced that God was working for his enrichment, not only in spite of all his difficulties, but even through them. In this part of the Apocalypse John's tears are being kissed into jewels.

We observe four main features in these verses before us.

The Profound Scroll

And I saw in the right hand of him who was seated on the throne a scroll written within and on the back, sealed with seven seals;

Revelation 5:1

Associated with God's throne there is a book or a scroll. Let us focus our attention upon this book. It is in God's right hand, that is, whatever the book contains, God's sovereign power controls it. It is written on both sides, which suggests that the book is entire, and there is no space for anything to be added. It was sealed with seven seals. This may indicate one of three things:

When a roll was completed it was held together with threads, and the threads were tied in knots and sealed. The common document that was sealed with seven seals was a will. Under Roman law the seven witnesses to a will sealed it with their seven seals, and it could only be opened when all seven, or their legal representatives were present. The roll may be what we might describe as God's will and testament, reminding us that God with sovereign power uses His prerogative to settle all the affairs of the universe.

It has been suggested that the scroll is a deed of purchase, and is the evidence of the Redeemer's sealed title deeds, His claim to His purchased people, His rights to His redeemed. That would demand more attention if the book closed at the end of Chapter 5, but with the opening of the seals and the revealing of the contents, the answer must be otherwise.

The other good suggestion is that it is the Book of Prophecy, or the Book of Destiny. But it would seem that the book is a comprehensive one, because it seems to contain past history as well as future prophecy. Prophecy is just history before it happens in time, and history is His story. God sees the end from the beginning; the scroll of history, explaining the past, enlightening the present and expounding the future, is in the hands of God.

Apart from God's gracious disclosure and majestic purpose, there can be no real explanation of the universe, no adequate interpretation of history, no elucidation as to where we have come from and where we are going to. God's scroll and God's Lamb help us to understand that the past, present and future are under divine control.

The Provocative Suggestion
The strong angel proclaimed with a loud voice:

Who is worthy to open the scroll and break its seals?

And no one in heaven or on earth was able to open the scroll and break its seals.
Revelation 5:2-3

This is the perplexing situation that exists today. Who is worthy? Who has the ability? Who has the integrity? Is there someone whom we can trust? Many people have slipped into deep depression because in their experience of life they have discovered that people are not dependable. Peter said, 'Lord to whom shall we go? You have the words of eternal life' (John 6:68).

Remember the recommendation of the Lord to the church in Sardis.

Yet you have still a few names in Sardis, people who have not soiled their garments; and they shall walk with me in white, for they are worthy.

Revelation 3:4

There are people who are worthy. They are true Christians. People who are resolute in faith, strong in courage, unwavering in endurance. When Satan attempts to discourage us through the actions of someone who is rude, critical, selfish and immature in the Christian church, we can immediately turn to others who are Christ-like, considerate and dependable, their lives focused on God. The way some folk talk, you would conclude that there are no worthy Christians. Banish the thought! God always has His people. There are always 7,000 who have not bowed the knee to Baal. Never allow the Evil One to depress us; if that happens, then we will have the experience of John.

The Perturbed Servant

. . . and I wept much that no one was found worthy to open the scroll or to look into it.

Revelation 5:4

John sheds tears. The Bible teaches him, and us, that tears are transient. Psalm 30:5 reminds us, 'Weeping may endure for a night, but joy comes in the morning'. We need the faith of the psalmist. He is daring to tell us that in this world of change and decay, in this world where our hearts are so often broken and our faces so often wet with tears, that joy may be a more abiding guest than sorrow. He does not promise exemption from sorrow. He makes no claim to the discovery of an ideal world. But what he does say is that while weeping may come in as a wayfarer and spend the night, that the unwelcome guest need not abide, that he need not establish himself upon our shoulders like an old-man-of-the-sea. He may remain for the night, but he cannot abide the dawning of the day. Tears may come, but they will be transient. With the rising of the sun they will vanish like the dew or be kissed into jewels by its splendour.

The Powerful Sovereign

'Then one of the elders said to me, 'Weep not; lo, the Lion of the tribe of Judah, the Root of David, has conquered, so that he can open the scroll and its seven seals'.

Revelation 5:5

The only person who is capable of fulfilling the purpose of God and who can execute perfectly His judgments is the Lord Jesus Christ. He is the Lion of the tribe of Judah. This title is taken from the blessing of Jacob, which Jacob bestowed on his sons just before his death

Judah, your brothers shall praise you; your hand shall be on the neck of your enemies; your father's sons shall bow down before you. Judah is a lion's whelp; from the prey, my son, you have gone up. He stooped down, he couched as a lion, and as a lioness; who dares rouse him up? The sceptre shall not depart from Judah, nor the ruler's staff from between his feet, until he comes to whom it belongs; and to him shall be the obedience of the peoples'.

Genesis 49:8-10

These verses describe Judah gaining prestige over his brethren. The sceptre and the staff are given to him because he is the ruler of the tribes. The prophecy was partially fulfilled when the Davidic dynasty came to power. David, as a member of the tribe of Judah, was anointed king over all Israel, and to him and to his posterity the promise of kingship was confirmed by God. The Gospel of Matthew introduces his genealogy by designating Jesus as the Son of David. He is heir to the throne of Israel and is the rightful ruler of the kingdom that God promised to His people. As the lion is the king of beasts, the embodiment of courage and strength, so Christ is the King of nations by divine appointment.

The second title, Root of David, is taken from a prophecy in Isaiah

There shall come forth a shoot from the stump of Jesse, and a branch shall grow out of his roots. And the Spirit of the Lord shall rest upon him, the spirit of wisdom and understanding, the spirit of counsel and might, the spirit of knowledge and the fear of the Lord. And his delight shall be in the fear of the Lord. He shall not judge by what his eyes see, or decide by what his ears hear; but with righteousness he shall judge the poor, and decide with equity for the meek of the earth; and he shall smite the earth with the rod of his mouth, and with the breath of his lips he shall slay the wicked.

Isaiah 11:1-4

The picture drawn by the prophecy is that of a tree which has been cut down, leaving only a stump rotting in the ground. Out of the stump, however, is growing a healthy young shoot in which the life of the tree is renewed, and which will in time restore its original glory.

Dr. Merrill C. Tenney reminds us of the political and historical background of this passage from Isaiah which assists us to understand its meaning. 'The preceding chapter describes the Assyrian invasion which devastated the northern kingdom of Israel and threatened the safety of the southern kingdom of Judah. The prophet indicated that the peril was a warning of more severe judgments to come, and that Jehovah would ultimately destroy the kingdoms of the land, including Judah. As the trees of the forest fell before the axe of the woodsman, so Judah would fall in judgment. Although the royal house of Judah as a ruling power perished in Babylonian captivity, the Messiah, or the 'Branch' as He is called in the prophecies, will yet come to restore its authority over His people. Our passage in Revelation 5:5 indicates by use of this phrase, 'the Root of David', that Christ, the ruler of the kings of the earth, is the lawful and lineal successor of David, who will restore the kingdom that has been destroyed by judgment.' Let us remember the words of the true Messiah:

'My kingdom is not of this world' (John 19:36). This kingdom is the Kingdom of God; its constituency are those who are 'born of God', and 'born from above'. True, this kingdom is now in the world in its rudiments and principles, in its citizens and representatives: those who, like their Lord, have been sent to accomplish the work of gathering out a people for His name. But, lest we fall into fatal error, let us not imagine that we are now reigning with Christ on earth, or that the Kingdom of God has been set up in the world. The Church's earthly career during the present age is the exact facsimile of her Lord's — a career of exile rather than of exaltation; of rejection rather than of rule; of cross-bearing rather than of sceptre-bearing. Grasping of earthly sovereignty for the Church while the Sovereign Himself is still absent has proved, as we should know, the most fruitful root of apostasy. We look forward to that day when the kingdoms of this world shall become the Kingdom of our God and His Christ and He shall reign for ever and ever.

THE GLORY OF THE LAMB OF GOD   Revelation 5:6-14

In the Acts of the Apostles there are recorded some of the exploits of the Apostle Paul. On one occasion when Paul was staying for a short time in Troas, a vision appeared to him in the night: 'There was a man of Macedonia standing beseeching him and saying, "Come over to Macedonia and help us" ' (Acts 16:9). Paul and his associates obeyed the vision, but when they moved into the West they found a woman, Lydia, who became the first convert in Europe. He saw a man in the vision, but when he saw in reality, there was an enterprising business-woman.

In Matthew 14 we read of how the disciples were caught in the teeth of a storm. They were terror-stricken. Jesus walked towards them on the water, but they were agitated and thought that He was an apparition, but immediately Jesus spoke they knew it was the Lord.

The passage before us says

Lo, the Lion of the tribe of Judah . . . I saw a lamb standing, as though it had been slain.

'Look, there is the lion!' But when the Seer looked up he saw the lamb. And instead of a lion, they saw a lamb. No contrast could be more absolute and startling than that between the Christ of Jewish expectation and the Christ of history. Instead of a prince coming from some royal palace they saw a carpenter from Nazareth. Instead of a person dressed in royal purple they saw a man in a seamless robe. Instead of one attended by a large retinue and with unlimited resources of command, they saw One who had nowhere to lay His head. Instead of a great commander giving His command to thousands, they saw one who did not strive, nor cry, nor lift up His voice in the streets. Instead of a soldier, they saw a preacher. Instead of a great warrior who summoned them out to fight against the oppressor they saw One who Himself was led like a lamb to the slaughter, and as a sheep before her shearers is dumb, so He opened not His mouth. Instead of a lion, a strong victorious lion, they saw a meek, gentle and suffering Lamb.

Observe the majesty of the Lamb. We speak about the majesty of the lion and the meekness of the lamb, but we shall speak about the majesty of the Lamb. Why? Because this is the most important symbol, not in the Apocalypse only, but in the whole Bible. Two words are used in the New Testament for lamb – *amnos* and *arnion*. The latter word is a diminutive and means lambkin or little lamb, and it is this word that is used on twenty-nine occasions in the Apocalypse, and nowhere else. The other word, *amnos*, is used twice in the fourth Gospel (John 1:29,36) and once in 1 Peter 1:19, so that in the New Testament, John, with the exception of the one reference by Peter, uses the designation 'Lamb' of Christ. The idea derives from Genesis 22:7-8 and Isaiah 53:7 which is related to God's plan of salvation, and Dr W. Graham Scroggie has reminded us that the most terrible phrase in all languages is 'the wrath of the little Lamb'.

There are three descriptive terms used of the Lamb. First, John sees the Lamb 'as though it had been slain'. The word slain means literally slaughtered, with its throat cut. It is used in Chapter 6:9 to describe those who were martyred for the witness of Jesus. In heaven, the Lamb bears the marks of humiliation. Fred Mitchell, who was a well-known Keswick speaker, related a great problem which faced him as a young worker for Christ in the poorer parts of a North of England city. Often visiting in poor homes and seeing children born to become the inheritors of disease and debt and sin, doubts arose in his mind as to the love and wisdom of God. Was it right that He should permit them to be born? The problem became acute and threatened his faith, until he happened to read a volume by an American theologian, Dr Henry Noble. This book, *Under the Redeeming Aegis*, steadied his faith and gave him mental peace and spiritual realisation. It reminded him that the Cross antedated the Creation. He had got the order wrong. He had been reading history like this: the Creation, the Fall and the Atonement; when really in the counsels of God, it is the Atonement first, then the Creation and then the Fall. He was slain before the foundation of the world. Salvation was provided before sin occurred; sin with all its consequences was fully anticipated, and because of this, though men and women are born into a fallen world, the eternal sacrifice makes it possible for them to be born a second time under a Covenant of Grace.

Secondly, the Lamb has seven horns. The horn is used in the Bible as a symbol of power, strength, honour and grandeur. Sometimes it is a good power, and sometimes an evil power. Sometimes it refers to the strength of a nation, other times to the ruler of a nation. Sometimes it refers to a position of elegance and popularity with pride.

A few passages from Revelation will help us to understand the significance of the symbolism. In 12:3 the figure represents Satan and his mighty power in controlling men. In 13:1 we have represented Satan's Antichrist who will have power over the nations. In 13:11 the type represents the false prophet. In 17:3-12 we have the evil powers of the world as represented in the ten kings.

The Lamb has seven horns. Seven, as we have noticed, represents perfection. The horns symbolise power. In the Lamb there is the wonderful combination of perfection and power. Some years ago Lord Acton said: 'All power corrupts; absolute power corrupts absolutely'. The mention of certain names in power-politics would be sufficient to prove this statement. But Christians would claim, 'Of men, this is true; but of one man it is not true'. There is one man whom power did not corrupt. He sought nothing for Himself, and He could be trusted with the interests of the others. The hands that were pierced refused power from wrong hands and for wrong purposes, and He could hold all power without fear.

Dr William Barclay reminds us, 'Here is the great paradox; the Lamb bears the sacrificial wounds upon it; but at the same time it is clothed with the very might of God which can now shatter and break its enemies'.

Thirdly, the Lamb has seven eyes. This picture (Plate 5) may seem to be grotesque, or, to use a word which seems to be on the tongue of every commentator, traumatic; that is to say, it comes with a violence that shocks the nervous system and shatters normal thinking patterns. That is why the chart, and Plate 5, present the Lamb in an abstract form. Perhaps John's vision came from God to him in an abstract form! Who can tell?

In Zechariah 4:10 we read that the seven lamps 'are the eyes of the Lord, which run to and fro through the whole of the earth'. They represent the all-seeing omniscience of God.

Let us take the three descriptive terms together. As the Lamb slain, there is the idea of perfect redemption, the seven horns symbolise perfect strength; the seven eyes convey the idea of perfect perception. Alexander MacLaren preached, 'Remember it is the slain Lamb that gives the Spirit . . . A maimed Christianity that has a Christ, but no slain Lamb, has little of the Spirit'.

The Meekness of the Elders

And when he had taken the scroll, the four living creatures and the twenty-four elders fell down before the Lamb, each holding a harp, and with golden bowls full of incense, which are the prayers of the saints;

Revelation 5:8

Notice that they fell down before the Lamb (verse 8). This is a further evidence of the deity of Christ. God the Father, God the Son – the Lamb, and God the Holy Spirit. The Apocalypse provides irrefragable evidence concerning the deity of Jesus Christ; for example in Revelation 1:8 He is God and the Almighty; in 3:14 He is the Amen or True One; in 15:4 the Lord; in 16:5 the Holy One; and in 19:13 the Word of God.

It is not idolatry to worship the Lord Jesus Christ. There is the equality of the Son with the Father and we should therefore worship Him who is here revealed.

The picture of the elders is interesting. They have harps. In the

Plate No. 5

tradition of the Jews, the harp was the instrument to which the psalms were sung – 'Praise the Lord with harp' (Psalm 33:2); 'sing praise upon the harp unto our God' (Psalm 147:7).

Golden bowls full of incense. Here is a wonderful thought – prayer on earth is incense in heaven. The bowls full of incense are the prayers of the saints. Once again we find ourselves back in the book of the Psalms – 'Let my prayer be counted as incense before thee (Psalm 141: 2). Let us set this truth in the routine of everyday living. Here is an old person who has given his energetic service for the Lord; now the body is weakened, robust activities are impossible, but the faithful veteran takes time to pray. Observe the wonderful situation. An elderly, lonely person prays and that prayer brings fragrance to heaven.

As evangelicals, we have claimed that when a sinner repents there is rejoicing in heaven, but we have forgotten that when a saint prays there is fragrance in heaven. This concept helps us to banish the theme of selfishness which normally characterises our personal prayers. How long has it been since you talked with the Lord and told Him about your troubles? Remember, prayer is a fragrant ministry.

The Music of the Myriads

And they sang a new song, saying, 'Worthy art thou to take the scroll and to open its seals, for thou wast slain and by thy blood didst ransom men for God from every tribe and tongue and people and nation, and hast made them a kingdom and priests to our God, and they shall reign on earth'.

Revelation 5:9-10

Christian Rossetti said, 'Heaven is revealed to earth as the homeland of music'. Dr Harry Whitley of Edinburgh relates his experience when he met the late Professor Karl Barth, one of the great theologians of the Christian Church. Barth said, 'Heaven will be a place filled with music. On Sundays, high days and holy days heaven will be filled with the music of Bach, but on weekdays we shall listen to Mozart'. Karl Barth was entitled to his opinion, but I have the impression that both Bach and Mozart will be outclassed by the musical genius of heaven.

As we analyse this great chorus, notice that there are three movements of praise. First, there is the praise of the four living creatures and the twenty-four elders. Here we see all nature and all the Church combining to praise the Lamb. Second, there is the praise of the myriads of angels, all singing praise to the Lamb. Third, he sees every creature, in every part of the universe, to its deepest depth and its widest circle and its farthest corner, singing in praise.

This innumerable choir sings a new song. The Apocalypse is characterised with 'new things'. There is the new name (2:17 and 3:12); there is the New Jerusalem (3:12 and 21:2); there is the new song (5:9 and 14:3); there are the new heavens and the new earth (21:1); and there is the breath-taking promise that God makes all things new (21:5).

The Greek language has two words for new. There is *neos*, which means new in point of time, but not necessarily new in point of quality. A new thing which is *neos* is a thing which has recently been produced; but it may be only a new sample of a kind of thing which has been in existence for a long time. There is *kainos*, which means new in point of quality. *Kainos* describes a thing which has not only been recently produced; it describes a thing the like of which has never existed before.

The importance of this is that Jesus Christ brings into life a new dimension and quality that has never existed before. He brings into life a new joy, a new thrill, a new strength, a new peace. Something begins to appear in the world and in life which Christless eyes have never seen and never can see.

Amid the discords of this life, it is an encouragement to think of heaven, where God draws after Him an everlasting train of music; for all thoughts are harmonious and all feelings vocal, and so there is round about His feet eternal melody. So, then, if your life has been discordant, get tuned into the majestic melody of heaven. Here is a spiritual uplift which shall have the value of tonic in your Christian experience.

In a day of deteriorating standards in Christian music, we ought to remember the Biblical exhortation found in Ephesians 5:18-19 —

'be filled with the Spirit, addressing one another in psalms and hymns and spiritual songs, singing and making melody to the Lord with all your heart'.

This means that church music must be actuated by the Spirit of God. When the Holy Spirit is ungrieved in the believer's life, there is both a restraining and constraining influence on all acts of worship and witness.

Furthermore, church music must be controlled by the Word of God.

Let the word of Christ dwell in you richly, as you teach and admonish one another in all wisdom, and as you sing psalms and hymns and spiritual songs with thankfulness in your hearts to God.

Colossians 3:16

In an age when the church seems to have majored on noise and irreverencies, we must constantly remind ourselves that there can be no true praise without sound spiritual perception.

Then, again, church music must be motivated by the glory of God.

Whatever you do, do all to the glory of God.

1 Corinthians 10:31

Since 'glory' (*doxa* in the Greek from which derives the word doxology) is the outshining of God's character, it follows that only music inspired by the Holy Spirit can honour the Lamb of God.

Examine the music and message of Revelation 5 in the light of Ephesians 5 and Colossians 3.

In 5:9-10 the four living creatures and the twenty-four elders sound the important theological notes that should appear in Christian praise.

The Note of Redemption. Our Lord died to fulfil the purpose of God. The object of that death was to restore that lost relationship between God and men. Christ died for our sins. People who attempt to expunge the death of Christ from theology cannot sing the new song, they are imperfect in their praise. If more Christians attended the Communion Service, there would be more song in their Christian experience!

The Note of Regeneration

[Ransomed] — from every tribe and tongue and people and nation, and hast made them a kingdom and priests to our God . . .

From time to time we have been shocked by the fruits of wrong relationships in our own country and in our own community. But we believe that men and women can be made anew, that is, born again by the power of the Holy Spirit.

The Note of Rule

And they shall reign on the earth.

The Christian's song is associated with triumph. His is the victory! 'This is not political triumph or material lordship. It is the secret of victorious living under any circumstances. In Christ there is victory over self, over circumstances, and over sin'.

An innumerable company of angels take up the praise of the Lamb. There is a seven-fold ascription of praise. These qualities belong to Jesus Christ. We have noticed that seven is the symbol of completion or perfection.

The Power. Christ is the power of God. All men seek power, but only one person has the incomparable power of God. Christ is the perfect expression of God's power.

The Riches. There is an infinite expression in the Bible which speaks of 'the unsearchable riches of Christ'. He is the multi-millionaire of this universe, but His riches are mainly spiritual. He has the resources to meet every circumstance.

The Wisdom. Christ is the wisdom of God. The Saviour has the insights and foresights of the purposes of God.

The Strength. Christ's power can assist the weakest sinner. That strength can raise the fallen sinner, resist and defeat the onslaughts of Satan. It is the believer's privilege to take up the words of Philippians 4:13 – 'I can do all things through Christ who strengthens me'.

The Honour. The One who is enthroned in the heavens deserves to be enthroned in the hearts of men.

The Glory. 'We beheld his glory, glory as of the only son from the Father, full of grace and truth' (John 1:14). Someone has put forward this definition, 'Glory is that which by right belongs to God and to God alone'. To say that Jesus possesses the glory is to do nothing less than to say that He is divine and He shares the rights and privileges of God.

The Blessing. Here is the culmination of it all. To Him belongs the blessing, – How can we give anything to Him that possesses all?

We have noticed that the heavenly praise has a seven-fold theme speaking of complete perfection. Now we listen to the third wave of music which involves all creation:

I heard every creature in heaven and on earth and under the earth and in the sea, and all therein.

It is significant that creation's praise is four-fold; four is the symbolic number that is representative of all creation.

To him who sits upon the throne and to the Lamb be blessing and honour and glory and might for ever and ever.

S. D. Gordon, many years ago, encouraged the Keswick Convention to study the choruses of Revelation. In Chapter 1 there is a solo from John himself on a major key –

To him who loves us and has freed us from our sins by his blood and made us a kingdom, priests to his God and Father, to him be glory and dominion for ever and ever.

But very quickly the soloist is joined by a quartet, that is the four living creatures of Chapter 4. The soloist and the quartet set the scene for the sextuple quartet, the twenty-four elders as presented in Chapter 5. An angel chorus is inspired by the sextuple quartet, and myriads and myriads take up the theme of praise. Eventually, creation changes from the minor to the major key and universe appears to be a music room. Chapters 7 and 14 present the martyrs' song and the virgins' chorus. The Apocalypse is a book of songfulness and we have a new song. No composer can estimate its value, no instrument can play its harmony, no voice can pronounce its beauty, no modulator can convey its height or its depth; this song is arranged to please the ear of God. At conversion, the Holy Spirit placed in our hearts a seed of celestial praise; in our Christian experience that seed germinates and grows, but it will not reach its fruition until that day when we stand in the presence of the Lamb.

And the four living creatures said, 'Amen!' and the elders fell down and worshipped.

Let us do likewise!

Chapter VI

In Chapter 1 of Revelation we saw the dazzling portrait of Jesus Christ. The seven churches of Chapters 2 and 3 alerted us to the fact that the Lord observes the spiritual condition of the seven churches, challenging and comforting them as the need arises. From Chapters 4 and 5 we have caught a vision of the throne and the Lamb of God.

It is our belief that the *parousia* has taken place at the commencement of Chapter 4, so that the Church is seen in heaven, represented by the twenty-four elders. Many Christians speak about the rapture of the Church, instead of the *parousia*, preferring the former Latin word to the latter Greek one. *Parousia* means both an arrival and a consequent presence. Rapture derives from the Latin word *raptus*, meaning to seize by force. The strength behind this word is seen in 1 Thessalonians 4:17

Then we who are alive, who are left, shall be caught up together with them in the clouds to meet the Lord in the air; and so we shall always be with the Lord.

The Greek word *harpazo* means to snatch away and is translated 'caught up' in the text of 1 Thessalonians 4:17. So then, when we speak about Christ coming for the Church, we are saying that His arrival and consequent presence has taken place and that the believers have been 'raptured' or snatched away.

After the Church has been 'raptured', a time of trouble will take place upon the planet earth. Our Lord's words will help us here:

For then there will be great tribulation, such as has not been from the beginning of the world until now, no, and never will be.

Matthew 24:21

Revelation 6-18 describes the Tribulation and there is no mention of the Church in this large section of Scripture, so, we believe this chapter relates to the Tribulation period and that the Church will be delivered from the Great Tribulation that is to come upon the earth.

Before we deal with the significance of the 'seven seals' it is essential for us to consider the different schools of interpretation which are related to the Revelation. They fall mainly into four groups.

The Praeterist View

This view maintains that the Apocalypse is an outline of the conditions of the Roman Empire in the first century, written by some Hebrew Christian who refused to submit to pagan tyranny. It is true that there are historical situations mentioned in the Apocalypse, especially with regard to the seven churches, but the praeterist view fails to deal with the content of the programme of the Apocalypse that is futuristic. For example, the praeterist view identifies the seven kings of Revelation 17:10 with the Roman Emperors Augustus, Tiberius, Caligula, Claudius, Nero, Galba and Otho. This view does not accept the predictive element in the Apocalypse.

The Historicist View

Sometimes called the continuous historical view, this view contends that 'the Apocalypse is a symbolic presentation of the entire course of the history of the Church from the close of the first century to the end of time'. The argument for the view is founded on the fact that two termini are mentioned: the day in which John the Seer lived, and the ultimate day of God's victory and the establishment of the Holy City.

No point between them can be identified with certainty as making a break in the sequence; therefore the process must be continuous. So they see in the Apocalypse the Goths, the Turks, and the Moslem Hordes. For example, if we accept this interpretation, the seven seals belong to the history of the Roman Empire during the second and third centuries. It should be said that this interpretation demands a highly educated reader and that many who hold this view are hopelessly in disagreement.

The Idealist View

This maintains that the Apocalypse represents the eternal conflict of good and evil which persists in every age, although here it may have particular application to the period of the Church. The symbols are set aside as having no immediate historic connection with any definite social or political events.

Dr. Merrill C. Tenney presents the following analysis of this view. 'There are five propositions which sum up the chief message of the book:

a.   It is an irresistible summons to heroic living.
b.   The book contains matchless appeals to endurance.
c.   It tells us that evil is marked for overthrow in the end.
d.   It gives us a new and wonderful picture of Christ.
e.   The Apocalypse reveals to us the fact that history is in the mind of God and in the hand of Christ as the author and reviewer of the mind!'

The idealist view has an attraction for Christians of all ages because they are aware of the spiritual conflict that is taking place. Its weakness is not so much in what it affirms as in what it denies. This view refuses to accept the biblical fact of predictive prophecy.

The Futurist View

Those who hold this view generally believe that all the visions from Revelation 4:1 to the end of the book are yet to be fulfilled in the period immediately preceding and following the second advent of Christ. Revelation 1:19 suggests a two-fold command — now write what is and what is to take place hereafter. Revelation 4:1 identifies the future visions as beginning at that point.

Dr. W. Graham Scroggie suggested that we may use an analogy, viewing the Apocalypse like a plant — 'It has a root - the past; a stem - the present; and a blossom - the future; and no one part of the plant is the plant. There is not only an element of truth in every responsible theory but also a subtle error. Comprehensiveness is safer than exclusiveness, and integration is sounder than disintegration. Relating to this Book, he who is praeterist, historicist and futurist is most likely to understand it.'

We shall be following the futurist view although it should be noted that this theory is open to elaborate systems which bring imbalance into the Christian's doctrine and experience. The futurist view helps us to get heaven's view of all events on earth. This is a world of storm-tossed souls, but those who hear and obey the prophetic voice of the Lord can face the storm with a victorious fortitude. The future is in God's hands. Nothing can move Him. Our destiny is secure!

In Revelation 6 the voice of thunder says, 'Come!' The Lamb had taken the book from the hand of the Almighty and standing in the middle of the throne and the vast assembled company, He began to unloose the seals and to reveal the dreadful contents of the scroll of God's purposes.

THE FIRST SEAL - THE WHITE HORSE

And I saw, and behold a white horse, and its rider had a bow; and a crown was given to him, and he went out conquering and to conquer.

Revelation 6:2

Is the first horseman a religious counterfeit? Some commentators have suggested that the rider on the white horse is Christ. They say that this symbolism represents Christ issuing forth in grace. This exegesis is faulty. 'The Apocalypse must be interpreted in consistency with itself, and this seal is not intended to describe the patient ministrations of God in grace, but the enforcement of His will by power'.

Others identify the rider on the white horse with the victorious Christ of Revelation 19:11-12 which tells of a white horse and on it a rider who is called Faithful and True, and who is crowned with many crowns. It is to be noted that the crown in the first seal is different from the crown in Revelation 19. Here the Greek word for crown is *stephenos* which is the victor's crown; in Revelation 19 the crown is *diadema* which is the royal crown. Moreover Revelation 6 describes one disaster after another and any picture of the risen and victorious Christ in it is inappropriate. This picture tells not of the coming of the victor Christ, but of the coming of the judgment of the wrath of God.

In Plate 6 we have the artist's impression of the Antichrist upon the white horse. The painting is suggesting that the impersonation of the true Christ is not a good one. It takes the expert eye to distinguish between reality and counterfeit. Those who have spiritual discernment find it difficult, if not impossible, to accept that this horseman is the true Christ.

This first seal seems to represent the principle of counterfeit religion supported by military force. When the Church has gone, ie been taken to heaven by the Lord, then a counterfeit religion backed by military power will be ready to take its place.

Some scholars believe that the rider on the white horse is the European Antichrist — the master statesman and charismatic character who will deceive many — but it is not possible to identify the rider with certainty.

Plate No. 6

Plate No. 7

THE SECOND SEAL — THE RED HORSE

And out came another horse, bright red; its rider was permitted to take peace from the earth, so that men should slay one another, and he was given a great sword.'

Revelation 6:4

Does this represent political strife? Human relationship is a precious blessing. The complete disintegration of all human relationships is a dark tragedy. One of the visions of the end of time conveys the picture of human relationships being destroyed in a seething cauldron of embittered hate.

No nation can afford a civil war. Political strife that issues in bloodshed wounds society, sometimes with a death blow, but let us never forget that when this power, symbolised by the red horse, is let loose, it will be given permission to take peace from the earth. In other words, this is a judgment of God upon the planet from which He has taken His Church.

It is not hard to guess which political philosophy is symbolised by the red horse. The political power must be international; it is essential for this strange power to be represented in all the nations of the earth. Communism aims at political domination and the conquest of the world, based on revolution. The red horse in Plate 7 is presented as an almost perfect animal. The equestrian is strong with ambition and determination to conquer.

THE THIRD SEAL — THE BLACK HORSE

And I saw, and behold, a black horse and its rider had a balance in his hand; and I heard what seemed to be a voice in the midst of the four living creatures saying, 'A quart of wheat for a denarius, and three quarts of barley for a denarius; but do not harm oil and wine'

Revelation 6:5-6

Is this a symbol of world famine? Black is the colour of mourning, but it also symbolises death and famine. The balance in the hand of the rider confirms the scarcity of food. According to the Old Testament, if food is measured or weighed, it denotes a shortage. Many people in the West find it difficult to accept that famine is a grim reality in other parts of the world.

The three main products of Palestine were corn, wine and oil, and it is these three which are always mentioned when the fruit and the crops of the land are being described. From the measures and the prices mentioned, it has been calculated that the cost of living had gone up 800 per cent. Here we have iniquitous inflation. We may conclude that some of the signs and events leading up to the end time will involve a tremendous increase in the cost of the necessities of life; a calculation from the narrative envisages a situation in which a man will use all of his wages to purchase a meagre food supply for his family.

It is interesting to note that oil and wine are not included in this third judgment. These were considered the rich man's luxuries, and it would seem that some people have manipulated a situation in which their luxuries were to remain intact, creating the situation that engenders class hatred and instigates civil war.

An analogy from the experience of mice may help us to understand the prophetic realities involved in the judgment of the black horse. Some experts see a parallel between rodent explosions and the social consequences of the human population explosion. In the history of Europe there have been occasions when mice have appeared in such incalculable numbers that complete crops have disappeared overnight. The cessation of the mice plague is always sudden. Apparently at the climax, there is a shortage of food which leads to tension, anxiety, fighting, cannibalism and disease. The decline is so swift that the plague terminates in an astronomical death rate.

Examine the horse in Plate 8. It does not look as strong as the red horse. It is predicting a famine that will have an effect on the animal kingdom, but it also reminds us that what happened to the mice will be the experience of the human race when men and women are too many and the food supplies too few. Pollution and population explosion are considered by the experts to be among the greatest problems which confront mankind. Solutions are being sought to these problems, but man's expertise will fall short – he cannot make it. Prophecy is against him. The judgment of God is against him!

THE FOURTH SEAL – THE PALE HORSE

And I saw, and behold, a pale horse, and its rider's name was Death, and Hades followed him; and they were given power over a fourth of the earth, to kill with sword and with famine and with pestilence and by wild beasts of the earth.

Revelation 6:7-8

Is Death 'the final absurdity of existence' as the existentialist claims? This picture is traumatic. The horse is described as pale in colour. The Greek word is *chloros*; 'it means pale in the sense of livid; the word is used of the face of a person who is paralysed with terror'. Examine Plate 9 and remember the awesome solemnity that it represents.

In the three preceding seals the riders are unnamed. Here the name of the horseman is Death. Death in connection with Hades is

Plate No. 8

mentioned in three places in the Apocalypse. In Chapter 1:18 our Lord has the keys of Death and of Hades. In Chapter 20:13 Death and Hades give up the dead which were in them, Death holding the body and Hades the spirit. And in Chapter 20:14 Death and Hades are cast into the lake of fire.

Ezekiel described the 'four sore acts of judgment' as the sword, famine, evil beasts and pestilence' (Ezekiel 14:21). These are closely associated in the four horsemen.

When war sweeps over a land, agriculture may be entirely abandoned while all able-bodied men take up the sword. In consequence, there is a scarcity of food and if the war is of long duration, the inevitable result is famine. For many who die without hope, death is the final absurdity of existence. Those who consider death as a terminus rather than an exit will awake to the shock that death, as they understood it, is not a final absurdity, but a doorway into a continuous absurdity, because they have been separated from God.

Death is a grim reality. But Hades follows death indicating that death is not the end of reality. Hades, since the Ascension of Christ is the region of departed spirits of the lost. None can escape the judgment of God.

The Christian who enjoys a personal fellowship with Christ, considering life and death, repeats the triumphant words

I consider that the sufferings of this present time are not worth comparing with the glory that is to be revealed to us . . . We know that in everything God works for good with those who love Him, who are called according to his purpose . . . Who shall separate us from the love of Christ? Shall tribulation, or distress, or persecution, or famine, or nakedness, or peril or sword? . . . No, in all these things we are more than conquerors through him who loved us. For I am sure that neither death, nor life, nor angels, nor principalities, nor things present, nor things to come, nor powers, nor height, nor depth, nor anything else in all creation, will be able to separate us from the love of God in Christ Jesus our Lord.

Romans 8:18-39

THE FIFTH SEAL – MARTYRDOM

'The blood of the martyr is the seed of the Church'. The first martyr in the New Testament was John the Baptist. He stood for righteousness and morality. He was decapitated. The first martyr of the Church was Stephen. He challenged the leaders of the Jewish religion, but his sermon was interrupted. The young preacher was hurried out of the city. The scene that follows was nothing more than a common lynching. These men were not able to resist his inspired logic. They had been publicly humiliated. They had their revenge. They crushed him with stones. His angelic face became bruised and blood-stained, a few minutes later he lay broken and still. He was the Church's first martyr. From Stephen to the martyrs of the present century, men and women have been faithful unto death. They have sealed their faith with their blood.

Plate No. 9

These thoughts about martyrdom lead us decisively into the interpretation of the fifth seal. When the fifth seal is removed, we are presented with an unusual situation.

I saw under the altar the souls of those who had been slain for the word of God, and for the witness they had borne; they cried out with a loud voice, 'O Sovereign Lord, holy and true, how long before thou wilt judge and avenge our blood on those who dwell upon the earth?' Then they were each given a white robe and told to rest a little longer, until the number of their fellow servants and their brethren should be complete, who were to be killed as they themselves had been.

Revelation 6:9-11

Each of the first four seals is connected with one of the living creatures, but the action which relates to these seals takes place on earth. The fifth seal is not associated with a living creature, or an equestrian, and the action is located in heaven.

Plate 10 represents the symbolism of the fifth seal. Many martyrs are in the presence of God. Their deaths are indicated by the use of red Maltese crosses. They have been slain because of their allegiance to the Word of God and their articulate testimony for God. The prayer they offer is primarily a Jewish prayer, crying for vengeance, whereas Christians are encouraged to pray for their enemies and, with the help of God, love those who ill-treat them. The expression 'O Sovereign Lord' occurs only here in Revelation and it has been suggested that this conveys the idea of landlord or head of the house.

The martyrs' interrogation is important. 'How long', they ask, 'before thou wilt judge and avenge our blood on those who dwell upon the earth?' They are reminded that there are others who will seal their testimony with blood. They are symbolised in the painting by the blue Maltese cross and when their martyrdom occurs these crosses will become red, thus completing the white circle of God's purpose; then they will all wear the white robe of purity and victory.

These martyrs of the Tribulation period are anxious that God should vindicate His righteous judgment, but they are encouraged to exercise patience. We are informed that they are under the altar, signifying that they have a standing with God based on the death of Jesus Christ on the Cross. Considering this call for patience from God to the martyr, Dr Donald Gray Barnhouse has paraphrased the divine message to them in this way; 'You have been martyred, but do not be impatient. I have the affair well in hand. I chose you before the foundation of the world for the very purpose you have just realised in your suffering bodies. You have been horribly treated, but I look upon it as having been suffered for the name of My Son, and I shall bless you for it forever. You are only the first of those whom I have thus chosen to die for my name. There are many others. I have marked them out for this purpose. I know all about them and about you. You may rest in peace'.

This 'call' to the Tribulation martyrs is relevant today. God invites us to live a disciplined life where there is a sober and consistent control of ourselves; where there is mastery over our frailties, our alarms, our moods of despondency and panic. With Christ's invincible might within us, we need not fear martyrdom.

THE SIXTH SEAL AND CHAOS IN CREATION

I looked, and behold, there was a great earthquake; and the sun became black as sackcloth, the full moon became like blood, and the stars of the sky fell to the earth as the fig tree sheds its winter fruit when shaken by a gale; the sky vanished like a scroll that is rolled up, and every mountain and island was removed from its place. Then the kings of the earth and the great men and the generals and the rich and the strong, and every one, slave and free, hid in the caves and among the rocks of the mountains, calling to the mountains and rocks, 'Fall on us, and hide us from the face of him who is seated on the throne and from the wrath of the Lamb; for the great day of their wrath has come, and who can stand before it?'

Revelation 6:12-17

This seal is frightening. As we read it the paralysis of fear grips our hearts. We do not like to face unpleasant things. In fact, there may be some people who object to the teaching of the Apocalypse, and under this pretext state, 'We prefer the teaching of Jesus'. Let us compare the teaching of Jesus our Lord with that of the sixth seal.

In Matthew 24:29-30 our Lord says, 'Immediately after the tribulation of those days', and gives us a striking parallel with Revelation 6. Consider the two sets of Scripture:

The sun will be darkened
The sun became black

The moon will not give its light
The full moon became like blood

The stars will fall from heaven
The stars of the sky fell to the earth

The powers of the heavens will be shaken
The sky vanished like a scroll that is rolled up

There can be no doubt that the teaching of our Lord and the Apocalypse are complementary. They agree that the end time will be characterised by a serious disturbance in the whole fabric of nature.

Plate No. 10

In the Old Testament we are informed by Amos, Ezekiel, Joel and Haggai that at the coming of the Lord the earth will tremble. The Bible is a book of seismic shocks. There are two important earthquakes in the gospels. One takes place at the Crucifixion, the other takes place at our Lord's Resurrection. We often speak of tears of joy and tears of sorrow. The tears are the same, but the emotion that gives birth to them is different. The earthquakes at the Death and Resurrection of Jesus Christ are the same, but the reasons for the earthquakes are different. At our Lord's Death the earth groans in an upheaval; at His Resurrection the earth leaps for joy. We repeat, the Bible is a book of earthquakes.

Plate 11 has captured the chaos of the sixth seal. It assists us to see the cataclysmic happenings of the Tribulation period. The great earthquake is having the effect of breaking up society, the sun is like a small island in a sea of darkness, the moon is like a massive blood clot, the stars have become displaced from their galaxies, the sky is in the process of becoming a scroll or turning back on itself as the atmosphere does in a nuclear explosion, mountains and islands are in motion and volcanic lava flows down in a mighty stream.

Men and women are possessed with reckless terror. But observe the painting carefully. Throughout the painting there is a white line. At the first impression it seems to add to the confusion, but a closer investigation reveals that the line reaches to the sun, touches the moon, is in close proximity to the star, penetrates the sky and the lava and hovers around the people who are panic-stricken; in other words, the line does not add to the confusion but reminds us that, in and through the confusion, God's purpose is being fulfilled and His sovereign will is being vindicated. Christ is the divine cohesive power of the universe and in God's time the universe will be a perfect fabric based on heaven's harmony.

Some scholars consider the sun, moon and stars as representative of individual authorities and government. The sixth seal is a symbolic presentation of a world without God and the universal disruption of society. Anarchy comes like a storm to the planet earth and all systems of government collapse. The literal interpretation of the sixth seal has science and weaponry on its side. It is feasible that what is presented here will actually happen.

In the fifth seal we observed a Jewish prayer,

O Sovereign Lord, holy and true, avenge our blood on earth!

Now in the sixth seal we have an atheist's prayer,

Fall on us and hide us from the face of Him who is seated on the throne, and from the wrath of the Lamb; for the great day of their wrath has come, and who can stand before it?

Someone has suggested that these people in their prayer are actually saying, 'Oh, dear God, please, please send us hydrogen bombs. We would rather deal with such things than with You. Your judgments are too terrible, we cannot stand them'.

Catastrophe can make atheists pray, but let us examine those who take part in this weird prayer meeting, where prayers are addressed to the rocks and mountains.

The Royalists - 'The Kings of the Earth'. The majestic wrath of the King of kings has flashed upon the royalists. The glory of His majesty causes them to panic. Imagine the ludicrous situation - kings praying to cold, inanimate, insensate rocks!

The Politicians and Scientists - 'The Great Men'. Who are the men of power and prestige of the world? Politicians and scientists are considered as the great power block. Now they are confronted with the One who has the government of the universe upon His shoulder and the Sovereign who is the Power of God.

The Military Personnel - 'The Generals'. The men responsible for military strategy have forsaken their training as tacticians. All orderliness is dispersed as the Captain of the Lord's hosts appears with power that makes a nuclear explosion appear like a damp squib.

The Industrialists and Business Tycoons - 'The Rich'. There is no time to place the situation before arbitration. There is no opportunity to present a bribe. The Lord Jesus Christ, the Lamb, does not have His price.

The Athletic - 'The Strong'. Men and women with physical prowess are helpless before revealed spiritual power. Flesh and blood cannot inherit the Kingdom of God. Flesh and blood cannot withstand the power of that Kingdom.

The Ordinary People - 'Everyone, Slave and Free'. Those who used Jesus Christ as a 'swear word'. Fearful people who did not want to step out of line in the office or workshop. Religious people, who

knew nothing about the new birth and experiencing salvation - they are all present.

Panic fills every heart as they cry

For the great day of their wrath has come, and who can stand before it?'

The Interlude

Chapter VII

In our consideration of the Apocalypse it is of interest to observe that there is a parenthesis between the sixth and seventh seals described in Chapter 7; another between the six and seventh trumpets (Chapters 10-11:13) and again another between the sixth and seventh bowls (Chapter 16:13-16).

Dr W. Graham Scroggie, after careful research on the chronology of the Book of the Revelation, observed: 'The trumpets, therefore, do not double back over all or some of the Seals, but lie under the Sixth Seal, and proceed from it. For this reason it is equally incorrect to speak of the Trumpets as following the Seals. They do not follow, but are the Seventh Seal'. He also makes the suggestion that 'The Bowls do not double back over Seal and Trumpet judgments; neither is it correct to say that they follow the Trumpet visitation. They do not follow because they are the Seventh Trumpet contents'. The parenthesis between the sixth and seventh seals reminds us that God is working out His purposes in spite of man's rebellion.

There are people today whose pessimistic attitude to God is sinful. They look around society in a superficial way and conclude that things are hopeless. Their conclusion is wrong because they are stating that 'God is not at work', or, in the language of some modern theologians, they are insinuating that 'God is dead'. At the death of our Lord, darkness covered the earth for three hours. Dread and horror filled many hearts. Had God forsaken the planet? No! What they did not recognise was that in and during that darkness over Calvary, God was in Christ reconciling the world unto Himself. This great act was central to God's fabulous future.

God is at work. His purposes move forward. We cannot tell the exact moment that the tide turns, but we know when it has turned. Sometimes we cannot really tell when the purpose and power of God have turned the tide in the affairs of men, but we know when the tide has been turned by God!

There are three movements of thought in this interlude. The first movement brings to our notice the 'seal of God' (verses 1-8). In the second, we have the statements made to God (verses 9-12). And thirdly we have the security that comes from God (verses 13-17).

THE SEAL OF GOD

After this I saw four angels standing at the four corners of the earth, holding back the four winds of the earth, that no wind might blow on earth or sea or against any tree. Then I saw another angel ascend from the rising of the sun, with the seal of the living God, and he called with a loud voice to the four angels who had been given power to harm earth and sea, saying, 'Do not harm the earth or the sea or the trees, till we have sealed the servants of our God upon their foreheads'. And I heard the number of the sealed, a hundred and forty-four thousand sealed, out of every tribe of the sons of Israel, twelve thousand sealed out of the tribe of Judah, twelve thousand of the tribe of Reuben, twelve thousand of the tribe of Gad, twelve thousand of the tribe of Asher, twelve thousand of the tribe of Naphtali, twelve thousand of the tribe of Manasseh, twelve thousand of the tribe of Simeon, twelve thousand of the tribe of Levi, twelve thousand of the tribe of Issachar, twelve thousand of the tribe of Zebulun, twelve thousand of the tribe of Joseph, twelve thousand sealed out of the tribe of Benjamin.

Revelation 7:1-8

In this section we are confronted with three numbers: 4 angels, 1 angel and a company of 144,000 people.

John sees in his vision four angels holding back the winds of the earth, like dogs in a leash, lest they should blow, and all destructive agencies are suspended. In the Bible there are two terms which we ought to note, these are 'the winds of heaven', and 'the winds of earth'. The winds of heaven in Scripture are the providential agencies of God 'employed by Him to execute His purposes', and the winds of earth are 'political and other troubles on earth'. The Old Testament teaches that the winds are the servants of God (Zechariah 6:1-5, 9:14; Nahum 1:3-4; Isaiah 66:15; Jeremiah 4:13). We are reminded in Job 37:10 that Elihu believed that the wind is the breath of God. Undoubtedly God controls the elements through His serving angels. When the number four is used in the Revelation, it is related to earth. In this section we have four angels at four locations holding the four winds of the earth. This may refer to the uttermost parts of the earth, or it may be confined to the Middle East which is of great importance in the unfolding of prophecy.

The angel that appears from the rising of the sun, that is, the East, conveys the divine message to the four angels who control the winds. The angel speaks like a conservationist! Land, sea and trees have to be conserved until the servants of God have been sealed. Judgment is temporarily suspended, and this comes as an order from the *living* God. This reminds us of the declaration of Chapter 1:18 'I am . . . the living One'. It may be that the jewels of the Urim and Thummim of the Old Testament have become dim; Bethel's ladder is fallen and the burning bush quenched, but our God is the Living One. The concept of a dead God is a cheerless supposition, a Satanic lie; God lives, so His harvest will be adequate, His plans will be fulfilled. Because He lives, our fears are terminated, the iron doors of our prison house are opened, we have seen the dawning of the eternal day.

The living God has a 'seal'; the Greek word *sphragis* suggests an emblem of ownership with the promise of security. W. E. Vine reminds us that when a person was sealed, 'he was secured from destruction and marked for reward'. In New Testament times soldiers were marked on the hand, and slaves were branded on the forehead. Sometimes the name of the god whom an individual worshipped was branded upon the worshipper. A seal indicated possession.

Dr William Barclay points out that in the early Church, sealing had a significant connection with two doctrines: 'It was connected with baptism. Baptism was regularly described as sealing. It is as if, when a person was baptised, a mark was put upon him to show that he had become the property and the possession of God. Paul regularly talks about the Christian being sealed with the gift of the Holy Spirit. The possession of the Holy Spirit is the sign and the proof and the guarantee that a man belongs to God'.

It is obvious that the sealing of the 144,000 involves a Jewish company. There are some, such as the Seventh Day Adventists and Jehovah's Witnesses who consider themselves to be in the privileged number, but the teaching of the Scriptures and the ethnic argument do not support such claims. There is a clear statement in this passage that 12,000 people are sealed from each of the 12 tribes of Israel, that is, 144,000 physical descendants of Abraham. Walter Scott makes this observation in his commentary: 'In the enumeration of the tribes throughout Scripture, of which there are about eighteen, the full representative number twelve is always given; but Jacob had thirteen sons, one of which is always omitted. Levi is more generally omitted than any other. In the apocalyptic enumeration, Dan and Ephraim are omitted. Both these tribes were remarkable as being connected with idolatry in Israel, the probable reason for the blotting out of their names here (Deuteronomy 29:18-21). But in the end grace triumphs, and Dan is named first in the future distribution of the land among the tribes (Ezekiel 48:2), but, while first named, it is the farthest removed from the temple being situated in the extreme north'.

Those who believe that the ten tribes of Israel were lost, ought to re-examine the Old Testament evidence. Ten tribes were taken into captivity by the Assyrians in 722 BC, and later in 586 BC the two tribes from the south were taken into captivity by Babylon. The books of Ezra and Nehemiah remind us that after seventy years of Babylonian captivity, representatives from the twelve tribes returned to the land and Ezra 2:70 states clearly 'The priests, the Levites, and some of the people lived in Jerusalem and its vicinity; and the singers, the gate keepers and the temple servants lived in their towns, and all Israel in their towns'. God is the efficient Registrar. He knows His chosen people, the Jews. He sovereignly and supernaturally places His seal upon this unique crowd and sets them apart for His service. They are witnesses to the world. And their effectiveness is outstanding, because in the face of intense persecution, an innumerable company believed their witness.

Dr. J. Dwight Pentecost, in his book *Will Man Survive?* asks a provocative question about Paul's claim in 1 Corinthians 15:8, 'Last of all, as to one untimely born, he appeared also to me'. What does Paul mean when he states that he was born prematurely? 'Comparing Revelation 7 with 1 Corinthians 15, we conclude that after the rapture of the Church, God will perform the same miracle He performed in Saul of Tarsus on the Damascus road 144,000 times over. The experience that Paul had on the road to Damascus is what these 144,000 will experience in that day when God sovereignly reveals Himself to these descendants of Abraham and brings them to Himself. God's strategy has all the expertise of the divine mind. In every nation of the world there are physical descendants of Abraham, knowing the language, culture and customs of the people, and as Hal Lindsay suggests, 'They will be like 144,000 Jewish Billy Grahams turned loose at once!'

THE STATEMENTS MADE TO GOD
After this I looked, and behold, a great multitude which no man could number, from every nation, from all tribes and peoples and tongues, standing before the throne and before the Lamb, clothed in white robes, with palm branches in their hands, and crying out with a loud voice, 'Salvation belongs to our God who sits upon the throne, and to the Lamb!' And all the angels stood round the throne and round the elders and the four living creatures, and they fell on their faces

before the throne and worshipped God, saying, 'Amen! Blessing and glory and wisdom and thanksgiving and honour and power and might be to our God for ever and ever! Amen.'

Revelation 7:9-12

This company is comprised of Gentiles. It is a cosmopolitan company. They were clothed in white robes. The robe is the character in which, as the result of his deeds, a man drapes himself, that of him which is visible to the world, the 'habit' of his spirit, as we say, and the word 'habit' means both custom and costume. White is the heavenly colour and the white is not dead but lustrous, like our Lord's garments on the Mount of Transfiguration, such white as sunshine smiting a snowfield makes. Later in the passage we are told why the robes are white: 'they are washed in the blood of the Lamb'. To our thinking the word blood means death, and it is an indisputable fact that the blood of Jesus Christ speaks of the death of Jesus Christ. But it must be noted that to the Hebrews the blood stood for life. That was precisely why the orthodox Jew never would, and still will not, eat anything which has blood in it. The blood is the life, and the life belongs to God, and the blood must always be sacrificed to God. 'The blood of Jesus, his Son, cleanses us from all sin' (1 John 1:7). It is the blood of Jesus Christ that makes propitiation for us (Romans 3:25). It is through His blood that we are justified (Romans 5:9). It is through His blood that we have redemption (Ephesians 1:7). It is through His blood that we have peace with God (Colossians 1:20). His blood purges our conscience from dead works to serve the living God (Hebrews 9:14).

Observe another important detail concerning this cosmopolitan company – they had palm branches in their hands. Among the Greeks and Romans the palm was a token of victory. That is usually taken to be the meaning of the emblem here. But it has been proved that there is no such use of the palm in the Old Testament. In the Jewish religion there was a very significant use of the palm branches. They were employed in the Feast of Tabernacles, when the people were bidden to take palm branches and 'rejoice before the Lord seven days'. This great multitude are rejoicing before the Lord. There is joy in the presence of the Lord!

There is also a loud voice crying

Salvation belongs to our God who sits upon the throne, and to the Lamb.'

Revelation 7:10

Salvation does not belong to a particular denomination. Salvation is not monopolised by one particular political philosophy. Salvation is not restrained by 'no-go areas'. This great doctrine of deliverance belongs to God and the Lamb. The throne is occupied and no one can de-throne God. We cannot fault the people because they cry with a loud voice!

Examine this great climax

And all the angels stood in a circle round the throne and the elders and the four living creatures, and they fell upon their faces before the throne and worshipped God saying, 'So let it be. Blessing and glory and wisdom and thanksgiving and honour and power and strength belong to our God for ever and ever.'

Revelation 7:11-12

Plate 2 shows the position of these concentric circles of the inhabitants of heaven around the throne. On the golden ring stand all the angels. Nearer the throne are the twenty-four elders, still nearer are the four living creatures; and before the throne are the white-robed martyrs. All heaven says 'Amen' – so let it be – to the martyrs' praise. But they make their own statement in God's presence. The statement is seven-fold.

Blessing

We are responsible for thanking God for all His goodness. He upholds creation by the word of His power. He has redeemed us. He lives for us.

Glory

God is king of this universe. We cannot afford to ignore the majesty of God. The Saviour is a close companion, but we must not forget that He is majestic, exalted far above every power and principality. Beware of the modern tendency of being too 'pally' with God.

Wisdom

In our Lord are hid all the treasures of wisdom and knowledge (Col.2:3). The fear of the Lord is the beginning of wisdom (Psalm 111: 10). If any man lacks wisdom, let him ask of God . . . (James 1:5).

Thanksgiving

Gratitude is a wonderful grace. It acts as a lubricant in the machinery of life and of the Church. It is enjoined in the New Testament that we should give thanks. Heaven will be a place of perpetual thanksgiving. We would not be so disgruntled if we gave thanks to God.

Honour

God is not someone to be used in our time of adversity, and neglected in the time of prosperity. We do not honour a friendship if we only communicate when we are in desperate trouble.

Power

All men seek power. Many have abused power. Archimedes using hyperbole declared, 'Give me a lever long enough and a prop strong enough, I can single-handed move the world'. There are people who would long to claim the responsibility for moving the planet. But all true power belongs to God.

Strength

Our strength is in the Lord. We can do all things through Christ who strengthens us (Phil. 4:13). The Lord is my strength and my salvation (Psalm 140:7). Strength belongs to the Lord.

This seven-fold statement reminds us that the Lamb is worthy. In heaven we shall be perpetually reminded that we owe everything to Calvary and to Him who was both victim and victor there.

THE SECURITY THAT COMES FROM GOD

Then one of the elders addressed me, saying, 'Who are these, clothed in white robes, and whence have they come?' I said to him, 'Sir, you know.' And he said to me, 'These are they who have come out of the great tribulation; they have washed their robes and made them white in the blood of the Lamb. Therefore are they before the throne of God, and serve him day and night within his temple; and he who sits upon the throne will shelter them with his presence. They shall hunger no more, neither thirst any more; the sun shall not strike them, nor any scorching heat. For the Lamb in the midst of the throne will be their shepherd, and he will guide them to springs of living water; and God will wipe away every tear from their eyes.'

Revelation 7:13-17

Here is an innumerable company from every nation. If the 144,000 are Jews then this company of people are Gentiles. One of the elders poses the question, 'Who are these clothed in white robes, and whence have they come?' The answer is given, 'These are they who have come out of the great tribulation. . .'

It is sometimes suggested that this multitude is identical with the Church, but the latter is depicted as enthroned, whereas the former stand before the throne. Walter Scott in his commentary of Revelation claims, 'Our venerable Authorised Version is at fault here. It reads, "These are they which came out of great tribulation!" But other versions give undoubtedly the Spirit's meaning 'come' not 'came' and 'The Tribulation', not simply 'Tribulation'. It is not the record of a past act, but they 'come out'. It is regarded as a characteristically present action. The tribulation points to a definite prophetic period, and not simply to tribulation in general in which all true believers share.'

Despite tribulation and icy fear, think of the security that comes from God. The multitude are

. . . before the throne of God and serve him day and night in his temple.

Dr. William Barclay indicates that there is a hidden fact here. The task of serving God day and night was part of the liturgy of the Levites and priests (1 Chronicles 9:33). Now those who are before the throne of God are Gentiles. Here, indeed, is a great reversal. In the Old Testament times, and also in the time of our Lord, any Gentile found within the inner precinct became liable to death.

... He who sits upon the throne will shelter them with his presence.

It is an exhilarating experience to know the covering presence of God's glory. Some time ago, I was speaking to a Christian whose mother had died after a lingering illness. His children wondered what had happened to grandma. 'Grandma is better', he answered, 'her illness is over, she is in good health'. That is true. The health-giving presence of God is the covering.

They shall hunger no more, neither thirst any more; the sun shall not strike them, nor any scorching heat.

Satisfaction in the Lord is the supreme blessing. Those who hunger and thirst after righteousness will be filled. Our Lord drew the curtain back and allowed us to look into the after-life in Luke 16. The man shut out of God's presence has an intolerable craving and longing. An eternal dissatisfaction is beyond our comprehension, but those who are separated from God's presence will experience it.

For the lamb in the midst of the throne will be their shepherd, and he will guide them to springs of living water; and God will wipe away every tear from their eyes.

Consider this strange combination of the future and the present. The Lamb will shepherd them in the future, but He guides them in the present. Christ's shepherdhood is eternal.

The Lord graciously guides them to the springs of living water; He will wipe every tear from their eyes. The Lamb who shed tears when upon earth, wipes away tears in heaven. At Bethany He wept for a friend, loved and lost; at Olivet, He wept for a great city doomed to death. It is fitting that the Lamb with a triumphant tenderness removes every tear from the eyes of His martyrs.

The Seventh Seal

Revelation 8:1-5

Chapter VIII

We have observed the Lamb of God removing six seals from the important scroll. The unveiling of the seals has been awe-inspiring, sometimes frightening, but definitely emphasising the fact that God is in control of every situation. As we approach the seventh seal we look forward to a great climax.

There are four important features associated with the seventh seal.

THE ELOQUENCE OF SILENCE

When the Lamb opened the seventh seal, there was silence in heaven for about half an hour.

Revelation 8:1

In the Book of Job, we have a very ancient story of the patriarch Job who lost all his possessions. Three friends, Eliphaz, Bildad and Zophar made arrangements to go and console Job in his suffering. When they saw him in the distance, they did not recognise him; and they raised their voices and wept. But here is an important disclosure, 'they sat with him on the ground seven days and seven nights, and no one spoke a word to him, for they saw that his suffering was very great.' (Job 2:13) Silence — and it has been suggested that it was the best advice they gave to Job — the eloquence of silence lasted for seven days and seven nights.

The study of the silences of Jesus is rich in application. When we come upon the statement, 'Jesus answered not a word', we observe the majesty of silence. In some ways the kingdom of the Bible is a realm of silences. Round many of the teachings of the Bible, there is an eloquence of silence; the Trinity of Persons in the Godhead, the Incarnation of the Lord of Glory, the Atonement of the Saviour on the Cross, the Father's sovereignty and how it harmonises with our freedom — such knowledge is infinite and when we request that God should solve the mysteries, He answers with silence.

'O Soul, keep silence on the mount of God.
Though cares and needs throb round thee like a sea;
From supplications and desires unshod,
Be still and hear what God shall say to thee.'

(Mary Roweles Jarvis)

Ten times in the Apocalypse an 'hour' is referred to and some of these references show that it means a short period of time, eg

So the four angels were released, who had been held ready for the hour, the day, the month and the year, to kill a third of mankind.

Revelation 9:15

And at that hour there was a great earthquake

Revelation 11:13

Fear God and give Him glory, for the hour of His judgment has come;

Revelation 14:7

And the ten horns that you saw are ten kings who have not yet received royal power, but they are to receive authority as kings for one hour, together with the beast.

Revelation 17:12

What then is signified in Chapter 8:1 is that there is an ominous connection between the seal and trumpet judgment — a very brief period of intense expectation.

To make out that the expression means thirty minutes would reduce the situation to ridicule; but regard the word as symbolic, as undoubtedly it is, and all is as dignified as it is dramatic. Silence in heaven for about half an hour. Many Christians are afraid of silence. That is why there are people who find it difficult to sit quietly before the Lord in a church during the service. Noisy evangelicals can learn something from the Quakers! There will be silence in heaven for a brief period of time. The music of heaven and the thunder of Revelation is stilled. The last seal being broken, the secret scroll now lies open, revealing the whole of God's purpose for earth.

THE IMPORTANCE OF STANDING

Then I saw the seven angels who stand before God, and seven trumpets were given to them.

Revelation 8:2

It was popularly believed by the Jews that there were seven 'presence angels', who were of the highest angelic order and comparable, for example, to the seven Persian princes referred to in Esther 1:4, who saw the king's face and ranked next to the monarch in status and power. 'It is obvious', says Dr. F.A. Tatford, 'that the heavenly state is not a democratic commonality but a sphere in which celestial orders tower one above another – Thrones, Lordships, Principalities, Authorities – Colossians 1:16, and in which the seven presence angels occupy a place of particular eminence and dignity. These sublimest ministers of God are the prime executors of the oncoming administrations.' The angels have been called 'the glorious septemvirate of celestial arch-regents'! These angels are 'standing' in the presence of God.

Other postures are mentioned in Scripture; for example, 'When I saw Him, I fell at His feet as though dead' (Revelation 1:17). 'When he said to them, "Iam He", they drew back and fell to the ground' (John 18:6). Many of us count it a privilege to fall at the feet of Jesus, but these seven angels have a standing before the Lord. Seven trumpets were given to them. The trumpet had a close association with Israel. With the sound of the trumpet, divine commands were given to the people. Its blast assembled them together, it controlled their movement in battle and it announced the year of jubilee. The trumpet was also used to announce God's judgment, and this is supported by the following Scriptures:

On the morning of the third day there were thunders and lightnings, and a thick cloud upon the mountain, and a very loud trumpet blast, so that all the people who were in the camp trembled.

Exodus 19:16

Blow the trumpet in Zion; sound the alarm on my holy mountain! Let all the inhabitants of the land tremble, for the day of the Lord is coming, it is near, a day of darkness and gloom, a day of clouds and thick darkness.

Joel 2:1

Is a trumpet blown in a city and the people are not afraid?

Amos 3:6

The seven trumpets play an important part in the unleashing of judgments upon the earth at the conclusion of this present age.

THE LANGUAGE OF SYMBOLISM

And another angel came and stood at the altar with a golden censer: and he was given much incense to mingle with the prayers of all the saints upon the golden altar before the throne; and the smoke of the incense rose with the prayers of the saints from the hand of the angel before God.

Revelation 8:3-4

There is an altar in heaven. The book of the Revelation frequently reminds us that the altar is of great importance.

I saw under the altar the souls of those who had been slain for the word of God and for the witness they had borne.

Revelation 6:9

I heard a voice from the four horns of the golden altar before God

Revelation 9:13

Then another angel came out from the altar, the angel who has power over fire . . .

Revelation 14:18

And I heard the altar cry, 'Yea, Lord God the Almighty, true and just are thy judgments'.

Revelation 16:7

In the Old Testament there are different kinds of altars, eg earthen, (Exodus 20:24); stone (Exodus 20:25); brazen (Exodus 27:1-2); golden (Exodus 30:1-3).

What about the altar in Revelation 8? 'The altar cannot be identified as the altar of burnt-offering, for there can be no animal sacrifice in heaven; the altar must be the altar of the incense. The altar of the incense stood before the Holy Place in the Temple. It was made of gold, and it was 18 inches square and 3 feet high. At each corner it had horns, it was hollow and was covered over with a gold plate, and round it, it had a railing to keep the burning coals from falling off it. In the Temple, incense was burned and offered before the first sacrifice of the day and after the last sacrifice of the day. It was as if the offerings of the people went up to God wrapped in an envelope of perfumed incense'. (Dr. William Barclay - *Daily Bible Readings.*)

Here is another important point. In the arrangements made for the priesthood in the Old Testament, the ordinary priest used a silver censer, but the High Priest used a golden censer to carry fire from the brazen altar to the golden altar of incense. The angel, therefore, is functioning as the High Priest. We are informed that much incense was given to him to add to the prayers of the saints upon the golden altar. Our Lord Jesus Christ is the High Priest associated with the heavenly sanctuary. Hebrews 8:1-2 provides the evidence that Christ is the 'minister in the sanctuary and the true tent which is set up not by man but by the Lord'. The Saviour is the only mediator. He sympathises with our weaknesses and utilises our prayers. As the unique High Priest, He reaches to the depths of our need. Man may reach to the lowest abysses of the ocean, but the Saviour can touch the depth of our profound loneliness and keenest temptation. He can reach out to the limit of our nature. Intellect, memory, conscience, imagination, will and emotion cry out for a separate satisfaction, and each of them finds it in the High Priest. Christ also touches the verge of our life. The various moods and experiences, our conflict and our calm, our work and our rest, our gladness and our grief – the High Priest upholds us through them all.

Plate 12 outlines the angel's face in the cloud formation; the golden censer is in the centre of the cloud.

We must not under-rate the potency of prayer and the ministry of thanksgiving that reaches to the heavenly sanctuary. Prayer is the neglected ministry of the Church. This seems to be a reflection on the personal prayer life of the believer. Our High Priest has set the example for prayer. Prayer and work were our Lord's maxims, but prayer always came first. To our Lord, prayer was life itself.

We ought to recognise that the neglected ministry of the individual Christian and the Church is the ministry of prayer. Many professing Christians have no prayer life. They are strangers to the quiet, personal confrontation of a holy God in the lonely and sacred place of prayer. Prayer is paramount in heaven. If you are embarrassed about prayer on earth, then what will your reaction be in the presence of God in heaven?

THE MAJESTY OF FIRE

Then the angel took the censer and filled it with fire from the altar and threw it on the earth: and there were peals of thunder, loud noises, flashes of lightning, and an earthquake.

Revelation 8:5

The angel filled the now empty censer with fresh fire from off the brazen altar and then cast it upon the earth. Plate 12 attempts to capture the intense drama and judgment which take place when the censer is emptied. The mushroom cloud and blood-like base remind us of the devastation that occurs when God intervenes in the affairs of the planet earth.

Walter Scott reminds us: 'As the altar was the expression of His holiness and righteousness in dealing with the sin of the people of old, so that same holiness and righteousness will search the earth and judge and punish it accordingly'.

This action has its sad and awful meaning. It challenges man's vain hopes. It rebukes man's fond and foolish dreams. Tribulation, anguish and wrath are being enacted by the priestly King.

The Fantastic Fanfare

Chapter IX

Few people realise that the Bible concludes with a dramatic spectacle. The last book of the Bible has been given a name which could be interpreted as 'the raising of the curtain'. As the curtain rises, we are confronted with happenings that out-dazzle the television musicals, eclipse spectacular films. Yes, the finale of the Bible supersedes all man-made productions. The heaven-made production, we recall, is seen by one man, located on a small island called Patmos.

Consider what we have in this extraordinary book. These are people who are called the stars. They are not television personalities, pop artists or people who have been awarded Oscars - they are people who preach the Bible. What a turn-up for the opinion polls - preachers looked upon as stars!

There is special lighting. Golden lamps convey a significant splendour, a diffusive light making the psychedelic lights look like candles in the strong sunlight. What are the golden lamps? – The Christian churches!

The sound effects are awe-inspiring - with flashes of lightning, rolling thunder, awesome voices, and heavenly choirs. The whole planet trembles.

Revelation 8 and 9 highlight one aspect of this great spectacular – The fantastic fanfare.

Before the angels can blow their trumpets to begin the judgments 'another angel' appears on the scene. He, the Lord Jesus, stands at the altar holding a golden censer filled with a special kind of incense – the prayers of saints. These He offers to God.

Observe carefully in Plate 12 the location of the seven trumpets in the cloud. Each trumpet blast has to do with the judgment of God upon the world. The Communist world which denies God and the

Western world which ignores Him cannot escape. God's son, Jesus Christ, has the leading role in this great and mysterious drama. His action is against the wrong-being and wrong-doing of mankind.

Before we enter into a detailed study of this important section of the Apocalypse, we must pose the question – Do the trumpet judgments prove that atomic warfare will destroy the planet earth?

Hal Lindsay, in his book *There's a New World Coming*, asserts: 'Although it is possible for God to supernaturally pull off every miracle in the Book of Revelation and use totally unheard of means to do it, I personally believe that all the enormous ecological catastrophies described in this chapter are the direct result of nuclear weapons. In actuality, man inflicts these judgments on himself. God simply steps back and removes His restraining influence from man, allowing him to do what comes naturally out of his sinful nature. In fact, if the Book of Revelation had never been written, we might well predict these very catastrophes within fifty years or less!'

In this persuasive statement, the writer is careful to point out that God has the supernatural resources to fulfil the prophecies in the Old and New Testaments regarding the final judgments upon the earth, but the main thrust of the interpretation is that man will destroy himself.

Dr. J. Dwight Pentecost, in his book *Will Man Survive* takes the opposite view: 'It must then be evident that these judgments that some say refer to atomic warfare, cannot be atomic warfare at all, because if someone in the Kremlin should push a button and send a warhead that landed somewhere in the United States and destroyed it, God would get no glory. Russia would. Or if, conversely, someone in this country (U.S.A.) should push a button and release a warhead that would destroy Europe . . . the United States military would receive the honour and the glory.'

Here we have two approaches to the literal interpretation of the judgments of the Apocalypse. Lindsay believes that God is passive, that is, He 'steps back' and allows the self-destruction of mankind. Pentecost highlights the sovereign intervention of God, so that it will be obvious to all that the glory belongs to the Lord. But is there a middle way? Surely God does not step back from the happenings on the earth! He takes the initiative. Some of the judgments could make use of man's weaponry and the planet's pollution, but there are some judgments that can only be described as the direct intervention of God rather than the use of man's diabolical devices.

The First Trumpet – Judgment on the Land.

And there followed hail and fire, mixed with blood, which fell on the earth; and a third of the earth was burnt up, and a third of the trees were burnt up, and all green grass was burnt up.

Revelation 8:7

Some people have mocked what they called 'the extravagant imagery' of the Bible. The description given after the first trumpet blast reads like a newspaper report of nuclear warfare, but we must not overlook the fact that this is a divine chastisement. Hail and fire are used in the Bible as symbols of judgment. The blood which is associated with the hail and fire indicates that there is violence and death.

The Second Trumpet – Judgment on the Sea.

And something like a great mountain burning with fire was thrown into the sea; and a third of the sea became blood, a third of the living creatures in the sea died, and a third of the ships were destroyed.

Revelation 8:8

This could be interpreted as a burning space-rocket, with nuclear warhead, plunging into the Mediterranean where ships are assembled ready for battle. If this is the meaning, the attack makes Pearl Harbour seem insignificant. The blood of the destroyed discolour a third part of the sea. What horror when oil slick and blood slick combine.

Of course, the great mountain burning with fire could be a meteor, used by God as a chastisement of the people. This is in harmony with the interpretation that God is sovereign and He always takes the initiative. Others maintain that the mountain represents a kingdom, the fire indicates that the political system is under punitive justice, the sea symbolises the nations and the ships organised religion. There is no valid reason to prevent us from understanding the second-trumpet judgment as a cataclysmic intervention of God accepting 'as something like a great mountain burning with fire' to be a literal meteoric mass from heaven that falls into the sea.

The Third Trumpet – Judgment on the Rivers

And a great star fell from heaven, blazing like a torch, and it fell on a third of the rivers, and on the fountains of water. The name of the star is Wormwood. A third of the waters became wormwood, and many died of the water, because it was made bitter.

Revelation 8:10-11

This passage raises the problem of pollution. Here is a mysterious device that, in exploding, will fill the atmosphere with 'noxious gases' that will be absorbed by the rivers and fountains of water, and poison them.

What is the great star? A thermonuclear weapon? A powerful political ruler? A religious dignitary who has been deposed? A heavenly mass from outer space burning as it enters the earth's atmosphere? The first answer indicates that man is responsible for pollution. In the second answer, we have the veiled suggestion that corruption in politics poisons mankind at the source. From the third answer we deduce that the apostate church propagates heresy that has a poisonous effect upon one third of the world's population. The fourth answer takes us back to the fact that God enacts the judgment. The meteorite descends and locates the exact spot that ensures the pollution of the waters.

The star is called wormwood — in Greek *apsinthos* — from which derives the English word 'absinth', indicating a deadly poisonous plant, which when placed in water has a toxicity making it lethal.

The Fourth Trumpet — Judgment in Space

And a third of the sun was smitten and a third of the moon, and a third of the stars, so that a third of their light was darkened; a third of the day was kept from shining, and likewise a third of the night.

Revelation 8:12

Here is a suggestion of cataclysmic happenings in space. Our planet is influenced by conditions on other planets, especially by the sun. Our Lord spoke about the sun and the moon, and in Luke 21:25-26 He makes a most important prophetic statement

And there will be signs in sun and moon and stars, and upon the earth distress of nations in perplexity at the roaring of the sea and the waves, men fainting with fear and with foreboding of what is coming on the world; for the powers of the heavens will be shaken.

Dr. Donald G. Barnhouse has made a penetrating analysis of our Lord's momentous words, 'The powers of the heavens will be shaken'. He reminds us that the Greek word for heaven is *ouranos*, from which we get our word 'uranium'. Furthermore, the word for powers is *dunamis* meaning explosive power, from which we get our word 'dynamite'. And the word which is used for shaken is *salevo* which means 'to set off balance'. The literal translation is very impressive: 'The explosive force of uranium shall be set off balance'. Dr. Barnhouse offers the following conclusion — 'I am willing to regard this as a coincidence, but it must be recorded as a coincidence that is so striking that it must be considered in the evidence when we discuss the prophecies of the Word of God. How wonderful for us who are believers to know that God is on the throne, that no weapon that is formed against us shall prosper, that God will always take care of His own, and He knows how to deliver the godly out of testing.'

We find it hard to comprehend the infinitude of the planets and galaxies. We gaze at the nearest fringe of the universe only to realise that beyond the fringe there are galaxies behind galaxies. These heavens teach us our limitations; we cannot bind the cluster of the Pleiades, or loose the bands of Orion, but God can and if He wants to He can, through His mighty power which abashes us, cause 'the explosive force of uranium to be set off balance.

The Eagle

Then I looked and I heard an eagle crying with a loud voice, as it flew in mid-heaven, 'Woe, woe, woe to those who dwell on the earth, at the blasts of the other trumpets which the three angels are about to blow'.

Revelation 8:13

Here is a dramatic pause; a stupendous 'selah'; an eagle, God's special agent, exhorts the world to prepare for the three judgments of woe. Those who are too fond of secular society, those who are dazzled by the sheen and sparkle of material wealth, those who are infected with their unbelief and those who are enslaved by their sins will be challenged, humbled and shattered with the direct judgment of God.

The Fifth and Sixth Trumpets Revelation 9

Chapter X

There are four salient features in the fifth-trumpet judgment. We cannot understand the impact of this woe unless we grasp the significance of 'the star fallen' (verses 1 and 11); 'the abyss opened' (verse 2); 'the locust-scorpion creatures' described in Verses 3-4 and 7-10 and mankind tortured (verses 5-6).

The Star Fallen from Heaven to Earth.

And the fifth angel blew his trumpet, and I saw a star fallen from heaven to earth, and he was given the key of the shaft of the bottomless pit;

Revelation 9:1

They have as king over them the angel of the bottomless pit; his name in Hebrew is Abaddon, and in Greek he is called Apollyon.

Revelation 9:11

In the third trumpet we suggested that the star that fell from heaven to earth was an unusual device that caused pollution in one third of the rivers. From the details given about the fallen star in the fifth trumpet there can be no doubt that the star is an individual possessing special powers.

Two important passages help to throw light on the star that is fallen. Isaiah 14:12-17 teaches us that the 'Day Star, son of Dawn' was cast out of heaven because he wanted to make himself 'like the Most High'. Our Lord makes a prophetic statement in Luke 10:18, 'And He said to them, "I saw Satan fall like lightning from heaven" '. The star of the fifth trumpet has a key, suggesting intelligent authority; he is described as king because he is commander-in-chief of the demonic forces. Other descriptive titles are given to this strange person: in Hebrew, he is *Abaddon* and in Greek *Apollyon*. The former means destruction and is the Hebrew word used in the phrase 'death and destruction'; the latter is derived from the Greek verb which means to destroy, and so we have linguistic authority to describe this evil person as 'destruction' and 'destroyer'. This person is none other than Satan himself. He is described by Christ as 'Beelzebub' (Matthew 12:27), that is, the genius who presides over corruption.

The Abyss Opened.

... he opened the shaft of the bottomless pit, and from the shaft rose smoke like the smoke of a great furnace, and the sun and the air were darkened with the smoke from the shaft.

Revelation 9:2

The Greek word for abyss is *abussos* and literally means bottomless. It occurs nine times in the New Testament, seven of which are found in the Apocalypse. Luke 8:31 throws more light on this word: the demons begged Jesus 'not to command them to depart into the abyss'. It is an unusual request as it suggests that they preferred to live in pigs rather than be consigned to the strange abyss.

Another passage, although it does not use the word abyss, gives further elucidation, 'And the angels that did not keep their own position, but left their proper dwelling have been kept by him in eternal chains in the nether gloom until the judgment of that great day' (Jude 6). It would seem then that the abyss imprisons some of the most malevolent creatures of the universe. Satan is permitted to release a demoniacal horde who, with envenomed attack, will startle the world. Smoke ascends from the abyss causing panic and pollution.

The Locust-Scorpion Creatures Described.

Then from the smoke came locusts on the earth, and they were given power like the power of scorpions of the earth; they were told not to harm the grass of the earth or any green growth or any tree, but only those of mankind who have not the seal of God upon their foreheads;

Revelation 9:3-4

In appearance the locusts were like horses arrayed for battle; on their heads were what looked like crowns of gold; their faces were like human faces; their hair like women's hair, and their teeth like lion's teeth; they had scales like iron breast-plates, and the noise of their wings was like the noise of many chariots with horses rushing into battle. They have tails like scorpions, and stings, and their power of hurting men for five months lies in their tails.

Revelation 9:7-10

Some students of prophecy have suggested that this description relates to the weaponry of modern warfare, such as helicopters, fighter bombers or some secret weapon. The passage before us does not teach that. We have before us a hellish species actuated by devilish instincts.

The locust in the Old Testament usually represents a divine judgment upon an evil world. These satanic locusts are unusual, as they are not permitted to attack the vegetation which ordinary locusts would do. In number they are like the swarming locust, but in effectiveness, they are like the poisonous scorpion. There is a combination of a double scourge. They seem to be human, with their heads shaped like a gold crown — they have long hair like a woman's, suggesting the power of attraction and they have teeth like a lion's, suggesting the power of destruction. Their mobility is symbolised by the wings and their protection by the breastplate. This army is energised by the powers of darkness.

Mankind Tortured

. . . they were allowed to torture them for five months, but not to kill them, and their torture was like the torture of a scorpion, when it stings a man. And in those days men will seek death and will not find it; they will long to die, and death will fly from them.

Revelation 9:5-6

This is not an indiscriminate judgment. Vegetation and foliage are protected; those who have the seal of God upon their forehead have immunity. It is significant that the torture lasts for five months as this coincides with the life-span of the locust. Verse 6 is most unusual. Suicidal attempts will be made without success. Atheists, who believe that death is the easy way out will find it impossible to die. It has been suggested that men and women will jump into the seas, lakes and rivers, seeking death by drowning, only to find their bodies will not sink; they may take poison, only to discover that it has been neutralised and is ineffective.

What we have considered is a plague-stricken world in discord, but there is no let-up in this intensity for we hear the ominous words of verse 12

The first woe has passed; behold, two woes are still to come.

THE SIXTH TRUMPET and Military Manoeuvre

Then the sixth angel blew his trumpet, and I heard a voice from the four horns of the golden altar before God, saying to the sixth angel who had the trumpet, 'Release the four angels who are bound at the great river Euphrates'. So the four angels were released, who had been held ready for the hour, the day, the month, and the year, to kill a third of mankind. The number of the troops of cavalry was twice ten thousand times ten thousand; I heard their number. And this was how I saw the horses in my vision: the riders wore breastplates the colour of fire and of sapphire and of sulphur, and the heads of the horses were like lions' heads, and fire and smoke and sulphur issued from their mouths. By these three plagues a third of mankind was killed, by the fire and smoke and sulphur issuing from their mouths. For the power of the horses is in their mouths and in their tails; their tails are like serpents, with heads, and by means of them they wound.

The rest of mankind, who were not killed by these plagues, did not repent of the works of their hands nor give up worshipping demons and idols of gold and silver and bronze and stone and wood, which cannot either see or hear or walk;

Revelation 9:13-20

Four important numbers are found in this passage: the four angels (verse 14); a third of mankind (verse 15); twice ten thousand times ten thousand (verse 16) and the five deadly sins (verses 20-21). If we can understand the significance of these numbers, we shall understand the meaning of the sixth trumpet.

The Four Angels

The four angels are said to be bound at the river Euphrates. Here the river is the literal and not the symbolic boundary. The Euphrates, according to Genesis 15:18, was the promised boundary of the territory of Israel. It is suggested that the Garden of Eden was located in this region. This river formed the boundary line between east and west.

Now we are informed that four angels were bound at the great river. Some students of prophecy believe that there are angels of punishment used by God to afflict and chastise mankind. Others suggest that God's good angels are not bound, and see the four angels as fallen evil angels that have been restricted by God's sovereign power. It can be argued from the Old Testament that God uses His angels as agents in judgment; for example, 2 Kings 19 makes it abundantly clear that one angel attacked the Assyrian encampment and 185,000 soldiers were killed, but this argument does not obviate the fact that the four angels were bound and that good angels are never described in this way. It would seem that the four angels are invisible instigators, emancipated to carry out a dastardly work.

A Third of Mankind

We have already noticed from the text of Revelation 6 that twenty-five per cent of the population was killed as a result of the four-horse judgment. Tim Lahaye makes the observation, 'According to today's population figures, that would be seven hundred million to one billion people . . . This one third would again involve a similar number of people, approximately six hundred or seven hundred million to one billion people.' Remember that according to the future projections of the statisticians, the world population will be seven billion by AD 2000. These figures help us to understand that the figures concerning death and massacre found in the Apocalypse can be calculated literally.

An Army of 200 Million

Is this a literal army? Walter Scott thinks not — 'A literal army consisting of 200 million of cavalry need not be thought of. The main idea in the passage is a vast and overwhelming army, or beyond human computation, and exceeding by far any before witnessed.' In Scott's day, it was thought impossible for any nation or nations to assemble an army of 200 million, but that is not so today; *Time Magazine* of May 1965 stated that Red China alone claims to have a man and woman militia of 200 million. It is no longer beyond the limit of human thinking to envisage an actual army of 200 million.

Some who have accepted the actual number have suggested that this large force is demonic and has come from the abyss which we studied in the fifth trumpet. Hal Lindsay, on the other hand, holds the opinion that the passage describes 'some kind of mobilised ballistic missile launcher'. Later in Revelation 16 and 19 we shall study in more detail the sixth-bowl judgment which tells us that this large army comes from the Far East and that at Armaggedon the Lord Christ will emerge from heaven to destroy the evil armies.

It is our opinion that this vast army is a literal one, but that the detailed description of breastplates, fire of sapphire, fire and sulphur will only be understood at the end of the age when the prophecy is fulfilled.

Five Deadly Sins

The remainder of mankind resisted God, refused to repent, intensified their resistance to God and continued in their abandonment to sin.

The first sin enumerated is *idolatry*. Worship is given to 'demons and idols of gold and silver and bronze and stone and wood'. The First Epistle of John concludes with a sentence that contains an eloquent shudder - 'Little children, keep yourselves from idols' (1 John 5:21). An idol is something or someone that takes the place of God and is intensified especially when the false worship is inspired by demonic forces.

Murder is listed as one of the prevalent sins during the Great Tribulation. A man usually becomes what he believes. Men who believe they cannot be held accountable to God can fulfil their murderous intent with impunity. When human life is held cheap, murderers enjoy the licence to kill.

Another of the listed sins is *sorcery*. This derives from the Greek word *pharmakeia*, from which we in turn get the word pharmacy. The root meaning has to do with the use of drugs. In the late 1930s Dr. Donald G. Barnhouse, commenting on this text maintained, 'I believe that the Bible teaches that drug addiction will indeed become very widespread'. How true! Addiction to drugs gives 'pleasures with a thousand faces, and none of them perfect; with a thousand tongues, and all of them broken; with a thousand hands and all of them scratching nails'. They fancied that drugs would be their friends and they discovered that they are their gaoler. The prison-house of drugs is distasteful, irksome, dreary.

Immorality is included in this catalogue of sins. The Greek word *porneia* represents all forms of sexual deviation such as homosexuality.

The final sin represents *theft*. Fraudulent practise abounds in high places. One scandal after another in society reminds us that the moral standards of the Bible have been disregarded and the only wrong seems to consist in getting caught.

Hebrews 3:13 reminds us that we can be hardened by the 'deceitfulness of sin'. Our society no longer speaks about sin. Clever men have changed the name of sin. They are like the old navigators who renamed the Cape of Storms as the Cape of Good Hope, and thought that they had worked a miracle by softening its tempestuousness, but they were so wrong! The Great Tribulation will be a time of storms and God will hold man accountable; 'the wages of sin is death'.

The Seventh Trumpet

Revelation 11:14-19

Chapter XI

The second woe has passed; behold the third woe is soon to come.

Then the seventh angel blew his trumpet, and there were loud voices in heaven, saying, "The kingdom of the world has become the kingdom of our Lord and of his Christ, and he shall reign for ever and ever." And the twenty-four elders who sit on their thrones before God fell on their faces and worshipped God, saying, "We give thanks to thee, Lord God Almighty, who art and who wast, that thou has taken thy great power and begun to reign. The nations raged, but thy wrath came, and the time for the dead to be judged, for rewarding thy servants, the prophets and saints, and those who fear thy name, both small and great and for destroying the destroyers of the earth."

Revelation 11:14-18

These words bring to us the accent of triumph. The positiveness is bracing and invigorating.

We see Christ in conquest. He is seen sweeping away popular philosophies, national conflicts and all unrelenting enemies and stupendous antagonists, annihilating their organised forces, establishing His reign over men. He is the undisputed Sovereign of the universe which is His by right of redemption.

We must listen to the fanfare. The solemn music has to do with life and death, or, to put it another way, it has to do with union and separation. In order to be prepared to meet God, we must understand the use of these great terms and what it really means to be a Christian through personal trust in Jesus Christ.

Physical life is union of the spirit with the body. Spiritual life is the union of the spirit with God. Everlasting life is the union perfected and consummated to all eternity.

Physical death is the separation of the spirit from the body. Spiritual death is the separation of the spirit from God. Eternal death is the perpetuation of this separation.

Our Lord spoke about a second birth — a spiritual birth — being made anew through His power. (John 3). For those who have not experienced a second birth, the second death becomes inevitable, for he who is only born once dies twice, while he who is 'born again' dies only once.

We cannot break the alliance between the infraction of law and the infliction of penalty. God links death and sin unbreakably. 'The wages of sin is death', yes, but the 'gift of God is eternal life' (Romans 6:23).

The Angel and the book of the Covenant

Revelation 10:11-13

Chapter XII

We have already noticed that there is an interlude or parenthesis between the sixth and seventh seals. Now we discover that there is another parenthesis between the sixth and seventh trumpets. This interlude is of major importance.

In this section there are three salient features which pose three questions:
The angel – Who is he?
The little scroll – What is it?
The two witnesses – Who are they?
The answer to these interrogations will lead us to a proper exegesis of this difficult section of the Word of God.

THE ANGEL OF THE COVENANT

Then I saw another mighty angel coming down from heaven, wrapped in a cloud, with a rainbow over his head, and his face was like the sun, and his legs like pillars of fire. He had a little scroll open in his hand. And he set his right foot on the sea, and his left foot on the land, and called out with a loud voice, like a lion roaring; when he called out, the seven thunders sounded. And when the seven thunders had sounded, I was about to write, but I heard a voice from heaven saying, 'Seal up what the seven thunders have said, and do not write it down.' And the angel whom I saw standing on sea and land lifted up his right hand to heaven and swore by him who lives for ever and ever, who created heaven and what is in it, the earth and what is in it, and the sea and what is in it, that there should be no more delay, but that in the days of the trumpet call to be sounded by the seventh angel, the mystery of God, as he announced to his servants the prophets, should be fulfilled.

Revelation 10:1-7

Observe some of the descriptive details. An angel dressed in a cloud; a multi-coloured halo resembling a rainbow is around his head; his face is resplendent as the sun and his massive legs burn like pillars of fire.

This portrait combines divine majesty – the shekinah glory of the cloud and the glowing solar orb — with the mercy of the rainbow. Strength, stability and sovereignty combine in the fiery legs and the feet that possess land and sea. There is no doubt in my mind that this picture presents the Lord Jesus Christ in His role as the Angel of the Covenant, such as we have in the Old Testament, technically called 'Christophanies'.

Some disagree with this conclusion. They suggest that 'The Angel of the Lord' describes our Lord in the 'Theophanies' of the Old Testament and that this is not His title in the New Testament. It is also asserted that the Lord Jesus will not come down to earth midway in the Tribulation, and another commentator suggests that the oath taken in verse 6 proves that the angel is not Christ.

These three objections can be answered satisfactorily. The word 'angel' in the Greek language can mean messenger, in fact the seven angels of the seven churches are the 'pastors' or the 'messengers'. In Chapter 1 the Lord is observed moving in and through the seven churches and they are in Asia, (verse 1). We can dismiss the third objection by pointing out that when God made a promise to Abraham, 'since he had no one greater by whom to swear, he swore by himself' (Hebrews 6:13).

Revelation 8:3-5 reminds us that an angel receives the prayers of the saints, but 2 Timothy 2:5 teaches that there is one mediator between God and man and this important teaching is given in the context of prayer.

Although a popular writer describes the angel as 'an ambassador from galaxy "H"' it remains my firm conviction that the angel is not a representative of the Lord, but the Lord Himself.

Donald Grey Barnhouse has made a penetrating observation about the 'special messenger'. 'The first appearance of this special messenger is in Chapter 7:2 where He holds back the sweeping judgments that are about to fall while God performs a special work of grace. Again in Chapter 8:5 He stands as the messenger of the covenant pouring out the fire of judgment upon earth. It should be noted that in the first instance, the messenger acts as *prophet*. In the second instance, he acts as *priest*. In this passage he acts as *king*.' We are inclined to believe that no mere creature would be used of God in such a high office.

In our Lord's hand a small scroll lay open, as we see in the painting. (Plate 13). This scroll seems to be the symbol of judgment and as His right foot is upon the sea and His left foot upon the land, it would seem that this is a judgment upon the Gentiles (sea) and the Jews (land). Our Lord's feet are upon all the nations, suggesting His sovereignty over the planet earth.

Plate No. 13

'Lion's roar and thunder's roll' combine to give us the impression of an authoritative, stentorian voice. In the Old Testament there are several occasions where the voice of Yahweh is compared to that of a lion.

The lion has roared; who will not fear? The Lord God has spoken; who can but prophecy?

Amos 3:8

They shall go after the Lord, He will roar like a lion; yea, He will roar, and His sons shall come trembling from the west;

Hosea 11:10

And the Lord roars from Zion, and utters His voice from Jerusalem, and the heavens and the earth shake. But the Lord is a refuge to his people, a stronghold to the people of Israel.

Joel 3:16

The lion's roar is a prelude to judgment. The seven-fold thunderclap gives resonance to the voice and thunder usually typifies the voice of God in judgment. God has not disclosed what was said in the thunderous roar. It is sacrilege to speculate.

The Angel raises His right hand and declares, 'there should be no more delay'. The translation in the Revised Standard Version is accurate and takes the Greek word *chronos* to mean that time has run out rather than a succession of chronological events. In the words of Jeremiah 1:12, God says, 'I am watching over my word to perform it.'

Varied interpretations have been given regarding the mystery of God in verse 7, such as the completion of the Church of God, the end of the age, the closing of the hidden workings of grace and the end of the veiling of God's glory in Christ. A. T. Robertson in *Word Pictures in the New Testament* suggests 'Here apparently the whole purpose of God in human history is meant.'

THE LITTLE SCROLL OF THE COVENANT

Then the voice which I had heard from heaven spoke to me again, saying, 'Go, take the scroll which is open in the hand of the angel who is standing on the sea and on the land.' So I went to the angel and told him to give me the little scroll; and he said to me; 'Take it and eat; it will be bitter to your stomach, but sweet as honey in your mouth.' And I took the little scroll from the hand of the angel and ate it; it was sweet as honey in my mouth, but when I had eaten it my stomach was made bitter. And I was told 'You must again prophesy about many peoples and nations and tongues and kings.'

Revelation 10:8-11

John is commanded to appropriate the open scroll in the angel's hand; in fact, he is told twice to take the scroll. There are two lessons here.

Note that God takes the initiative; it is He who opens and offers the scroll. God's servant is given the responsibility of taking the opened book. The Lord will not do for us what we can do for ourselves.

Having obeyed the two-fold command, John has a two-fold experience; the scroll is bitter to his stomach but sweet to his mouth. This is not a unique experience. Ezekiel the prophet was also instructed to eat a scroll (Ezekiel 2:8 - 3:3). Life is bittersweet. Prophecy is bittersweet. The Apocalypse pursues this twin theme. There is bitterness for those who resist the will of God, but there is sweetness for those who have been caught up in the purpose of God through their personal faith in Jesus Christ:

Note then the kindness and the severity of God: severity toward those who have fallen, but God's kindness to you, provided you continue in his kindness; otherwise you too will be cut off.

Romans 11:22

This quotation gives an inspired definition. John had a foretaste of the unfolding message of the Lord. It contained kindness and severity. Someone came to me after listening to my sermon on the seals and said, 'The Book of the Revelation terrifies me.' I concurred that certain parts of the Apocalypse scare me, but I advised the young Christian to see the whole of the Revelation, especially chapters 20-22. We cannot escape the bittersweet experience.

The Two Witnesses of the Covenant

Revelation 11:1-13

Chapter XIII

Then I was given a measuring rod like a staff, and I was told: 'Rise and measure the temple of God and the altar and those who worship there, but do not measure the court outside the temple; leave that out, for it is given over to the nations, and they will trample over the holy city for forty-two months. And I will grant my two witnesses power to prophesy for one thousand two hundred and sixty days, clothed in sackcloth.' These are the two olive trees and the two lampstands which stand before the Lord of the earth. And if any one would harm them, fire pours from their mouth and consumes their foes; if any one would harm them, thus he is doomed to be killed. They have power to shut the sky, that no rain may fall during the days of their prophesying, and they have power over the waters to turn them into blood, and to smite the earth with every plague, as often as they desire. And when they have finished their testimony, the beast that ascends from the bottomless pit will make war upon them and conquer them and kill them, and their dead bodies will lie in the street of the great city which is allegorically called Sodom and Egypt, where their Lord was crucified. For three days and a half men from the peoples and tribes and tongues and nations gaze at their dead bodies and refuse to let them be placed in a tomb, and those who dwell on the earth will rejoice over them and make merry and exchange presents, because these two prophets had been a torment to those who dwell on the earth. But after the three and a half days a breath of life from God entered them, and they stood up on their feet, and great fear fell on those who saw them. Then they heard a loud voice from heaven saying to them, 'Come up hither! And in the sight of their foes they went up to heaven in a cloud. And at that hour there was a great earthquake, and a tenth of the city fell; seven thousand people were killed in the earthquake, and the rest were terrified and gave glory to the God of heaven.

Revelation 11:1-13

It is obvious that for some commentators this chapter is considered *crux interpretatorum.* They actually see the Church in this chapter and the temple is a symbolism of the Church. No wonder they are confronted by problems! Chapter 11 is describing the Great Tribulation. The Church is in heaven, but on earth the temple has been built in Jerusalem and specific instructions are given regarding its measurement.

163

Today, there is much speculation regarding the building of the temple in Jerusalem. It has been suggested in my hearing, without proof, that plans have been drawn up for the rebuilding of the temple. But upon the original temple site there stands the Mosque of Omar which was built in AD 682. I have stood inside this mosque which is known as the Dome of the Rock and have observed the mechanical and ecstatic devotion of Moslem men and women as they pray to Allah. Muslims believe that Muhammad ascended from the rock on his white steed. There is a hoof mark on the rock as proof. Some devout Jews will not enter this area lest they should walk unwittingly over the spot which was the original Holy of Holies. Before the Israelites can rebuild their temple, they will have to demolish the Dome of the Rock. This action would precipitate a major conflict in the Middle East. It is difficult to ascertain how the Mosque of Omar will be removed, but it could happen in fulfilment of the prophetic jest of Eldad the Israeli historian who said in answer to a question about the removal of the mosque, 'Perhaps there will be an earthquake'. But it should be noted that Israel promised religious freedom to all who live in Jerusalem; it was promised also that they would restore the Dome of the Rock if it were damaged.

God speaks of His two witnesses. They are depicted on the left-hand side of the painting (Plate 14). Their power of witness is symbolised in the white scroll in the right hand. Power over the elements is represented by the left hand holding the cloud. Although dressed in sackcloth, they have an effective ministry suggested by the two olive trees and the two lampstands. Their ministry covers a period of 1,260 days. The 3½ circles represent the length of their ministry. This is equal to the 42 months when the Gentiles will trample over the Holy City. It is important to our understanding that the days and the months represent a period of 3½ years, that is, one half of the Tribulation period of 7 years of Daniel 9:27. John F. Walvoord makes the observation, 'From the fact, however, that the two witnesses pour out divine judgments upon the earth and need divine protection lest they be killed, it implies that they are in the latter half of the seven years when awful persecution will afflict the people of God, as this protection would not be necessary in the first three and one half years'.

An Identification Parade! Who are the two witnesses?
The two witnesses are seen by some as symbolising 'an adequate witness of the Church', but this is unacceptable as we have already noticed that the Church is in heaven and will not pass through the Tribulation.

Others suggest that the two witnesses symbolise the 'entire remnant' of the Tribulation period. Against this suggestion there stand the facts that the witnesses perish simultaneously (Chapter 11:7), but the witness of the remnant continues to the end of the Tribulation. Some expositors believe that the two witnesses are from a former era. It is supposed that they are Moses and Elijah, although Enoch has been preferred to Moses.

Observe how the Lord describes them —

These are the two olive trees and the two lampstands which stand before the Lord of all the earth.

Revelation 11:4

This refers to the teaching of Zechariah 4 where Zerubbabel and Joshua are identified as the witnesses of the Lord. The main point of the exegesis in Zechariah 4 is that the source of the power and authority associated with their witness is the Spirit of God. J. Dwight Pentecost in his monumental volume, *Things To Come,* suggests, 'They [the two witnesses] in all probability, are not men who lived before and have been restored, but are two men raised up as a special witness to whom sign-working power is given.' God's two witnesses in Revelation 11 have a similar power which is dramatised in the fascinating narrative.

We look upon the witnesses as God's special agents. They have divine protection for three and a half years; 'if any one would harm them, thus he is doomed to be killed'.

They have a marvellous meteorological ministry; divine authority gives them power over the weather and especially the rainfall. 'They have power to shut up the sky'.

They have an ecological expertise. If they wish they can bring about epidemics and pollution that will instigate crises on the earth. Their deaths are a monstrous martyrdom. The beast emerges from the abyss and kills the two witnesses. This action is obvious from the painting. Notice how the bodies lie on the street of Jerusalem for three and a half days. Again the three and a half circles in the painting represent this time factor.

Their dead bodies will lie in the street of that great city which is spiritually called Sodom and Egypt, where their Lord was crucified.

Revelation 11:8

By means of television the world could gaze upon the death of the Lord's witnesses and celebrate the event by exchanging presents. These celebrations would be short-lived. The international party becomes a non-event. Once again God's intervention shocks the world! The dead witnesses are made alive by the power of God. After three and a half days, the witnesses stand on their feet. Here is a major miracle and it is seen by the populace of the world. A voice from heaven commands the witnesses, 'Come up hither!' Now we have an actual ascension – 'In the sight of their foes they went up to heaven in a cloud'. The painting with a subtle touch gives an outline of the two witnesses ascending to heaven.

Following this drama of strange events, there was a great earthquake, a tenth of Jerusalem fell, as highlighted in the painting, seven thousand people were killed and many possessed with a reckless terror find themselves giving glory to God.

Events are taking place that indicate that the Lord God is soon to govern His own planet. This is expressed beautifully in verse 15 –

The kingdom of the world has become the Kingdom of our Lord and of His Christ and He shall reign forever and ever.

The twenty-four elders express themselves in worship.

We give thanks to thee, Lord God Almighty, who art and who wast, that thou hast taken thy great power and begun to reign. The nations raged, but thy wrath came, and the time for the dead to be judged, for rewarding thy servants, the prophets and saints, and those who fear thy name, both small and great, and for destroying the destroyers of the earth.

Revelation 11:17-18

God's temple in heaven was opened. The Ark of the Covenant was seen in heaven as we have it at the right-hand side of the painting. From the Old Testament we learn that this ark was made of wood and covered with gold. Typologists have a tacit agreement that the wood represents the humanity of the Lord Jesus and the gold typifies His deity; in other words, the Ark of the Covenant is a vivid representation of the Lord Jesus Christ. Israel's high priest never approached the earthly Ark of the Covenant without blood and our Lord Jesus has made atonement through the shedding of His precious blood – eternally efficacious in heaven.

Flashes of lightning, seen striking at the head of the beast, remind us that our sovereign Lord is continuously active in the fulfilment of His divine will.

Israel; Persecuted and Protected

Chapter XIV

In this remarkable chapter the points are illustrated in two ways: linguistically by alliteration and visually by a tableau. An alliterated address, or sermon, has each keyword commencing with the same letter. In this passage we have six key words – woman (v.1), war (v.7), woe (v.12), wings (v.14), wilderness (v.14), water (v.15). This is not a manipulated alliteration for the observant reader has no difficulty in detecting these important words.

A tableau is a vivid representation of a scene in history, literature, art or prophecy by a group of persons appropriately dressed or posed. The significant thing about a tableau is that it is a living picture. In the main, the picture is of a woman. She is not the only woman mentioned in the Apocalypse, for in Chapter 2 the church in Thyatira is afflicted by the neurotic teachings of a 'Jezebel of a woman' who claimed to be a prophetess. However, the Lord gives her a scathing rebuke that reminds us of the words of Jeremiah 23:21, 'I did not send the prophets, yet they ran; I did not speak to them, yet they prophesied'. While in Chapter 17 there is an exposure of 'the great harlot' – the apotheosis of the Satanic system.

WHO IS THE WOMAN?

And a great portent appeared in heaven, a woman clothed with the sun, with the moon under her feet, and on her head a crown of twelve stars; she was with child and she cried out in her pangs of birth, in anguish for delivery. And another portent appeared in heaven; behold, a great red dragon, with seven heads and ten horns, and seven diadems upon his heads. His tail swept down a third of the stars of heaven, and cast them to the earth. And the dragon stood before the woman who was about to bear a child, that he might devour her child when she brought it forth; she brought forth a male child, one who is to rule all the nations with a rod of iron, but her child was caught up to God and to his throne, and the woman fled into the wilderness, where she has a place prepared by God, in which to be nourished for one thousand two hundred and sixty days.

169

Ponder on the inspired imagery of the painting (Plate 15). It is important for the interpretation of the Apocalypse to identify the woman and the male child.

A wild claim was made by Mary Baker Glover Patterson Eddy, the founder of Christian Science, that she is the woman of Revelation Chapter 12. Her interpretative suggestions are that the 'man-child' she gave birth to is Christian Science while the dragon is 'mortal mind' which is the antagonist of her new teaching.

Plate 15 represents accurately the teaching of the passage, unlike the painting of Bartolome Murillo, the Spanish artist, which portrays the Virgin Mary in her pregnancy, but located in heaven ready to give birth to the Saviour. This cannot be the true interpretation. The woman is not the Virgin Mary. The historical facts are against such an idea. She was never persecuted, and although she went to Egypt with Joseph and Jesus, she did not flee to a wilderness and was not given special care for 1,260 days.

Some scholars have used the allegorising principle of interpretation and depicted the woman as the Church in travail, bringing Christ to the nations. But Dr J. Dwight Pentecost in his eschatological master-piece, *Things To Come* makes this incisive statement, 'The church did not produce Christ, but Christ the Church. Since the Church is not seen on earth in chapters four through nineteen of Revelation, the Church cannot be represented by this woman'. It was Dr H.A. Ironside's contention that 'if the interpreters are wrong as to the woman and the man-child they will be wrong as to many things connected with them'.

Here, then, is a personage full of significance. The translation of the Revised Standard Version states 'a great portent appeared in heaven'. This translation of the Greek word *semeion* as portent is not the best translation. A portent is 'a thing of grave significance', but *semeion* means more than that, it is 'a great sign'. It is this word that is used to describe our Lord's miracles in John's Gospel. When God speaks of a great sign, we must be earnest in our study of its importance. Let us, therefore, consider this passage in greater depth.

The Woman's Clothing
The woman is clothed with the sun, the moon is under her feet and on her head there is a crown of twelve stars. This luminous clothing confirms our identity of the woman, as in the Old Testament the sun, moon and stars are associated with the nation Israel. These following Scriptures demand our study.

Plate No. 15

Then he dreamed another dream, and told it to his brothers, and said, 'Behold, I have dreamed another dream; and behold, the sun, the moon, and eleven stars were bowing down to me'.

Genesis 37:9

Thus says the Lord, who gives the sun for light by day and the fixed order of the moon and the stars for light by night, who stirs up the sea so that its waves roar – the Lord of hosts is his name. 'If this fixed order departs from before me, says the Lord, then shall the descendants of Israel cease from being a nation before me for ever'.

Jeremiah 31:35-36

Then spoke Joshua to the Lord in the day when the Lord gave the Amorites over to the men of Israel; and he said in the sight of Israel, 'Sun, stand thou still at Gibeon, and thou Moon in the valley of Aijalon'. And the sun stood still, and the moon stayed, until the nation took vengeance on their enemies. Is this not written in the Book of Jashar? The sun stayed in the midst of heaven, and did not hasten to go down for about a whole day. There has been no day like it before or since, when the Lord hearkened to the voice of a man; for the Lord fought for Israel.

Joshua 10:12-14

From heaven fought the stars, from their courses they fought against Sisera.

Judges 5:20

Once for all I have sworn by my holiness; I will not lie to David. His line shall endure for ever, his throne as long as the sun before me. Like the moon it shall be established for ever; it shall stand firm while the skies endure.

Psalm 89:35-37

In all of these passages it is obvious that the sun, moon and stars have a close relationship with the history of Israel.

The number twelve suggests the twelve tribes and the use of the term woman corresponds to passages of the Old Testament where Israel is spoken of as a woman. For example in Jeremiah 4:31

For I heard a cry as of a woman in travail, anguish as of one bringing forth her first child, the cry of the daughter of Zion gasping for breath, stretching out her hands, 'Woe is me! I am fainting before murderers.'

The Woman's Child
Secondly, consider the woman's child.

She brought forth a male child, one who is to rule all the nations with a rod of iron, but her child was caught up to God and to his throne.

Revelation 12:5

The man-child is the Messiah. Two aspects of the Messiah's experience are highlighted, namely, the Incarnation and the Ascension. There is no mention of the thirty-three years between the Incarnation and the

Ascension, but we are informed about the rule of the Messiah upon the earth and the words remind us of Psalm 2 which contains strong Messianic emphases.

The Woman's Conflict

A red dragon appears. We are informed in verse 9 that the dragon is Satan. There are two words in the New Testament Greek for red — *eruthros* denotes the normal colour of red and is used to describe the Red Sea; *purrhos* suggests a fiery red. It is only used twice in the New Testament, describing the red horse of Revelation 6 and the red dragon of Revelation 12. Its use here indicates the fire and fierceness associated with Satanic opposition. The red dragon has seven heads and ten horns and on each of the heads there is a diadem. Satan has an authority and power which he brings against Israel and the Messiah. The dragon's tail brings down one third of the stars. On the basis of Isaiah 9:15, 'The elder and honoured man is the head, and the prophet who teaches lies is the tail', we may conclude that the tail of the dragon represents false teaching.

THE WAR

Now war arose in heaven, Michael and his angels fighting against the dragon; and the dragon and his angels fought, but they were defeated and there was no longer any place for them in heaven. And the great dragon was thrown down, that ancient serpent, who is called the Devil and Satan, the deceiver of the whole world — he was thrown down to the earth, and his angels were thrown down with him. And I heard a loud voice in heaven, saying, 'Now the salvation and the power and the kingdom of our God and the authority of his Christ have come, for the accuser of our brethren has been thrown down, who accuses them day and night before our God. And they have conquered him by the blood of the Lamb and by the word of their testimony, for they loved not their lives even unto death. Rejoice then, O heaven and you that dwell therein! But woe to you, O earth and sea, for the devil has come down to you in great wrath, because he knows that his time is short!

Revelation 12:7-12

This passage describes a spiritual warfare. (Remember that the Ascension of our Lord took place 1900 years ago, but Satan's final expulsion and Israel's final tribulation have yet to take place.) This is not an underground resistance — it is an overhead war and takes place in the heavens.

Some may find it difficult to realise that there is a spiritual and invisible conflict taking place now which will reach its culmination in the fulfilment of the prophecies of the Apocalypse. We are given a salutary reminder in Ephesians 6:11-12 about our involvement in the spiritual war.

Put on the whole armour of God, that you may be able to stand against the wiles of the devil. For we are not contending against flesh and blood, but against the principalities, against the powers, against the world rulers of this present darkness, against the spiritual hosts of wickedness in the heavenly places.

Christians are not called to a playing field but a battlefield. The spiritual warfare is taking place now. The war that is going on in heaven can be traced back to Satan's sin. Fallen angels and demonic forces combine to overthrow purity and goodness under the leadership of Satan.

In this conflict, Michael is presented as the commander-in-chief over the angels of God. Daniel 12:1 is of tremendous significance,

At that time shall arise Michael, the great prince who has charge of your people. And there shall be a time of trouble, such as never has been since there was a nation till that time; but at that time your people shall be delivered, everyone whose name shall be found written in the book.

Michael has a special relationship with Israel. It was Michael, according to Jude 9, who, 'contending with the devil disputed about the body of Moses; he did not presume to pronounce a reviling judgment upon him, but said, 'The Lord rebuke you'. Again, we observe this remarkable association with God's earthly people, the Jews. Jude 9 suggests that Michael was responsible for the funeral arrangements of the leader of Israel, Moses.

God's victory is most effective. Satan and his angels are thrown down to earth. Heaven rejoices. There is a great celebration as the 'accuser of our brethren' is ejected from heaven.

HOW CAN WE UNDERSTAND THE WOE?

Rejoice then, O heaven and you that dwell therein! But woe to you, O earth and sea, for the devil has come down to you in great wrath, because he knows that his time is short!

Revelation 12:12

Although there is singing in heaven, there is sighing on earth. Earlier, in Revelation 6:16-17 we are reminded of 'the wrath of the Lamb' and 'the great day of their [The Trinity] wrath has come, and who can stand before it?' Now we are informed that 'the devil has come down to you in great wrath'. He is unable to overcome the Lord Jesus Christ, so he turns his fury upon the nations, especially Israel. There is a reckless urgency in the actions of the evil one. Seven words are given to us in an earnest exclamation, 'He knows that his time is short!'

How can we understand this heart-rending woe? First of all we must distinguish between the wrath of the Lamb and the wrath of

Satan. In the former *orge* and in the latter *thumos* is used. *Orge* is the stronger of the two words. The wrath of the Lamb is not to be compared with the great wrath of the devil. *Orge* is 'an emotional rather than a rational state', observes Dr. John F. Walvoord.

The time factor helps us to understand the woe that comes from Satan. 'His time is short,' indicates that Satan has approximately three and a half years to enact his dastardly plans. The timetable is referred to in verse 14 '. . . where she is to be nourished for a time, and times and half a time', that is, three and a half years.

Christians should remind themselves of the statements in 1 Thessalonians 1:10, 'Jesus who delivers us from the wrath to come', and 1 Thessalonians 5:9, 'For God has not destined us for wrath, but to obtain salvation through our Lord Jesus Christ.' The Tribulation period, especially the latter part, will be a time of great wrath. Thank God that the Church will escape this terrible judgment.

THE WINGS AND THE WILDERNESS

And when the dragon saw that he had been thrown down to the earth, he pursued the woman who had borne the male child. But the woman was given the two wings of the great eagle that she might fly from the serpent into the wilderness, to the place where she is to be nourished for a time, and times, and half a time.

Revelation 12:13-14

Let us consider the following questions: Is there a special significance associated with the two wings? Where is the wilderness?

There can be no doubt that 'the wings' and the 'wilderness' have played a significant part in the history of the Jews. Deuteronomy 32:9-12 combines the wilderness and the wings of the eagle in the experience of Israel.

For the Lord's portion is his people, Jacob his allotted heritage. He found him in a desert land, and in the howling waste of the wilderness; he encircled him, he cared for him, he kept him as the apple of his eye. Like an eagle that stirs up its nest, that flutters over its young, spreading out its wings, catching them, bearing them on its pinions, the Lord alone did lead him, and there was no foreign god with him.

Observe the juxtaposition. There is 'the howling waste of the wilderness' and the eagle 'spreading out her wings'. This is the birth of the nation, the emergence of Israel at the beginning of their history. At the end of their history we have the same analogies – the wings and the wilderness.

Satan's persecution of Israel is curbed by the direct intervention of God. It is apparent that many Israelites die but God protects a remnant. The wings of the eagle remind us of the means of their escape and the wilderness the destined area of safety. Some prophetic students believe that the wings represent an air-lift, in which large planes, such as Jumbo-jets will be involved. Who can tell? But the facts are there. Israel will be taken to safety by means of wings.

But what about the destination? Where is the wilderness? Some people think that they know. In Plate 15 the wilderness is represented by the use of colour in the top left-hand corner. There is a mystique about this wilderness! God provides it. He sustains the fugitives for three and a half years. But is it possible to identify the location of the wilderness? Students of prophecy have suggested that Petra will be the place of refuge. Petra was a trading town during the reign of King Solomon and is located in the mountains, in the crater of a volcano. There is one entrance – 'through a narrow, winding canyon twelve to forty feet in width, the sides of which are precipitous and at times so close together they almost shut out the sky above.'

No one can be so dogmatic about the location of the wilderness that God provides, although William E. Blackstone had some of the copies of his book *Jesus is Coming* buried in Petra so that Jews who flee there might discover them and be persuaded to accept Jesus as their Messiah!

WHY IS WATER USED BY THE SERPENT?

The serpent poured water like a river out of his mouth after the woman, to sweep her away with the flood. But the earth came to the help of the woman and the earth opened its mouth and swallowed the river which the dragon had poured from his mouth. Then the dragon was angry with the woman, and went off to make war on the rest of her offspring, on those who keep the commandments of God and bear testimony to Jesus. And he stood on the sand of the sea.

Revelation 12:15-17

Three quotations may help us to grasp the difficulties surrounding an exegetical approach regarding the water from the serpent's mouth and the earth that swallows up the river of water.

Walter Scott suggests that the earth is symbolic of other nations who support Israel, 'the settled government of that day who befriend the Jew, and providentially frustrate the efforts of the serpent'. This presupposes that the serpent's water is an army determined to exterminate Israel.

Dr. F. A. Tatford offers the interpretation, 'The flood that pours forth from the serpent's mouth can be viewed as symbolic of the false teachings which are directed to the spiritual corruption of the people.'

This gives us the imagery of a Niagara of falsehood, streams of spurious teaching, flooding Israel; but it also maintains that another strong teaching will counteract the heresy.

Dr. William Barclay attempts a naturalistic approach. 'Nature itself is on the side of the man who is faithful and loyal to Jesus Christ. In the last analysis the world and nature are contrived, not to destroy, but to aid goodness, and so, the symbolism is that in the greatest hour of need nature itself comes to the aid of goodness.' This is a literal interpretation based on the observation that under certain geological conditions in Asia Minor and elsewhere, rivers disappear underground only to reappear at the surface some distance downstream.

In this study we have seen that the tail of the dragon symbolises false teaching. Surely it is not wrong to accept the suggestion of Dr. F. A. Tatford that the river from the serpent's mouth symbolises evil heresy.

Despite prolonged persecution, the Lord will preserve His remnant who will maintain a strong witness.

The First Beast and the Miracle
The Second Beast and the Mark

Chapter XV

The rich vocabulary of New Testament Greek enables the significance of spiritual truth to be expressed accurately and fully. We have already noticed that there are two words for lamb.

Amnos is the normal word used in John 1:29 and 31. But in the Apocalypse the word translated lamb is *Arnion* which is the diminutive, meaning lambkin. Similarly, there is a distinct difference between the two words *stephanos* and *diadema* that can be translated crown. *Stephanos* means a laurel wreath, representing victory at the games, while *diadema* is the ruler's crown — so in Revelation 19:12 we are informed that many diadems are on Christ's head.

Two important words highlight the meaning of new: *neos* means new in point of time, but not necessarily new in point of quality; *kainos* describes a thing, the like of which has never existed before. The latter is used to describe the New Song, the New Jerusalem, etc.

In the Apocalypse there are two Greek words which the Authorised Version translates beast. It is essential, as we noticed in our study of Chapter 4, that we differentiate between these two words. *Therion* means wild beast and occurs thirty-nine times in the Apocalypse. *Zoon* occurs twenty times and means living creatures. *Zoon* is used to depict the four magnificent sentinels around God's throne. *Therion* represents evil systems, kingdoms and individuals. It is this word that is used of the two beasts in Chapter 13.

And I saw a beast rising out of the sea, with ten horns and seven heads, with ten diadems upon its horns and a blasphemous name upon its heads. And the beast that I saw was like a leopard, its feet were like a bear's, and its mouth was like a lion's mouth. And to it the dragon gave his power and his throne and great authority. One of its heads seemed to have a mortal wound, but its mortal wound was healed, and the whole earth followed the beast with wonder. Men worshipped the dragon, for he had given his authority to the beast, and they worshipped the beast, saying, 'Who is like the beast, and who can fight against it?'

Revelation 13:1-4

The two beasts of Revelation 13 are effectively presented through the beautiful oil painting, Plate 16.

THE FIRST BEAST

Observe the details that are given to help us understand the significance of the beast that emerges from the sea. This beast resembles a leopard, has bear's feet and the mouth of a lion. The painting (Plate 16) indicates the teaching of the passage that one of the heads seems to have a mortal wound. This wound is miraculously healed by the power of the dragon. The wonder-working authority of the dragon through the beast evokes worship and adoration. They have witnessed a hecatomb and a resuscitation that leads them to an obsession that issues the challenge, 'Who is like the beast, and who can fight against it?' (verse 4).

It is interesting to notice the numerology used here: ten horns, seven heads, with ten diadems upon its horns. The painting represents the horns and diadems in a triple-symbolism. Here the artist has depicted the horns as representing strength and the diadems rulership. He has portrayed the diadem on the horn as an indication that each power has a military or nuclear ability.

Before dealing with the triple symbolism of horns, heads and diadems we ought to consider the imagery of the body like that of a leopard, the paws of a bear and the mouth of a lion. Daniel 2:31-35 can help us in our understanding:

You saw, O king, and behold, a great image. This image, mighty and of exceeding brightness, stood before you, and its appearance was frightening. The head of this image was of fine gold, its breast and arms of silver, its belly and thighs of bronze, its legs of iron, its feet partly of iron and partly of clay. As you looked, a stone was cut out by no human hand, and it smote the image on its feet of iron and clay, and broke them in pieces; then the iron, the clay, the bronze, the silver, and the gold, all together were broken in pieces, and became like the chaff of the summer threshing floors; and the wind carried them away, so that not a trace of them could be found. But the stone that struck the image became a great mountain and filled the whole earth.

The prophet Daniel reminds Nebuchadnezzar about his dream. Four kingdoms are represented in the gold, silver, bronze and iron. Daniel, inspired by the Holy Spirit, declares that the Babylonian kingdom is represented by the head of gold. Three other empires are mentioned: the Medo-Persian, symbolised by the breast and arms of silver; the Greek, typified by the belly and thighs of bronze, and the Roman, symbolised by the legs of iron. At our Lord's incarnation the Roman Empire was the great world power. About four hundred years after the

Plate No. 16

death of our Lord, the Roman Empire was divided into two kingdoms - East and West, with capital cities at Constantinople and Rome. It should be noted that the two legs of iron represent the divided Roman Empire. By the eighth century the Roman Empire had completely disintegrated. In God's divine plan, the old empire will be revived. This revival is symbolised in the feet and toes of clay and iron. The ten toes represent ten nations.

Daniel Chapter 7 throws further light on this prophecy. In the first section of the chapter, we are informed about a lion representing Babylon; a bear representing Persia and a leopard representing Greece. Later in the passage a fourth beast is described having ten horns and this represents the Roman Empire.

The first beast of Revelation 13 represents the culmination of Gentile dominion during the Great Tribulation period. All the powers and glories of four former kingdoms combine in this great climax. It is important to remember that the ten toes of Daniel 2 and the ten horns of Revelation 13 represent the same ten kingdoms that exist simultaneously.

Examine the actions of the Antichrist in Revelation 13, especially in relationship to the beast and the miracle. It has been suggested that Satan is neither innovator nor inventor; he is an imitator. In the intriguing book *Will Man Survive?* Dr J. Dwight Pentecost points out that there are two possible interpretations of the word Antichrist on the basis of the original text. 'The prefix anti means 'against' and it emphasises Satan's programme to oppose Christ. It also means 'in place of' or 'instead of', one who comes as a substitute for Christ.'

W. R. Newell in his commentary follows this line in his exegesis. He propounds that the dragon, that is Satan, imitates the death and resurrection of the Lord Jesus. As Satan takes the place of God our Father, so the beast who is wounded and resuscitated takes the place of God the Son. The word *sphatto,* to slay, is used of the Lamb of God and of the beast. God allows men to believe an illusion because they have rejected the truth. 2 Thessalonians 2:9-12 explains the acceptance of the strong delusion.

The coming of the lawless one by the activity of Satan will be with all power and with pretended signs and wonders, and with all wicked deception for those who are to perish, because they refused to love the truth and so be saved. Therefore God sends upon them a strong delusion, to make them believe what is false, so that all may be condemned who did not believe the truth but had pleasure in unrighteousness.

Men and women approach Satan through the beast. The latter is the mediator; the former does not openly reveal himself. Verse 4 makes it clear, 'Men worship the dragon, for he had given authority to the beast'. The beast's ministry lasts for three and a half years. He blasphemes the name and the dwelling of God. Persecution becomes more intense for the faithful upon earth and the rulership of the beast becomes more expansive: 'And authority was given it over every tribe and people and tongue and nation . . .' (verse 7).

This suggests that the influence and authority of the ten-nation confederacy would be considerable. Can we identify the ten kingdoms that are symbolised by the ten horns? The Scriptures do not provide sufficient data for such an identification. It could be that the European Common Market would emerge as that confederacy, but we must not dogmatise.

The question has been asked, especially by Americans, 'Where does the United States fit into this prophecy?' Some have reached the conclusion that the United States will be exterminated by nuclear warfare. Others maintain that the great nation will be chastised by being overrun by Communism. A further question raised by Dr J. Dwight Pentecost in his book *Will Man Survive?* is 'Now what is our origin? (i.e. Americans) Politically, socially, economically and linguistically, we have come from nations that originally belonged to the old Roman Empire. Our customs and laws have all come from that European background, from nations that have emerged out of the Roman Empire . . . The United States may well cast her lot with Europe and come into this confederation of nations and be a part of that western confederacy that will be drawn into this conflict and will be judged by the Lord at His second advent.'

The beast, who leads the United States of Europe, persecutes those who oppose him. Three and a half years is the length of the persecution and that is one half of the seven years which is called the Great Tribulation.

THE SECOND BEAST AND HIS MARK

Then I saw another beast which rose out of the earth; it had two horns like a lamb and it spoke like a dragon. It exercises all the authority of the first beast in its presence, and makes the earth and its inhabitants worship the first beast, whose mortal wound was healed. It works great signs, even making fire come down from heaven to earth in the sight of men; and by the signs which it is allowed to work in the presence of the beast, it deceives those who dwell on earth, bidding them make an image for the beast which was wounded by the sword and yet lived; and it was allowed to give breath to the image of the beast so that the image of the beast should even speak, and to cause those who would not worship the image of the beast to be slain. Also it causes all, both small and great, both rich and poor, both free and slave, to be marked on the right hand or the forehead, so that no one can buy or sell unless he has the mark, that is, the name of the beast or the number of its name. This calls for wisdom: let him who has understanding reckon the number of the beast, for it is a human number, its number is six hundred and sixty-six.

Revelation 13:11-18

The painting, Plate 16, depicts the lamb emerging from the land. Here the same word *arnion* found in Chapters four and five is used. In other words, it is the idea of lambkin — but this tender lamb has two horns! The lamb speaks like a dragon. Sound effect is not possible in a painting, but the artist has represented the dragon's influence over the lamb by giving the latter the tail of the former.

'I saw another beast' (verse 11) demands our interest. Dr Donald Grey Barnhouse enjoins us in his commentary on Revelation to examine the importance of the use of the word 'another' in the Greek. Two Greek words are translated 'another' in English. The two words appear to be the same in English but in Greek they express two radically different meanings. Dr Barnhouse uses the illustration: 'We purchase a fountain pen and find that it leaks and is generally unsatisfactory. We return it saying, 'I want another pen'. This means that we want one quite different from the one we have had. Then we find this to be the best pen we have ever had, and it is so much admired by a friend that we decide to give him a present. We go to the salesman and say, 'This is the best pen I have ever had, I want another'. In this case we mean that we want one exactly like the one we have. In the Greek language there are two different words which express these different ideas. Just as the Lord Jesus said, "I will send you another, absolutely alike, Comforter", so this passage says, "And I saw another - absolutely alike wild beast coming up out of the earth". There can be no doubt that this beast is a Satanic representation.

As the dragon represents God the Father, and the beast who leads the ten-nation confederacy imitates the Son of God as Mediator, so the second beast mimics the ministry of the Holy Spirit. We have an evil trinity! This wicked unity attempts to frustrate the purposes of the Holy Trinity. The second beast is usually described as 'the false prophet'. His traits are highlighted in the Scriptures. Notice how he rose out of the earth, had two horns, was like a lamb, and spoke like a dragon.

The Earth

The word 'earth' occurs at least eighty times in the Apocalypse. On most of these occasions it is used in a literal sense. The first beast rises out of the sea — which symbolises many turbulent nations, but the second beast comes out of the earth. What is the symbolism? In certain Scriptures, Israel is represented by the earth. Some scholars believe that the second beast, the false prophet, will come out of Israel and will be closely associated with the ruler of the United States of Europe. Daniel 9:27 predicts that the leader of Israel will make a covenant with many, that is the ten-nation confederacy.

And he shall make a strong covenant with many for one week; and for half of the week he shall cause sacrifice and offering to cease; and upon the wing of abomination shall come one who makes desolate, until the decreed end is poured out on the desolator.

At the present time the West supports Israel. This supportive policy will give Israel a status for a short time in the middle of an extremely cold war, that is, in the earlier part of the Great Tribulation.

The Two Horns

We have already noted that the horn denotes strength and power. There is a twin authority associated with the false prophet. We know that he has a religious authority for he promotes idolatry. Men are encouraged to make an image of the first beast. This becomes an articulate and animated idol. It could be an authentic miracle used to delude millions, or it could be the culmination of technological achievement which astounds innumerable people.

We know, too, that the false prophet, has political and economic authority:

It causes all, both small and great, both rich and poor, both free and slave, to be marked on the right hand or the forehead, so that no one can buy or sell unless he has the mark, that is, the name of the beast or the number of its name.

Revelation 13:16-17

The Lamb

It is obvious that the second beast wants to give the impression of being gentle and submissive like the diminutive lamb. He is a good cover-man for the first beast. He represents all that is spurious. His aberrations are accepted as normal and authentic by unsuspecting multitudes.

The Voice like the Dragon

His oratorical power is overwhelming. The dynamism of his speeches creates a scintillating persuasiveness that only God's elect can resist. Satan's voice is not quiet today. Discerning Christians ought to recognise his teaching. During the Tribulation the dragon's voice will be heard as an aweful authority that must be obeyed.

Economic and commercial authority will reside in the false prophet. People are forced into a situation that demands their identification with, and support of, the second beast. A mark is given. It is placed on the right hand or the forehead. This may be a parody of the sacred Jewish custom of wearing a phylactery (a small leather box containing scriptural scrolls), on the left arm or forehead whilst in prayer. The false prophet demands conformity and orthodoxy from everybody. They must have his mark. In this context the word *charagma* meaning 'to engrave' is used. It suggests a permanent marking. The false prophet does not issue membership cards — he marks his followers on their person.

The Number of the Beast

. . . let him who has understanding reckon the number of the beast, for it is a human number, its number is six hundred and sixty-six.

Revelation 13:18

What is the significance of the beast's number? One thing is clear; the number 6 has a symbolic significance in the Bible and it means the number of man or humanity. It is obvious that 666 is the total of the numerical value of the beast's name. The numerical value of the name of Jesus in the Greek is 888. This is the number of resurrection, or new things.

It has been suggested that we have in the name of Jesus the perfect octave. If that be true, perhaps we have in 666 the inharmonious combination that is the sum total of a devilish discordance!

Identification of the beast and the interpretation of his name and number are legion. Emperor Nero, the Pope and Mussolini have all been put forward. During the Second World War it was suggested that if our alphabet was evaluated as A = 100, B = 101, C = 102, and so on, then the following equation could be obtained:

H	=	107	E	=	104
I	=	108	R	=	117
T	=	119			
L	=	111			

How surprising! The total is 666. Of course, this is not sound exegesis, but we admire the ingenuity of the person who thought out such an equation when the free world thought that Hitler was a beast.

We have observed in this chapter that there is an unholy trinity, that is, the dragon, beast and false prophet. Hal Lindsay in *There's a New World Coming,* takes up the principle that as number 6 in the Bible stands for humanity, then the meaning of 666 is man trying to imitate the trinity of God (three sixes in one person). This may not be an accurate interpretation but it is in harmony with Satan's attempt to counterfeit the Christian faith.

Six Channel Viewing

Chapter XVI

Imagine a television with six channels. It is a coloured set, but is somewhat special as we can view six pictures simultaneously on the one
screen.   There is movement, sound and song, message and meaning.
The six channels focus on the overwhelming conviction of one message – God is supreme!

The artist's impression of this chapter, Plate 17, gives us a 'wide
screen'. It is living colour. Mount Zion is the nerve-centre from which
there is transmitted the wonder and the woe of God's revelation.

Our reception depends upon our faith.   The gift of the faith-
antenna gives us confidence in the prophetic word and trust in God's
ability to bring order out of chaos.

CHANNEL 1 Rev 14: 1-5

Then I looked, and lo, on Mount Zion stood the Lamb, and with him a hundred
and forty-four thousand who had his name and his Father's name written on their
foreheads.   And I heard a voice from heaven like the sound of many waters and
like the sound of loud thunder; the voice I heard was like the sound of harpers
playing on their harps, and they sing a new song before the throne and before the
four living creatures and before the elders. No one could learn that song except
the hundred and forty-four thousand who had been redeemed from the earth.
It is these who have not defiled themselves with women, for they are chaste; it
is these who follow the Lamb wherever he goes; these have been redeemed from
mankind as first fruits for God and the Lamb, and in their mouth no lie was found,
for they are spotless.

There are four salient features in this first picture.

Mount Zion
The lamb is standing on Mount Zion. Geographically and historically
Mount Zion is the lower eastern hill of Jerusalem, the city captured by
King David from the Jebusites (2 Samuel 5).

Spiritually it is important as the dwelling place of the Lord:

For the Lord has chosen Zion; He has desired it for His habitation; this is my resting place forever; here I will dwell for I have desired it.

Psalm 132: 13-16

Prophetically it is important because it is at the centre of what will happen on this earth in the fulfilment of God's predictions. Psalm 48 relates how the Kings of the earth have gathered together at Zion, but they are astounded, they tremble and are in anguish. Why? Because it is the time of Armaggedon, the end of the age. This psalm calls Zion the 'city of the great King' but that had not taken place and cannot take place until our Lord Jesus Christ comes to the earth to establish His Kingdom and the millennial reign.

In this passage in Revelation, therefore, John is giving us a fore-taste of the beginning of Christ's millennial reign.

What is the significance of the number?

Christ stands on Mount Zion accompanied by 144,000. In Chapter 7 we are informed that the 144,000 is comprised of 12,000 from each of the twelve tribes of Israel. The amazing fact about the number is that despite persecution and opposition it remains intact. None has been lost. God's protection has preserved them.

What is the purpose of the name?

The Father's name was written on their forehead. At the beginning of the Tribulation period the Father's name is given (Chapter 7). Now we see the same group at the end of the Tribulation still displaying the power of that wonderful name. The name guaranteed safety.

What is the meaning of the new song?

The song is one of praise from the 144,000 who have been redeemed from the earth. It reaches to the throne of God to the four living creatures and the Church. The large choir of 144,000 are the first-fruits of the Tribulation who will inhabit the earth during the millennial reign. These people are chaste in character. Their purity, honesty, loyalty and dedication are honoured by their God.

CHANNEL 2 Rev 14: 6-7

Then I saw another angel flying in mid-heaven, with an eternal gospel to proclaim to those who dwell on earth, to every nation and tribe and tongue and people; and he said with a loud voice, 'Fear God and give him glory, for the hour of his judgment has come; and worship him who made heaven and earth, the sea and the fountains of water.

The second phase of the painting symbolises the angelic proclamation in the two-edged sword which is directed from heaven to earth. Red runs parallel with the sword reminding us that the eternal gospel is based upon the redemptive act of our Lord Jesus accomplished on Calvary, declared and complemented by the resurrection. The cloud in the second picture reminds us that the angel makes the proclamation from mid-heaven.

Why is the gospel described as eternal? An explanation is given in the painting and is highlighted in the idea of the balance. The hour of judgment has come. It is God's time for reckoning. Here is a gospel that has an eternal significance. Judgment is eternal. Blessing is eternal. There is an awesome permanence in the everlasting gospel. 'This is an ageless gospel in the sense that God's righteousness is ageless. Throughout eternity God will continue to manifest Himself in grace towards the saints and in punishment toward the wicked.' (John F. Walvoord). God's justice symbolised in the balance, is an eternal concept.

CHANNEL 3 Rev 14: 8-11

Another angel, a second, followed, saying, 'Fallen, fallen is Babylon the great, she who made all nations drink the wine of her impure passion.' And another angel, a third, followed them, saying with a loud voice, 'If any one worships the beast and its image, and receives a mark on his forehead or on his hand, he also shall drink the wine of God's wrath, poured unmixed into the cup of his anger, and he shall be tormented with fire and brimstone in the presence of the holy angels and in the presence of the Lamb. And the smoke of their torment goes up for ever and ever; and they have no rest, day or night, these worshippers of the beast and its image, and whoever receives the mark of its name.

In the second picture we have considered the message of the first angel; now the third picture conveys the indisputable fact that Babylon is fallen – the message of the second angel – followed by a message of judgment declared by a third angel.

Notice the colours the artist has used to symbolise Babylon (Plate 17). There is a dark smoke haze through which we catch a glimpse of idolatry and the image of the beast. In the Bible, Babylon is used as a composite title. This is seen in prophecy where Babylon can be a literal city, a political power or a religious system. In verse 8 the impure passion of the Babylonian system is exposed. Dr Donald Grey Barnhouse developed a statement of the noted German writer, Thomas Mann, who analysed Europe's danger of 1930s as 'mass drunkenness' that relieves the individual of responsibility – 'mass hysteria' which is the evidence of having drunk the wine of impure passion.

The television news reports on political extremists reveal their hysterical chants, their threatening gestures. We can only describe it as drunkenness, when they are temporarily deprived of self-control, through political and military brainwashing. Those who have been intoxicated by Babylon's impure passion will be compelled to drink 'the wine of God's wrath.'

Eternal Judgment

Some commentators side-step the stern teaching of this section which explicitly states that those who worship the beast or receive his mark are destined for an agonising judgment. It is a mind-shattering experience to learn

... he shall be tormented with fire and brimstone in the presence of the holy angels and in the presence of the Lamb. And the smoke of their torment goes up forever and ever ...

Revelation 14: 10-11

We are confronted with the concept of eternal judgment. This is a dread reality conveyed by the terms 'tormented', 'fire' and 'brimstone'. God uses expressions known to us and through them refers to realities beyond the grave. Christians ought to stand against sentimental attitudes toward the divine wrath. Watered down doctrine follows the sentimental approach. Some people, labouring under a misapprehension, suggest that we should forget about the Apocalypse and get back to the teaching of Jesus, imagining that there is a softness in His approach. But is that so? There are fifty-six occasions of the word 'hell' in the teaching of our Lord. All of these are translated as 'hell' in the Authorised Version. On examination we discover that most of these translations are from the Hebrew *sheol* and the Greek *hades* meaning the 'grave' and 'the unseen state' respectively. But there are ten passages in which our Lord uses the word *Gehenna* which, taken together with other verses, refers to the future state of the people that refuse to accept the mercy and forgiveness of God in Jesus Christ. We have no right to be broader-minded than Christ. We have no right to nurture false hopes which have no basis in His teaching.

When we consider the judgment of God, the word retribution is to be preferred to punishment. Why this distinction? Because the Bible teaches that the fate of the Christ-rejector is not arbitrary, but the necessary consequence of their own sins. Our Lord spoke with certainty about retribution.

Plate No. 17

193

But I say to you that every one who is angry with his brother shall be liable to judgment; whoever insults his brother shall be liable to the council, and whoever says, 'You fool!' shall be liable to the hell of fire.

Matthew 5:22

Christ speaks of causeless anger and careless condemnation of others as placing us as being 'liable to the hell [Gehenna] of fire'. In verses 29 and 30 of the same chapter, He pronounces a similar warning concerning the sin of lust. It must not be overlooked that these passages are in the Sermon on the Mount, which is the most generally accepted part of Christ's teaching.

In our Lord's own explanation of the parable of the weeds found in Matthew 13: 41-42, He declared,

The Son of man will send his angels, and they will gather out of his kingdom all causes of sin and all evildoers, and throw them into the furnace of fire; there men will weep and gnash their teeth.

Again, in the same gospel, our Lord speaks of the hypocritical Pharisees as 'children of hell' [Gehenna], showing that their conduct had fitted them for it. In verse 33 of the same chapter He interrogates them, 'How are you to escape being sentenced to hell?' [Gehenna]. Hell, or Gehenna, has not been prepared for human beings. This is stated categorically in Matthew 25:41:

Depart from me, you cursed, into the eternal fire prepared for the devil and his angels.'

We may conclude that if Gehenna is not prepared for human beings, then human beings prepare themselves for it!

Does our Lord's teaching relate to the teaching in the Apocalypse about torment, fire and brimstone, or in other words, what did our Lord say about the character of future retribution? In Mark 9:43-48 He speaks about being thrown into Hell [Gehenna], and reminds us that in that terrible place 'their worm does not die', and 'the fire is not quenched'. In so doing, our Lord utilised the common Jewish metaphors for Gehenna. These were taken from the valley of Hinnom where the refuse was destroyed by fire, and the worms fed upon the unburied corpses that were thrown there. It is obvious that the undying worm and the unquenchable fire are metaphorical, yet these dramatic figures of speech must be symbolical of a terrible reality. We must never forget that in Luke 16 the Lord, Himself, speaks about a man being in torment, and in anguish, and that taking place in Hades. The moral torture of an acutely sharpened conscience cannot be grasped by us, but we must ponder the circumstances of the moral torment where intensified lusts and passions find no means of gratification. Think about that — the pleasure gone while the power remains! The symbols used by our Lord in His teaching and the statements we find in the Apocalypse do not present pious fiction but plain facts.

We may be agreed about our Lord's teaching about the certainty and character of future retribution, but what about the continuity of future retribution? Does our Lord agree with the statement that 'they have no rest day and night'? One writer suggests that this teaching in the Apocalypse is sub-christian, but that cannot be if our Lord gave similar teaching.

Aionias is the Greek word which is translated 'everlasting' or 'eternal'— literally it means age-long. It occurs no less than twenty-five times in the New Testament. It is used twice of the Gospel, once of the Gospel Covenant, once of the consolation brought to us by the Gospel, twice of God's own being, four times of the future of the unregenerate, and fifteen times of the present and future life of the believer. No one thinks of limiting its duration in the first four cases and the last. Why then do so in the other one?

So, then, the teaching of our Lord and the teaching of the Apocalypse are not contradictory but complementary. Both our Lord and John the seer are agreed in the inspiration of the Holy Spirit that as there is no final restoration for the devil and his angels, so there can be no final restoration of those who die in their sins without Christ.

CHANNEL 4 Rev 14: 12-16

Here is a call for the endurance of the saints, those who keep the commandments of God and the faith of Jesus. And I heard a voice from heaven saying, 'Write this: Blessed are the dead who die in the Lord henceforth.' 'Blessed indeed,' says the Spirit, 'that they may rest from their labours, for their deeds follow them!' Then I looked, and lo, a white cloud, and seated on the cloud one like a son of man, with a golden crown on his head, and a sharp sickle in his hand. And another angel came out of the temple, calling with a loud voice to him who sat upon the cloud, 'Put in your sickle, and reap, for the hour to reap has come, for the harvest of the earth is fully ripe'. So he who sat upon the cloud swung his sickle on the earth, and the earth was reaped.

The call for endurance is issued. A voice from heaven summons John the Seer to be his amanuensis. Beatitudes can mean 'beautiful attitudes', and this beatitude in Revelation is no exception. Blessing is promised to those who, during the Tribulation, die in the Lord. This part of the narrative is represented in Plate 17 in the triangle of gold; the triangle draws the eye upward to that vision which has compelled the Seer to look up.

John sees a white cloud. A person sits upon the cloud and appears as the son of man. There is the absence of the resplendent glory that our Lord said would accompany the Son of man when he returned to the earth:

Then will appear the Son of man in heaven and all the tribes of the earth will mourn, and they will see the Son of man coming on the clouds of heaven with power and great glory.

Matthew 24:30

Some scholars have argued that this one who is like the Son of man is an angel and not the Lord Jesus Christ. But it should be remembered that in Revelation 1 John saw the Lord as 'one like a son of man'. It is true that the One seated upon the white cloud does not seem to have the accompaniment of overpowering glory, but it is also true that the person has a golden crown on his head and a sharp sickle in his hand. The crown combines the symbols of deity and victory. The crown (Greek, *stephanos*,) is the laurel wreath as we have already seen in our study, but here we are informed that the crown is gold.

The victorious Christ, in His deity, exercises His authority in the use of the sickle. The word 'sickle' occurs twelve times in the Bible and seven of these are contained in Chapter 14 of Revelation. The sickle is described as *oxus* – meaning 'sharp'. This word sharp is characteristic of the Revelation. Six times this word is used – three times of the sickle and three times of the sword that proceeds from our Lord's mouth in searching judgment: Revelation 1:16; 2:12 and 19:15.

Our Lord's sharp sickle reaps a harvest, represented by the strip of golden grain between the dark blue sky and the golden triangle. An angelic voice signals that the time is right and the harvest is over-ripe. The Greek word translated ripe is *exeranthe* and means over-ripe, almost dry. We are reminded of the words of our Lord, 'For if they do this when the wood is green, what will happen when it is dry?' (Luke 23:31). The final state is dry; it is obviously a harvest of judgment.

CHANNELS 5 and 6 Rev 14: 17-20

And another angel came out of the temple in heaven, and he too had a sharp sickle. Then another angel came out from the altar, the angel who has power over fire, and he called with a loud voice to him who had the sharp sickle, 'Put in your sickle, and gather the clusters of the vine of the earth, for its grapes are ripe'. So the angel swung his sickle on the earth, and gathered the vintage of the earth, and threw it into the great wine press of the wrath of God; and the wine press was trodden outside the city, and blood flowed from the wine press, as high as a horse's bridle, for one thousand six hundred stadia.

Notice the artist's use of colour and symbolism. In the top right-hand corner is the portraiture of the angel in gold, and beneath the angel, authoritative hands reap the grapes so that they fall into the wine-press. In the bottom right-hand corner there is the ominous black, speaking of judgment and associated with the human blood that spurts from the wine-press.

The idea of the great wine-press of the wrath of God makes us shudder, but the symbol of the blood in the sixth channel represents the scriptural statement that blood flowed freely for 'one thousand six hundred stadia'; that is, approximately two hundred miles; it is hard, if not impossible, to imagine. If this is symbolism, what is the reality like? If this is literal, what will the battle be like?

It is a salutary warning. None can afford to spurn God's mercy. None can get away with flouting God's holiness. Examine the six-channel viewing in the painting and narrative. Be certain that Jesus Christ is your Saviour and Lord.

Chapter XVII

'Everyone is criticising and belittling the times,' asserted Emerson, 'yet I think that our times, like all times are very good times, if only we knew what to do with them'.

From time to time waves of disillusionment break over us, leaving us shattered and dazed. 'If only we knew what to do with them!' What can we do about the anarchy, brutality, selfishness and thoughtlessness of man? Humanity seems to be obsessed with futile, feckless trivialities, alternating between terror and hope. What is the answer? Christians believe that the only answer is the direct intervention of God.

It is said, 'A Christian has no right to be discouraged in the same world as God'. This part of the Apocalypse makes an ominous reference to terror, but it also presents the overtones of hope, indeed, this chapter presents another proof of God's sovereignty.

ANOTHER SIGN   Rev 15:1

Then I saw another portent in heaven, great and wonderful, seven angels with seven plagues, which are the last, for with them the wrath of God is ended.

We meet the same word here that we found in Chapter 12 of the Apocalypse – *semeion* – indicating not just a portent but a significant sign; in fact, the Seer explains that it is a great and wonderful sign. Its greatness is shown by the seven angels with seven judgments; it is wonderful because with these judgments the wrath of God is ended.

AN ALTERED SEA   Rev 15:2

And I saw what appeared to be a sea of glass mingled with fire, and those who had conquered the beast and its image and the number of its name, standing beside the sea of glass with harps of God in their hands.

In the geometrical chart, representing chapters four and five of the Apocalypse, Plate 3, we considered the sea of glass before the throne of

God. Now, in Chapter 15, the same sea of glass is mingled with fire. What is the significance of this? Turn again to the geometrical chart, and notice that before God's throne there are also seven torches of fire. Here, therefore, either the fire and water have inter-mingled, or the seven-fold flame is on, or above, the crystal sea which in turn reflects the glowing fire. The significant alteration seems to emphasise judgment.

Celestial fire cleanses and purges; it is the symbol of judgment. Never forget the Godhead's burning flame!

The Father — 'Our God is a consuming fire' (Hebrews 12:29)
The Son — 'I came to cast fire upon the earth' (Luke 12:49)
The Spirit — 'There appeared to them tongues as of fire' (Acts 2:3)

Christians will escape the wrath of God as depicted in the Apocalypse, but we cannot escape the glow of the Godhead's burning flame. Take heed of Paul's words to the Corinthians:

Now if any one builds on the foundation with gold, silver, precious stones, wood, hay, stubble — each man's work will become manifest; for the Day will disclose it, because it will be revealed with fire, and the fire will test what sort of work each one has done. If the work which any man has built on the foundation survives, he will receive a reward. If any man's work is burned up, he will suffer loss, though he himself with be saved, but only as through fire.

1 Corinthians 3: 12-15

This fire is a testing, not a tormenting, fire.

Also in the vision are victors standing 'beside' the sea, although the Greek preposition could be translated 'upon' or 'over'. These believers have overcome the satanic system. In their hands are harps. We are about to enjoy a musical interlude!

ANOTHER SONG Rev 15:3-4

And they sing the song of Moses, the servant of God, and the song of the Lamb, saying,
'Great and wonderful are thy deeds, O Lord God the Almighty!
Just and true are thy ways, O King of the ages!
Who shall not fear and glorify thy name, O Lord? For thou alone art holy.
All nations shall come and worship thee, for thy judgments have been revealed.'

There are two songs combined here: the Song of Moses and the Song of the Lamb. The former (Exodus 15:1-18) celebrates a political emancipation; the latter celebrates a spiritual emancipation. The Lamb is greater than Moses, but both fulfilled the purposes of God in leadership for the people of God.

The Lord's deeds are great and wonderful. He is the Almighty! There is no injustice in the ways of God. The last part of verse 3 has an

Plate No. 18

interesting history in our translations; 'King of the saints' is how it is translated in the Authorised Version; the Revised Version scholars chose 'the King of the Nations', but the Revised Standard Version has 'King of the Ages', which is preferred by many of the scholars who researched the manuscripts. God, alone, is the ruler of eternity. All the nations will come and acknowledge His sovereignty.

AN AMAZING SANCTUARY Verses 5-7

After this I looked, and the temple of the tent of witness in heaven was opened, and out of the temple came the seven angels with the seven plagues, robed in pure bright linen, and their breasts girded with golden girdles. And one of the four living creatures gave the seven angels seven golden bowls full of the wrath of God who lives for ever and ever.

These verses introduce us to the painting, Plate 18. Notice the blend of colours the artist has used. In the Old Testament the 'tent of witness' curtains and the veil were made of fine linen with the colour scheme of 'blue, purple and scarlet'. (Exodus 36:8 and 35).

Cherubim were skilfully worked into the curtains and veil. Our painting incorporates these colours, but instead of the angelic creatures being embroidered on the colour scheme, we have seven angels emerging from the heavenly sanctuary. These sinless beings come from the Holy of Holies representing the radiance of God's righteousness and the power of His absolute justice. They are clothed in white linen, representing purity. They have golden girdles and the gold reflects the deity of the Godhead. One of the four living creatures gives the angels seven golden bowls. This leads us to another startling fact.

THE SYMBOL OF SMOKE Rev 15:8

. . . and the temple was filled with smoke from the glory of God and from his power, and no one could enter the temple until the seven plagues of the seven angels were ended.

There is smoke in the heavenly sanctuary as the angels enact the judgment of the planet Earth.

In the Bible the symbol of smoke on most occasions represents the presence or the purity of God. The word 'smoke' (*kapnos* in the Greek) occurs thirteen times in the New Testament. Only one of these references occurs outside the Apocalypse — in Acts 2:19. In the Old Testament we find that there was smoke on Mount Sinai because the Lord descended upon it (Exodus 19:18). At his 'call', Isaiah saw the temple filled with God's glory, but we are reminded that the house was filled with smoke (Isaiah 6:1-4). Whilst Aaron, on the Day of Atonement, had to make sure that the cloud of the incense covered the Mercy Seat (Leviticus 16:12-13).

AWESOME SEVERITIES
. . . seven golden bowls full of the wrath of God who lives forever and ever.

These severities are further described in Chapter 16.

The Judgment of God

Revelation 16

Chapter XVIII

Let us consider, with the help of the artist's illustrative and interpretative skills, the judgment of God.

THE FIRST BOWL OF GOD'S WRATH Rev 16:2

So the first angel went and poured his bowl on the earth, and foul and evil sores came upon the men who bore the mark of the beast and worshipped its image.

Observe the representation of this terrible judgment, Plate 19. Beneath and slightly to the left of the red dragon, there is a semi-abstract, grotesque face. This epitomises the foul and evil sores that come upon those who have the mark of the beast. What causes the epidemic? The question is not *who?* for it is God who pours out the judgment, but *what?* is used. It is here that we can, with restraint, use our imagination. Look at that face again. Sores are on the surface of the body, but they are the result of an internal condition. When the bloodstream is impure, the poison breaks out into spots and sores. Man's corruption becomes apparent during this judgment. His inward moral corruption is seen in an outward physical way.

When someone has smallpox and is covered with sores, we isolate the patient for at least two reasons. Firstly, the disease is infectious and society demands the ostracism of the victim. Secondly, it is a most unpleasant experience to look at someone who is literally disfigured with sores and scabs, so we hide the poor creature from the soft sophistication of society. But this first judgment is extensive and public. All those who have the mark of the beast suffer. There is no escape.

THE SECOND BOWL OF GOD'S WRATH Rev 16:3

The second angel poured his bowl into the sea, and it became like the blood of a dead man, and every living thing died that was in the sea.

Scrutinise the bottom right-hand corner of the picture. The red effect symbolises the sea that has turned red. Again, we pose a question : 'What causes the sea to become like blood?' We know that our oceans and seas are being polluted. It is not beyond the scope of our imagination to visualise what will happen when all the creatures in the ocean die. What happens when a fish dies? It floats on the surface of the water. Think of it! Billions of sea creatures – whale, shark, tuna, cod, haddock, herring, crab, lobster – floating upon the waters, the result of a universal pollution of the oceans and the seas. An appalling sight and nauseous stench such as this will have a terrible effect upon men and women.

THE THIRD BOWL OF GOD'S WRATH Rev 16:4-7

The third angel poured his bowl into the rivers and the fountains of water, and they became blood. And I heard the angel of water say, 'Just art thou in these thy judgments, thou who art and wast, O Holy One. For men have shed the blood of saints and prophets, and thou hast given them blood to drink. It is their due!' And I heard the altar cry, 'Yea, Lord God the Almighty, true and just are thy judgments!'

Focus your attention on the bottom left-hand corner of the painting. Here is a representation of the rivers and fountains becoming blood. Following the corrupting sores and the blood-red oceans and seas we have the total pollution of the waters. It is no wonder that the angel of the water makes a pronouncement! He reminds the human race that they are reaping what they have sown.

The 'altar cry' takes us back to the fifth seal when the martyrs exclaimed, 'O Sovereign Lord, holy and true, how long before thou wilt judge and avenge our blood on those who dwell upon the earth?' (Rev 6:9-11). Here, in Chapter 16, the blood of the martyrs is avenged.

THE FOURTH BOWL OF GOD'S WRATH Rev 16:8-9

The fourth angel poured his bowl on the sun, and it was allowed to scorch men with fire; men were scorched by the fierce heat, and they cursed the name of God who had power over these plagues, and they did not repent and give him glory.

The artist has given a spotlight effect to the sun. Through carelessness many people have experienced sunburn rather than suntan – A most unpleasant experience! Violet rays are welcome in moderation only. Now we learn the terrible fact – 'men were scorched by the fierce heat'. Is this a sun-induced heatwave or is it atomic radiation? Remember that heat causes dehydration; water is necessary to replace the fluids of the body, but if there is no water available, the body becomes

a syndrome of pain; agony with red-hot iron shoes walks along every nerve. Men's reaction to this judgment is swift — 'they cursed the name of God'. Observe the two men in the painting. They represent humanity — judged, agonised, and in its lost state cursing God.

THE FIFTH BOWL OF GOD'S WRATH Rev 16:10-11

The fifth angel poured his bowl on the throne of the beast, and its kingdom was in darkness; men gnawed their tongues in anguish and cursed the God of heaven for their pain and sores, and did not repent of their deeds.

It is obvious from the Scriptures that Satan has his throne on earth, but where is it located? Recall the teaching of Revelation 2:13 'I know where you dwell, where Satan's throne is, [Pergamum] ; you hold fast my name and you did not deny my faith.' The Antichrist has his literal headquarters upon earth. But we should not dogmatise about its location. We know that he shall assume authority. Administratively he shall control men and women for Satan. People will be held in this satanic sway, and will look to his capital as the religious and commercial centre of the world. The first beast of chapter 13 is actually dethroned and displaced by God.

The darkness covering the Beast's kingdom is depicted in Plate 19 by the black sky. The Scriptures abound with teaching about darkness. There is literal and spiritual darkness. Both are combined in this judgment. The one who is called 'the angel of light' (2 Corinthians 11:14) now has a kingdom of darkness. The dragon in the painting suggests the Satanic consternation as the Lord God makes a direct intervention upon his quasi-spiritual domain.

Let us remember that there are those on earth who have not been controlled by the Beast. We see them in our picture, lifting their hands to God, praying and praising the One who rules from heaven. In contrast men 'gnawed their tongues in anguish'. When the tongue is bitten accidentally, the discomfort can be considerable, but in this case the men deliberately gnawed their tongues. The Greek word *masomai* only occurs here in the New Testament and means to chew. It is not easy to grasp the excruciating pain that these people have to bear, but despite the disfigurement of the tongue, they curse God. Note that the bowl judgments are cumulative: 'they cursed the God of heaven for their pain and sores'; the latter takes us back to the first bowl.

THE SIXTH BOWL OF GOD'S WRATH Rev 16:12-16

The sixth angel poured his bowl on the great river Euphrates, and its water was dried up, to prepare the way for the kings from the east. And I saw, issuing from the mouth of the dragon and from the mouth of the beast and from the mouth of the false prophet, three foul spirits like frogs; for they are demonic spirits, performing signs, who go abroad to the kings of the whole world, to assemble them for battle on the great day of God the Almighty. ('Lo, I am coming like a thief! Blessed is he who is awake, keeping his garments that he may not go naked and be seen exposed!') And they assembled them at the place which is called in Hebrew Armageddon.

The river Euphrates was mentioned during the judgment of the sixth trumpet; now it is used in the prophecy of the sixth bowl. Trumpets and bowls are complementary. An army of 200 million is associated with the sixth trumpet but the sixth bowl reminds us that when the army marches from the Far East towards the Middle East, the river will be dried up through the direct intervention of God.

In Genesis 15:18, God made a covenant with Abram: 'To your descendants I give this land, from the river of Egypt to the great river, the river Euphrates.' Devout Jews are aware of this promise. It could be that during the Great Tribulation, Israel's borders will reach the Euphrates. If that should happen, there will be a most significant geographical alteration. Study the map on Plate 22. Two thirds of Syria would be annexed. Possibly Jordan and part of Iraq would become Israeli territory. If this takes place, then we can grasp the significance of the Euphrates being dried up. It removes the natural defence line between Israel, or those who occupy Israel at that time, and the large army led by the kings of the East.

In the sixth-bowl judgment, three foul spirits like frogs emerge from the mouth of the dragon. The frog can clearly be seen in Plate 19 and represents demonic spirits. The climax of demonism is part of the eschatology of the New Testament. No doctrine of the last things can afford to neglect biblical demonology.

Now the Spirit expressly says that in later times some will depart from the faith by giving heed to deceitful spirits and doctrines of demons, through the pretensions of liars whose consciences are seared, who forbid marriage and enjoin abstinence from foods which God created to be received with thanksgiving by those who believe and know the truth.

1 Timothy 4:1-3

Much of the depravity around us is instigated by demons. The sophisticated, modern church refuses to recognise the existence of evil supernatural forces. This unbelief does not obviate the facts. Some books, films and personalities seem to be produced and directed by these emissaries of Satan. Let us remember that the demonic spirits perform signs and work miracles. At this particular time in prophecy we see them assembling the nations for battle on the great day of God the

Almighty. The site of the battle is called Armageddon. We shall analyse the strategies that lead to this battle later.

Before we leave the sixth-bowl judgment, examine the important parenthesis in verse 15. The Lord is coming like a thief. When He comes like a thief, it should be understood that the Lord is coming for those who do not belong to Him. They shall be taken for judgment. A thief comes unexpectedly to take what does not belong to him – so will the Lord.

THE SEVENTH BOWL OF GOD'S WRATH Rev 16:17-21

The seventh angel poured his bowl into the air, and a great voice came out of the temple, from the throne, saying, 'It is done!' And there were flashes of lightning, loud noises, peals of thunder, and a great earthquake such as had never been since men were on the earth, so great was that earthquake. The great city was split into three parts, and the cities of the nations fell, and God remembered great Babylon, to make her drain the cup of the fury of his wrath. And every island fled away, and no mountains were to be found; and great hailstones, heavy as a hundred-weight, dropped on men from heaven, till men cursed God for the plague of the hail, so fearful was that plague.

There are three consecutive ends of ages spoken of in the New Testament:

'He has appeared once for all at the end of the age to put away sin by the sacrifice of Himself' (Hebrews 9:26). Christ's first coming terminated the Jewish system in the judgment and rejection of the House of Israel, and opened the door of grace to the Gentiles. This age finished with dramatic solemnity. The temple veil was rent, the earth shook, the sky was darkened and from the cross our Lord ended the age with the mighty cry 'it is finished!'

'So it will be at the end of the age. The angels will come out and separate the evil from the righteous' (Matthew 13:49). At Christ's second coming, the dispensation of grace will be terminated, the apostate church will be judged and Israel restored. In the midst of the lightning, loud noises, peals of thunder and earthquake, the voice of God with earnest eloquence will announce 'it is done!'

"Then comes the end, when he delivers the kingdom to God the Father after destroying every rule and every authority and power' (1 Corinthians 15:24). This takes place when the first earth and first heaven have passed away, when death, sorrow and crying have been abolished and the Millennium has ended. Again God speaks 'It is done! I am the Alpha and the Omega, the beginning and the end' (Revelation 21:6).

Our hearts ought to burst with praise as we hear the voice of our God finalising His plans.

The word 'great' occurs five times in this passage (verses 17-21). As we have just seen there is a 'great voice'. This proceeds from the throne. There is also a 'great earthquake'. It is well known that the river Jordan flows along a rift valley – a geological fault which extends into Africa and around the Pacific rim. There is no doubt that this final earthquake will be the greatest in the history of the planet earth. In Plate 19 the artist has depicted the flashing lightning in the sky above and the devastating earthquake on the earth below.

Next, we read of the 'great city' – 'great Babylon'. Here the artist has divided the painting into three sections to portray the words of verse 19 – 'the city was split into three parts'. What panic, horror and fear there will be from such devastation, especially when the cities of the nations fall, all the islands disappear or drift, and all the mountains begin to disintegrate.

Finally, consider the 'great hailstones' (shown in the painting as a spiked hailstone to the left of the picture just above the frog). These hailstones weigh as much as 7 stone or 112 pounds! Considered literally this means the extermination of everything; taken figuratively, it suggests that the destruction of the earth will be complete. Either way, rebellious man cannot win. This precipitation of hail is a prelude to the falling of the great stone from Heaven prophesied by Daniel:

And in the days of those kings the God of heaven will set up a kingdom which shall never be destroyed, nor shall its sovereignty be left to another people. It shall break in pieces all these kingdoms and bring them to an end, and it shall stand for ever; just as you saw that a stone was cut from a mountain by no human hand, and that it broke in pieces the iron, the bronze, the clay, the silver, and the gold. A great God has made known to the king what shall be hereafter. The dream is certain, and its interpretation sure.

Daniel 2:44-45

This stone that struck the image became a great mountain and filled the whole earth. It is a sobering thought.

Remember the words of Hebrews 10:31 'It is a fearful thing to fall into the hands of the living God.'

Chapter XIX

Trends in the fields of technology, weaponry, politics and religion during the past three or four decades have proved that a literal fulfilment of the prophetic teaching of Revelation is not an extreme figment of the imagination. All the prophecies of Revelation are capable of being literally fulfilled. In particular there are three major trends that indicate that we are approaching the end of the age.

1. THE EMERGENCE OF ISRAEL AS A NEW STATE

Here we have the political miracle of the twentieth century. This fact of Israel becoming a nation was foretold by many of the Old Testament prophets. At the beginning of the century there were no more than 25,000 Jews in the land of Palestine. In 1976 there are over 3 million Jews in Israel. This is a miracle indeed. It is the modern Exodus involving three times as many people who left Egypt under the leadership of Moses.

The Zionist movement began at the end of the nineteenth century, and made slow progress into the twentieth century. By 1917 the Balfour Declaration was issued and gave the impression that the British government was willing to give support for the Jews' return to their homeland, Palestine. This decision was rescinded by the British government soon after the First World War.

By the year 1938 the number of Jews in Palestine had increased to 400,000. A decade later — 14 May 1948 — the State of Israel was recognised by the United Nations Organisation. The struggle, bloodshed and pathos of the conflict between Arab and Jew is detailed accurately in *O Jerusalem!* by Larry Collins and Dominique Lapierre.

The Six Day War of June 1967 brought about the annexation of Jerusalem by Israeli forces. Jerusalem had not been in their possession since 586 BC. Another miracle had happened! Announcing the Israeli victory General Moshe Dayan, Commander-in-chief of the Israeli forces, made it clear that Israel was in Jerusalem and would never leave it again.

Israel's economic development has surprised the world; irrigation systems, improved methods of farming, industry and the new modern cities of Haifa and Tel Aviv, including the tourist trade euphemistically described as 'pilgrimages', provide irrefutable evidence of a progressive nation.

2. THE MOVE TOWARDS WORLD GOVERNMENT

The world powers Russia and America are attempting by means of *détente* to end the era of strained relations between East and West. Remembering the failure of the League of Nations after the First World War, the leaders of the nations are working hard to establish good relationships within the United Nations Organisation. The Common Market has proved that the concept of a United Nations of Europe is viable. We have noticed previously in Revelation 13:7 that the Antichrist is given authority 'over every tribe and people and tongue and nation'. God's sovereign purpose is working out that situation which will bring the nations to the point of saying, 'Peace and security!' After this, there will be swift destruction. A system of world government is forecast in the Bible.

3. THE GROWTH OF A WORLD CHURCH

The visible church has always been divisive. In AD 313, Constantine the Great, by the Edict of Milan, decreed full legal toleration for Christianity. Constantine adopted Christianity, but his motives have been hotly debated. He considered himself as 'the servant of God', having the same status as the church leaders and sometimes authority over them. Constantine was the *pontifex maximus* in the garb of Christianity. Church and State had come together with a semblance of unity, despite the protests of the Donatists — the dissenters of the fourth century. Division between the Eastern and Western Churches took place in the eleventh century. This Great Schism of AD 1054 meant that the Eastern Orthodox Church refused to accept the authority of the Pope and the Roman Church. The Reformation, which arose about AD 1500 and reached its climax around the mid-seventeenth century, brought about a radical rupture. Protestantism eventually became fragmented with many denominations and thousands of independent churches.

During the past fifty years ecumenicalism has been discussed within the context of the possibility of a world church, that is, a visible unity of Christendom. The World Council of Churches was formed in 1948 and is dedicated to the cause of Church unity amongst Protestantism, the Roman Catholic and the Greek Orthodox Church.

From the standpoint of prophecy, a world church is inevitable, but it will not reach its culmination until Christ comes for His true Church. Revelation 17 presents a picture of the World Church becoming the Apostate Church. To assist you in the understanding of the counterfeit church, examine the painting (Plate 20) which includes most of the details found in the narrative.

The Apostate Church

Chapters 17 and 18 are closely related and give a graphic description of the system that is called Babylon. In Chapter 17 the ecclesiastical destruction of Babylon is described while in Chapter 18 the political destruction of the system is represented — though both aspects are interfused.

The name Babylon is derived from the Hebrew word *'Babel'.* Enshrined in this name is the meaning 'the gate of God'. The ending *-el* is a derivation of *Elohim* meaning God. It is found in other Hebrew names, for example Bethel, meaning the house of God; Rachel - the lamb of God; Daniel - God is my judge, and Joel which affirms Yahweh is God. We must ask the question, 'Why did the people call the tower Babel?' (Genesis 11:9)

Babel is the source of false religion and idolatry. Babel or Babylon is associated with astrology.   The Chaldeans were the aristocratic priesthood of the Babylonian Empire. These priestly astrologers exercised great authority, almost equal in prestige to the King of Babylon himself. Giant observatories called *ziggurats* were built by the King. When we study Revelation 17, it is obvious that Babylon is a descriptive term for the world religion. It is necessary to differentiate between Christianity and religion. It has been said 'Religion is the process of man trying to achieve goodness, perfection and acceptance with God by his own efforts. Christianity, on the other hand, is God saying that man cannot reach Him except through the one path He has provided — through the acceptance of His Son, Jesus Christ.'

Revelation 17 is the culmination of the Babylonian system in the religious setting. The true Church of Christ has been taken from the earth. The Apostate Church is on her own. She is described as the harlot.

Compare the painting with the Scripture.

Then one of the seven angels who had the seven bowls came and said to me, 'Come, I will show you the judgment of the great harlot who is seated upon many waters, with whom the kings of the earth have committed fornication, and with the wine of whose fornication the dwellers on earth have become drunk.' And he carried me away in the Spirit into a wilderness, and I saw a woman sitting on a scarlet beast which was full of blasphemous names, and it had seven heads and ten horns. The woman was arrayed in purple and scarlet, and bedecked with gold and jewels and pearls, holding in her hand a golden cup full of abominations and the impurities of her fornication; and on her forehead was written a name of mystery: 'Babylon the great, mother of harlots and of earth's abominations.' And I saw the woman, drunk with the blood of the saints and the blood of the martyrs of Jesus.

Revelation 17:1-6

We note five salient characteristics of this monstrous woman.

1.   The Disloyalty of the Harlot Church

She is described as the 'great harlot'. The overall impression of the narrative and the painting suggest that you dare not trust this woman, that is, the system of apostasy. She is not a demimonde being treated like someone who has been ostracised from society, but is the gay deceiver, the majestic minx, misdirecting mankind under the name of religion. We dare not trust her! She is disloyal, like the concubine who, taken by the Levite of Judges 19, played the harlot against him. So it is with the apostate church, the kings of the earth committed fornication with her.

Dr. Francis A. Schaeffer, in his book *The Church Before the Watching World,* has a chapter entitled 'Adultery and Apostasy' — the bride and the bridegroom theme! He maintains that it is spiritual adultery for the church to be unfaithful to Christ. Paul wrote to the church in Corinth, 'For I am jealous over you with godly jealousy: for I have espoused you to one husband, that I may present you as a chaste virgin to Christ.' Many Christians are guilty of spiritual adultery. They have 'intimate' fellowship with those who derogate Christ. This is unfaithfulness. There is a doctrinal permissiveness in the church; she will tolerate anything! This harlot system is the epitome of spiritual adultery.

The Person of Christ is the touchstone of fellowship. We dare not trust the person or the system that demeans Christ. The deity of our Lord, His unique mediatorship, supreme kingship and position as judge are some of the criteria for Christian togetherness.

2.   The Drunkenness of the Harlot Church

She made the dwellers on earth drunk. John asserts, 'I saw the woman, drunk with the blood of the martyrs of Jesus'. Addicted to blood!

Plate No. 20

What an indictment! Normal drunkenness means that the person is temporarily deprived of self-control, but the harlot's drunkenness is of a permanent nature. She is controlled by Satan and she has a devilish addiction. The receptacle from which she drinks is significant. The artist has made a feature of the golden cup which is 'full of abominations and the impurities of her fornication'. Abominations suggests idolatrous practises. The impurities indicate that there is a lack of moral standards.

Study the painting. Examine the face of the drunkard. She is insensitive, harsh and unmerciful, her eyes are out of focus and her mouth is distorted. From the death of Stephen, the first Christian martyr, until our time, many true believers have been murdered by others who posed as religious people; like the harlot, they lacked true insight and projected distorted teaching.

3.   The Dictatorship of the Harlot Church
There are two key statements here. The first is that she is seated upon many waters — verse 1. The explanation is given in verse 15: 'The waters that you saw, where the harlot is seated, are peoples and multitudes and nations and tongues.' The second statement, verse 3, is most significant: 'I saw a woman sitting on a scarlet beast which was full of blasphemous names, and it had seven heads and ten horns.' It is apparent that the religious power is controlling the political authorities at this time. During a part of the Tribulation period the ecclesiastical system will appear supreme, but that supremacy will be short-lived.

Our narrative and painting depict the harlot sitting on, that is, controlling, the beast and the ten-nation confederacy. The woman has authority over the waters, that is, the many nations. The apostate church has political dominion. There is a subtle circle on the painting that holds the Church and politics together.

4.   The Dress of the Harlot Church
Another examination of the painting will imprint upon our minds the adornment of the apostate church. Purple and scarlet are recognised as her colours. These colours are associated with ecclesiastical pomp, especially in the Roman Catholic and Greek Orthodox churches. This colour scheme will characterise the world church at the end of the age and indicates the grandiose concept of imperial power. Apostasy is presented as having great riches — 'bedecked with gold and jewels and pearls, holding in her hand a golden cup . . . ' The church and mammon are one. Gold is apparent in her hair, on her clothes, around

her person. She is the final expression of mammon, and 'you cannot serve God and mammon' is the categorical teaching of our Lord. The cylinder of gold beneath the harlot's left hand signifies the emptiness and nothingness of apostate riches.

We examine the head-dress of the harlot with its golden effect, but beneath the head and on the forehead there is written a name of mystery — 'Babylon the great, mother of harlots and of earth's abominations'. It was the custom of the common prostitute to have her name upon her brow. Her posterity is responsible for world-wide idolatry. In this harlot church we have apostate Roman Catholicism, heretical Protestantism, mystical paganism — all religious systems that do not have the true God. Remember, our Lord chose twelve disciples, but one of them was an apostate. Judas was a counterfeit. When he knelt in prayer, he was collaborating with the powers of darkness. He kept company with Jesus, but did not know the Lord as his Saviour.

Arithmetical Calculation
Before we consider the destiny of this great apostate super-church, it is necessary to examine verses 7-14.

But the angel said to me, 'Why marvel? I will tell you the mystery of the woman, and of the beast with seven heads and ten horns that carries her. The beast that you saw was, and is not, and is to ascend from the bottomless pit and go to perdition; and the dwellers on earth whose names have not been written in the book of life from the foundation of the world, will marvel to behold the beast, because it was and is not and is to come. This calls for a mind with wisdom: the seven heads are seven hills on which the woman is seated; they are also seven kings, five of whom have fallen, one is, the other has not yet come, and when he comes he must remain only a little while. As for the beast that was and is not, it is an eighth but it belongs to the seven, and it goes to perdition. And the ten horns that you saw are ten kings who have not yet received royal power, but they are to receive authority as kings for one hour, together with the beast. These are of one mind and give over their power and authority to the beast; they will make war on the Lamb, and the Lamb will conquer them, for he is Lord of lords and King of kings, and those with him are called and chosen and faithful.'

Here is a combination of history and prophecy. This comes over clearly from the words — 'The beast that you saw *was*, and *is* not, and *is* to ascend from the bottomless pit'. Past, present and future are caught up in this statement. As verse 9 says, only a mind with divine wisdom can grasp the supreme significance of this teaching.

Scrutinise the painting very carefully. Seven heads are represented. The Scriptures teach that these seven heads have a dual symbolism; that is, they typify seven hills and seven kings. What about the seven hills? A tacit agreement exists amongst most expositors that the seven hills refer to Rome. History bears witness to the fact that Rome is the city of the seven hills. Rome is destined to be the seat of ecclesiastical power at the end of the age. The super church will have its geographical centre at Rome; in other words, the spiritual or religious Babylon will not have headquarters at the river Euphrates, but at the river Tiber.

Consider the puzzles associated with verses 10-11. 'They are also seven kings, five of whom are fallén, one is, the other has not yet come, and when he comes he must remain only a little while, (verse 10). What are the five kingdoms, or empires, that have fallen? Going right back to Old Testament times, contemporaneous with Abraham, was the great Chaldean civilisation. This was succeeded by the Egyptian Empire and reminds us of Moses and the great Exodus. Egypt was a great political power, but it practised syncretism and perpetuated the Chaldean religion. The Babylonian Empire followed Egypt. In Babylon we have the culmination of astrology. It is here that we find the very apex of the pinnacle of paganism. Babylon was replaced by the Medo-Persian Empire which in turn was succeeded by the cultured Greek Empire. Observe that five kingdoms have fallen, but one is in existence during the days of John, and, of course, this is the Roman Empire. The other that is the seventh has not yet come. This refers to the ten-nation confederacy of chapter 13 with Antichrist as ruler.

Now notice 'the beast that was and is not, it is an eighth but it belongs to the seven and it goes into perdition' (verse 11). In Chapter 13 we were told how the beast is mortally wounded, that is the seventh ruler, but he is resuscitated; now he belongs to the seventh, nevertheless he is the eighth with a new sovereign power and 'the whole earth followed the beast with wonder'. We are instructed that the beast is destined for perdition and this prediction is fulfilled in Revelation 19:20 where the beast is 'thrown alive into the lake of fire that burns with brimstone'.

Our arithmetical calculation takes us to verse 12 where the ten-nation confederacy is mentioned. The ten kings will receive power for a limited period of time. Although they will make war upon the Lamb, He will conquer them.

5. The Destruction of the Harlot Church

And he said to me, 'The waters that you saw, where the harlot is seated, are peoples and multitudes and nations and tongues. And the ten horns that you saw, they and the beast will hate the harlot; they will make her desolate and naked, and devour her flesh and burn her up with fire, for God has put it into their hearts to carry out his purpose by being of one mind and giving over their royal power to the beast, until the words of God shall be fulfilled. And the woman that you saw is the great city which has dominion over the kings of the earth.'

Revelation 17:15-18

These verses act like a launching pad and shoot us into orbit with commercial Babylon in Chapter 18. The political system turns against the religious one. In the painting (Plate 21) we see the horror of the total destruction. Our artist, with a touch of spiritual ingenuity, has recognised that when the political power destroys the religious system, the action brings about self-destruction. Notice how the harlot's bracelet turns into a manacle. She is chained to the beast but as he destroys the apostate church, it entails the total destruction of both systems. The enchantress is doomed.

The late Arnold Toynbee, the famous historian, offered a bracing philosophy of history in terms of struggle, crisis and victory within the major civilizations of the world. He believed that a society rises by encountering a challenge – physical, moral or military. Emerging from the crisis, there is a creative minority which offers moral and spiritual leadership. Toynbee maintained that the breakdown of society occurs when the society's creative leadership loses its spiritual vision.

Toynbee's emphasis on religion as the adhesive that holds civilisation together has been appreciated by most Christian historians. He suggested that religion ascended throughout history and eventually a universal Kingdom of God would appear made up of the big four religions – Christianity, Hinduism, Islam and Mahyana Buddhism. If we substitute Christendom for Christianity, we have what Toynbee dreamed about – a universal church, acting as a cohesive principle, although the true Church has been removed. When the Antichrist attacked religion, he removed the adhesive force of the culture, resulting in complete disintegration.

Compare the operative words of the narrative with the painting: 'desolate', not defiant; 'naked', the purple and scarlet, the gold and jewels are stripped from her – she becomes the most horrific nude in human history. 'Devour' – notice the relish of the political system as the woman is 'put in her place'. The 'Fire' projects on the screen of our imagination the strangest cremation service of modern times. As the apostate burns, we are reminded that God's purpose is sovereign – 'God has put it into their hearts to carry out His purpose . . . until the words of God shall be fulfilled.'

Yes, God's fabulous future is secure.

An Economic and Political Upheaval

Chapter XX

We have noticed that Revelation 16 indicates that the seven bowls of judgment will end in the war of Armageddon. That is the military aspect of the end of the age. (We shall analyse this military campaign and final conflict in Chapter 19). In our study of Chapter 17, we have seen the super-church represented by the harlot riding upon the beast. There we have the religious aspect of the finale of the world's history. Now, in Chapter 18, we come back to the same world, but we are considering it from the economic and political aspect. It is a startling fact that there is apparently no mourning over the destruction of the religious Babylon in Chapter 17, but in our study of the commercial Babylon we discover panic and protest as the markets of the world crumble with a resultant massive trade recession and economic catastrophe.

Five strands of teaching are interwoven in this section of God's word. The introductory sentence is surprising:

After this I saw another angel coming down from heaven, having great authority; and the earth was made bright with his splendour.

Revelation 18:1

This is the same angel of Chapter 17. Spiritual splendour and absolute authority have been given to this celestial being.

THE STRAND OF CONDEMNATION
Verses 2 and 3 could be described as a 'doom song'. They contain great poetry which expresses intense passion and grim foretelling, and anticipates the victory of good over evil.

And he called out with a mighty voice, 'Fallen, fallen is Babylon the great! It has become a dwelling place of demons, a haunt of every foul spirit, a haunt of every foul and hateful bird; for all nations have drunk the wine of her impure passion, and the kings of the earth have committed fornication with her, and the merchants of the earth have grown rich with the wealth of her wantonness.'

Revelation 18:2-3

The repetition of the word 'fallen' has been interpreted as two different stages of the fall of Babylon. The religious system has capitulated and now the city of Babylon, the centre of commerce is destroyed.

The mention of demons, foul spirits and hateful birds takes us back to the painting (Plate 21). On the right-hand side of the painting we observe the weird bird. What does it mean to be a 'haunt' of every emissary of Satan? This is significant in the Greek. The word is *phulake* and derives from *phulasso* which means 'to guard'. Sometimes the word is translated as keeping watch, but invariably it means 'prison'. This throws further light on the passage, for it suggests that Babylon is imprisoned with satanic agencies and there is no way of escape. Isaiah 34:11-17 describes the desolation of the nations that have experienced God's anger, and tells how God stretches the line of confusion over the crisis and provides a title that is applicable to the destruction of Babylon – 'No Kingdom There'.

Will there be a literal city of Babylon? In Chapter 17 we discovered that ecclesiastical Babylon had headquarters at Rome, but will a great commercial centre be built at the river Euphrates? The ancient city of Babylon was destroyed according to Old Testament prophecy, but will another city be rebuilt at the Euphrates and become the commercial capital of the world? It may be so. Consider the wealth of the Arabic countries. Oil has brought prosperity to the Middle East. There is a surplus of wealth and it is feasible that the Arabic States could build a modern Babylon. It is important that the destruction of Babylon causes the disruption of the commerce of the earth. Today, if Africa and the Middle East cut off all oil supplies, industry would grind to a halt. Despite the discovery of oil in the North Sea, we are faced with the possibility that the oil capital of the world could be built at the river Euphrates or in the Middle East.

THE STRAND OF SEPARATION

Then I heard another voice from heaven saying, 'Come out of her, my people, lest you take part in her sins, lest you share in her plagues; for her sins are heaped high as heaven, and God has remembered her iniquities. Render to her as she herself has rendered, and repay her double for her deeds; mix a double draught for her in the cup she mixed. As she glorified herself and played the wanton, so give her a like measure of torment and mourning. Since in her heart she says, 'A queen I sit, I am no widow, mourning I shall never see,' so shall her plagues come in a single day,

pestilence and mourning and famine, and she shall be burned with fire; for mighty is the Lord God who judges her.

Revelation 18:4-8

There has always been a rivalry between the city of God and the city of man. The voice from heaven commands God's people, during the Great Tribulation, to come out of the Babylonian system. This separation is two-fold: first, by separation from the system, they will not share in the sin; and second, they will escape the plagues inflicted on the atheistic system which are enumerated in Chapter 16.

Separation has been taught since Old Testament times. Examine the following Scriptures and recognise the need for being different:

Depart, depart, go out thence, touch no unclean thing; go out from the midst of her, purify yourselves, you who bear the vessels of the Lord.

Isaiah 52:11

Flee from the midst of Babylon, and go out of the land of the Chaldeans, and be as he-goats before the flock. For behold, I am stirring up and bringing against Babylon a company of great nations, from the north country; and they shall array themselves against her; from there she shall be taken. Their arrows are like a skilled warrior who does not return empty-handed.

Jeremiah 50:8-9

Ho! Ho! Flee from the land of the north, says the Lord; for I have spread you abroad as the four winds of the heavens, says the Lord. Ho! Escape to Zion, you who dwell with the daughter of Babylon.

Zechariah 2:6-7

Let us not forget that we are also challenged by the Lord to live a life of spiritual separation. Consider some of the statements found in 2 Corinthians 6:14-15:

Do not be mismated with unbelievers. For what partnership have righteousness and iniquity? Or what fellowship has light with darkness? What accord has Christ with Belial? Or what has a believer in common with an unbeliever?

We are enjoined to experience insulation not isolation. Christians are involved with the world but they should not be influenced by the world. Separation has been defined as 'a certain aloofness of spirit maintained in the very heart of the world's traffic'.

Literal separation is expected in this passage of Revelation. 'Her sins are heaped high as heaven', suggests an end-time Tower of Babel — iniquities 'welded together', stretching up to the very throne of God. The burning fire of the painting depicts the intensity of the judgments. None can escape.

THE STRAND OF LAMENTATION

And the kings of the earth, who committed fornication and were wanton with her, will weep and wail over her when they see the smoke of her burning; they will stand far off, in fear of her torment, and say, 'Alas! alas! thou great city, thou mighty city, Babylon! In one hour has thy judgment come'. And the merchants of the earth weep and mourn for her, since no one buys their cargo any more, cargo of gold, silver, jewels and pearls, fine linen, purple, silk and scarlet, all kinds of scented wood, all articles of ivory, all articles of costly wood, bronze, iron and marble, cinnamon, spice, incense, myrrh, frankincense, wine, oil, fine flour and wheat, cattle and sheep, horses and chariots, and slaves, that is, human souls. The fruit for which thy soul longed has gone from thee, and all thy dainties and thy splendour are lost to thee, never to be found again!' The merchants of these wares, who gained wealth from her, will stand far off, in fear of her torment, weeping and mourning aloud, 'Alas, alas, for the great city that was clothed in fine linen, in purple and scarlet, bedecked with gold, with jewels, and with pearls! In one hour all this wealth has been laid waste'. And all shipmasters and seafaring men, sailors and all whose trade is on the sea, stood far off and cried out as they saw the smoke of her burning, 'What city was like the great city?' And they threw dust on their heads, as they wept and mourned, crying out, 'Alas, alas, for the great city where all who had ships at sea grew rich by her wealth! In one hour she has been laid waste.

Revelation 18:9-19

Three different types of people lament. The kings of the earth are represented in the top left-hand corner of the picture behind the beast. It is significant that they speak of a particular city. Descriptive words are very important. The city of Babylon is 'great' and 'mighty'. From the Greek we learn that the use of the definite article underlines how important the city was to the rulers — 'the city the great, Babylon the city the mighty'.

The merchants of the earth and all shipmasters and seafaring men are located by the artist on the right-hand side of the painting, above the weird bird (Plate 21). Trade is paralysed. There is the cessation of the cash flow and raw materials are unobtainable. It is unusual for a shopping list to appear in the Bible, but this one tabulates luxury goods; priceless jewels, fine fabrics, expensive furnishings, exotic perfumes and wholesome food. But the last item is alarming — 'slaves, that is, human souls'. Slavery has never been abolished completely. Godless philosophy and totalitarianism envisage man as 'a protoplasmic mass on the way to the manure pile'. Man is a non-person. It is not surprising that the traders throw dust on their heads and say with pathos, 'In one hour she has been laid waste'.

THE STRAND OF EXULTATION

Rejoice over her, O heaven, O saints and apostles and prophets, for God has given judgment for you against her!

Revelation 18:20

Contrast the three classes expressing the exultation with the three classes associated with the lamentation: saints with kings, apostles with merchants and prophets with shipmasters. Here we have the spiritual and the material, heaven and earth, the Kingdom of God and the satanic system. God's holy ones and spiritual leaders rejoice over the judgment and doom of earth's geniuses and capitalists. God out-thinks and outlasts His enemies!

THE STRAND OF DESOLATION

Then a mighty angel took up a stone like a great millstone and threw it into the sea, saying, 'So shall Babylon the great city be thrown down with violence, and shall be found no more; and the sound of harpers and minstrels, of flute players and trumpeters, shall be heard in thee no more; and a craftsman of any craft shall be found in thee no more; and the sound of the millstone shall be heard in thee no more; and the light of a lamp shall shine in thee no more; and the voice of bride-groom and bride shall be heard in thee no more; for thy merchants were the great men of the earth, and all nations were deceived by thy sorcery. And in her was found the blood of prophets and of saints, and of all who have been slain on earth.

Revelation 18:21-24

The final obliteration of Babylon is represented with dramatic action. Acted parables are found in the Old Testament and used with great effect by Isaiah, Jeremiah and Ezekiel. These acted parables contain the truth and are neither jocular nor superficial.

Babylon's judgment is graphically portrayed in our painting (Plate 21). The mighty angel stands with authority presiding over the despair and chaos of the Babylonian system. Then Babylon is thrown into the sea like a great millstone, seen in the bottom left-hand corner of the painting. This acted parable is proleptic. Babylon is assumed destroyed before it is so. This is the sure word of prophecy. Babylon 'shall be found no more'.

The cessation of activities is symbolised by the broken candle in the bottom right-hand corner of the painting. It is a significant commentary that the great, flamboyant, prosperous empire of Babylon is eventually the extinguished candle — 'and the light of the lamp shall shine in thee no more' (verse 23). It is a culture without music, the throb has gone out of the industrial giant, the floating economy has sunk, darkness pervades society and love and marriage are meaningless. Civilisation without God is crippled and condemned. Now God is supreme! The stage is set for the King to return.

The Singing Saints

Chapter XXI

Two themes are drawn together in this chapter. Christ is recognised as the Bridegroom at the wedding celebration; He is also the Commander-in-Chief of the armies of heaven. We have the Church from the music room and carnage at the battlefield. Singing and sighing are combined in the narrative. Our Lord, once despised and rejected, is the absolute Sovereign. We see the end of the Great Tribulation and witness the beginning of the Millennium. The storm is abating, clouds are lifting and God's reign is about to commence in a new way.

THE MAJESTIC INSPIRATION
The mighty voice of a great multitude in heaven are inspired to give this great paean which includes four resounding 'Hallelujahs!'

Phase One of the Paean
After this I heard what seemed to be the mighty voice of a great multitude in heaven, crying, 'Hallelujah! Salvation and glory and power belong to our God, for his judgments are true and just; He has judged the great harlot who corrupted the earth with her fornication, and He has avenged on her the blood of His servants.'
Revelation 19:1-2

There are four Hallelujah's in the New Testament and all of them are in this chapter. 'Hallelujah' is a compound word in Hebrew meaning 'praise Yahweh'. The first mention of the word in the Bible was used when the Ark of God was installed in the midst of Zion (1 Chronicles 16:4). God's presence was symbolised in the Ark of the Covenant. In Christ, the Old Covenant and the New Covenant are fulfilled. He is not the symbol of God's presence, He is God! The planet earth is being invaded by the King; it is no wonder that we hear this pulsating 'Hallelujah!'.

Three words are associated with this great burst of praise — salvation (Greek - *soteria*), glory (Greek - *doxa*) and power (Greek -

dunamis) – these belong to our God! Consider what this means: deliverance from sin; the supremacy of the doxology and spiritual dynamism. When these blessings are known, the heart becomes a home of music that recognises the truth and justice associated with God's judgment. Gratitude, reverence and trust flow from the heart that accepts Christ as Saviour and Lord.

Phase Two of the Paean

Once more they cried, 'Hallelujah! The smoke from her goes up for ever and ever.'
Revelation 19:3

Rejoicing takes place because the Babylonian system has been destroyed. Those who made a satanic onslaught on the law of God did not break it; they illustrated the strength of it!

Phase Three of the Paean

And the twenty-four elders and the four living creatures fell down and worshipped God who is seated on the throne, saying 'Amen. Hallelujah!'
Revelation 19:4

The Church represented by the twenty-four elders, and living creatures takes the humble place and exclaims, 'Amen. Hallelujah!' Amen adds a new dimension to Hallelujah. Our Lord, in His public ministry, used the expression frequently. This was His method of solemnly announcing the truth. Praise cannot be acceptable unless it is true. Some songs are not blessed by the Holy Spirit because they violate the teaching of 'the sword of the Spirit'. Humanly devised ditties cannot expect divine anointing. Because words are set to music they cannot be exonerated from the crime of distorting God's word. Music from the throne of God reminds us that truth ought to have the primacy in praise, in other words, Amen and Hallelujah are doctrinally inseparable.

Phase Four of the Paean

And from the throne came a voice crying, 'Praise our God, all you his servants, you who fear Him, small and great.' Then I heard what seemed to be the voice of a great multitude, like the sound of many waters and like the sound of mighty thunderpeals, crying, 'Hallelujah! For the Lord our God the Almighty reigns. Let us rejoice and exult and give Him the glory, for the marriage of the Lamb has come, and His Bride has made herself ready; it was granted her to be clothed with fine linen, bright and pure' – for the fine linen is the righteous deeds of the saints.
Revelation 19:5-8

This is a sheer shout of joy. 'The Lord our God the Almighty reigns.' God is already reigning. The Kingship of God is one of the cardinal and bracing convictions of the Bible. 'The Lord reigns; let the earth rejoice', sings the author of the ninety-ninth Psalm. Some of us find it difficult to believe in God's sovereign Kingship. We believe that the horns of circumstance have got entangled in our stomach, leaving us sick and ready to die. Associated with our personal problems we have national and international problems. Biased blindness has made us demand a celestial despot instead of a kingly father. The fatherhood of God is not detached from sovereignty, but we must wait for the Lord's time!

THE MEANINGFUL INVITATION

And the angel said to me, 'Write this: Blessed are those who are invited to the marriage supper of the Lamb'. And he said to me, 'These are true words of God.'
Revelation 19:9

This invitation relates to verse 7 and 8. Exquisite joy overflows with the announcement that the marriage of the Lamb has come, and that His Bride has made herself ready. The Bride is bright and pure, clothed in the righteous deeds of the saints.

Now let us examine the beautiful expression 'the marriage supper of the Lamb'. Dr. F.A. Tatford emphasises the point that the normal order is reversed: 'On earth it is customary to speak of the marriage·of the bride, here it was the marriage of the Bridegroom.' Most weddings emphasise one aspect of the wedding by proclaiming 'Here comes the bride!' But the Bible makes a reversal of that order by exclaiming 'Behold the Bridegroom! Come out to meet him.' (Matthew 25:6).

In our culture we divide the wedding celebration into two parts: the ceremony and the reception. Usually the wedding of Biblical times had three aspects:
1   Parents arranged the marriage contract of their children.
2   When the couple became adults, the bridegroom, accompanied by his friends would go to the bride's house and escort his bride to his home.
3   Having brought his bride home, he would invite his friends to the marriage supper.
Dr. John F. Walvoord suggests that this ancient custom has its parallel in the experience of the Bride — the Church of Christ, and the Lamb — the Bridegroom. The wedding contract is arranged when the Church is redeemed. Every true Christian is joined to Christ by a valid contract registered at Calvary. The second stage of the wedding is consummated

when Christ comes to receive His Bride. The marriage is culminated at the wedding feast or the marriage supper. It is not the wedding union that is announced in Revelation 19, but the wedding feast.

THE MISTAKEN IDENTITY

Then I fell down at His feet to worship Him, but he said to me, 'You must not do that! I am a fellow servant with you and your brethren who hold the testimony of Jesus. Worship God.' For the testimony of Jesus is the spirit of prophecy.

Revelation 19:10

Some outstanding Christians have lacked cognisance in the time of crisis. Mary Magdalene thought the risen Lord was the gardener. Luke reminds us that Cleopas and his wife were kept from recognising the living Christ as they walked towards Emmaus — they thought Jesus was a passover pilgrim. Even the disciples could not discern between an apparition and the Lord. John made the other mistake — he thought that the angelic messenger was the Lord Jesus Christ and fell down at his feet to worship. The angel gave the timely warning, 'You must not do that!' Do what? Put anyone in the place of the Lord. Worship is for God alone. There was a tendency in the early Church to worship angels — in the sense that they were intermediaries. Judaism had constantly emphasised the transcendence of God — there was an immeasurable distance between God and man; because of that, it was felt that man needed angelic intermediaries. Angels became prominent. Christ is greater than the angels and is the only mediator between God and man. We must oppose all the teaching that suggests a plurality of mediators — there is only one.

Consider verse 10: 'for the testimony of Jesus is the spirit of prophecy.' This statement has been expressed in different ways. One paraphrase is 'the possession of the prophetic spirit will always manifest itself in a witness to Jesus'; while another states 'prophecy at its very heart is designed to unfold the beauty and loveliness of our Lord and Saviour Jesus Christ'. Another analysis suggests that there is a double meaning: 'the witness which the Christian bears to Jesus Christ', and 'the witness which Jesus Christ gives to men'. Perhaps the experience of John the Seer is the answer to this suggestion. He received the Revelation, or witness from Jesus Christ and has passed the supreme disclosure of that witness to men.

A deep explanation comes from an older commentary: 'The testimony of Jesus in the Apocalypse is of a prophetic character, 'referring to His public assumption of governmental power to be displayed in the

Kingdom'. Prophecy emphasises the Kingship and rule of Christ. Perhaps a modern writer on prophecy is not too extreme when he suggests 'Prophecy is a person'; in other words, those who reject prophecy are rejecting Christ himself!

Armageddon and The Conquering Christ

Chapter XXII

It is helpful at this point to take in the drama of the painting (Plate 23) which represents this passage of Scripture. From the first impression it is apparent that all has been dark, but out of the blackness emerges the conquering Saviour. In this painting we have the end of the greatest war of all time. It is obvious that Christ died for something. Someone has suggested that most of us die of something, be it disease, accident or old age. But very occasionally there appears a man who dies for something. Our Lord died for someone — the Church. He died for the sinner. This emergence of Christ in conquest ought to be related to His own words, 'Was it not necessary that the Christ should suffer these things and enter into His glory?' (Luke 24:26). The glory of Christ's appearing is captured by the painting. All hail, mighty Conqueror! He invades the planet at the time of Armageddon. This takes us back to Revelation 16:16, 'And they assembled them at the place which is called in Hebrew Armageddon'. In between, in Chapters 17 and 18, we have seen the religious, economic and commercial developments which lead to the climax of history and the fulfilment of prophecy.

Before we examine the painting of the conquering Christ in detail, let us study the map (Plate 22). This represents the findings of those scholars who believe in a literal fulfilment of prophecy regarding the nations that will be involved in the campaign and final conflict at Armageddon.

Geographically, the nations at the end of the age will be divided into four distinct areas — north, south, east and west. Central to our understanding of Armageddon is the nation of Israel. The Middle East is the bridgehead of three important continents — Asia, Africa and Europe. Israel is located in the centre of that bridgehead and has a major role in the fulfilment of prophecy.

THE KING OF THE NORTH

The king of the north plays a significant role in the Armageddon campaign. Ezekiel 38 and 39 describe some of the crises and conflicts that will involve the great northern kingdom. Whilst it is difficult to dogmatise about exact details, especially regarding chronological happenings, there is no doubt that the king of the north can be identified, and the major issues clarified.

Most people, when they read a book about the Bible, do not check the references that are given for study. It is essential that we read carefully Ezekiel Chapters 38 and 39. The king of the north is also mentioned in Daniel 11.

At the time of the end the king of the south shall attack him; but the king of the north shall rush upon him like a whirlwind, with chariots and horsemen, and with many ships; and he shall come into countries and shall overflow and pass through. He shall come into the glorious land. And tens of thousands shall fall, but these shall be delivered out of his hand: Edom and Moab and the main part of the Ammonites. He shall stretch out his hand against the countries, and the land of Egypt shall not escape. He shall become ruler of the treasures of gold and of silver, and all the precious things of Egypt; and the Libyans and the Ethiopians shall follow in his train. But tidings from the east and the north shall alarm him, and he shall go forth with great fury to exterminate and utterly destroy many. And he shall pitch his palatial tents between the sea and the glorious holy mountain; yet he shall come to his end, with none to help him.

Daniel 11:40-45

The argument from geography is important. Ezekiel 38:6 indicates that the armies of the great leader come from 'the uttermost parts of the north'. In other words, these armies originate from the extreme north. Examine the map (Plate 22). Locate the position of Israel. The Mediterranean is to the West, Egypt is in the South, Jordan, Arabia and Iraq are to the East. Now draw a line northward to 'the uttermost parts' and you will come to Russia. This argument from geography is formidable.

The argument from linguistics is convincing. In Hebrew 'the chief prince' is literally 'the prince of Rosh' (Ezekiel 38:3). Dr. John F. Walvoord has made it clear that in the study of how ancient words come into modern language there is the practise of keeping the consonants permanent although the vowels may be changed. Examine the word 'Rosh'. If we change the vowel from 'o' to 'u', we have the root - Rush of the modern word Russia, especially when the suffix is added. 'Genesius, the famous lexicographer, gives the assurance that this is a proper identification, that is, that Rosh is an early form of the word from which we get Russia.'

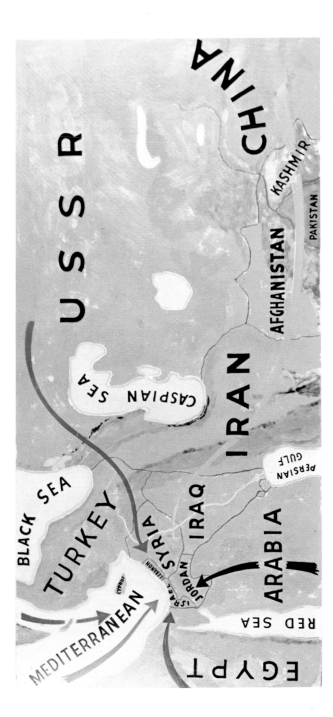

The etymology of 'Meshech' and 'Tubal' (Ezekiel 38:3) is most remarkable. Moscow is similar to Meshech and the modern province of Tobolsk in Russia derives from Tubal.

This mighty power, Russia and her satellites, will invade Israel.

THE KING OF THE SOUTH

The Old Testament provides much evidence to prove conclusively that Egypt is the kingdom of the south. In Genesis 12 we have the first mention of Egypt. A large part of Genesis 37-50 describes how Jacob and his family went to Egypt. 'Israel', through the miraculous intervention of God, escaped from the bondage of Egypt.

Daniel 11 refers to Egypt as 'the king of the south'. There are at least ten references to the king of the south in this chapter. These refer to different princes of the king of the south, but verses 40-45 are dealing with Egypt 'at the time of the end'. Here is a suggested plan of campaign. Prior to Christ's coming to earth, Egypt attacks 'him', that is, the recognised world ruler of the ten-nation confederacy described in Daniel 11:36-39. The Hebrew word for attack in verse 40 means 'to thrust at'. Egypt attacks the ruler of the ten nations through Israel who has enjoyed the protection of the great ruler. This thrust of Egypt is represented on the map by the brown arrow. It is possible that other Arab states will assist Egypt and possibly some African states indicated by the black arrow on Arabia. Now the king of the north rushes upon the king of the south like a whirlwind. The red arrows represent the movement of forces. This northern power, Russia and her satellites, will be completely destroyed.

I will summon every kind of terror against Gog, says the Lord God; every man's sword will be against his brother. With pestilence and bloodshed I will enter into judgment with him; and I will rain upon him and his hordes and the many peoples that are with him, torrential rains and hailstones, fire and brimstone. So I will show my greatness and my holiness and make myself known in the eyes of many nations. Then they will know that I am Lord.

Ezekiel 38:21-23

It is of paramount importance to our understanding that Russia and her supporters will be destroyed.

THE KINGS OF THE EAST

We have seen in the sixth trumpet and the sixth-bowl judgment the importance of the vast army of 200 million and the drying up of the river Euphrates. For many years, students of prophecy were faced with the problem that Russia and China were both communist states. It was expected that a break would take place, probably after the Rapture of the Church. These same students were surprised that the rift took place before the Rapture. Today, Russia and China are far apart. Political experts have asserted that Russia and China's differences are irreconcilable.

The kings of the east are those from 'the sunrising'. Here are leaders who originated in the Orient. China is the only nation that has the manpower to provide the large army. Of course, at 'the time of the end' this could involve Japan and other countries from the Far East. The yellow arrow on the map represents the movement of that large army. Russia, apparently, is destroyed before the eastern forces reach the Middle East.

THE TEN-NATION CONFEDERACY
In Chapter 13 we studied the significance of the United States of Europe. They are represented on the map by the purple arrow. Moving from the west they invade the Middle East and are confronted by the kings of the east. Israel is the battlefield, with special significance given to the plain of Megiddo.

Observe how the people of Israel have been gathered from many nations — Ezekiel 38:8. This prophecy could only be fulfilled subsequent to 1948 when Israel became a nation. Careful study of Ezekiel 38 will produce the amazing facts that Israeli cities would be rebuilt without walls. That is, as we build them today, that the small restored nation's economy would be sound and that she would live at peace. This cannot be applied to Israel at this point in time,but in the future, after the Church has been taken to heaven and during the early part of the Great Tribulation, Israel will be protected by the leader of the ten-nation confederacy.

I have given a brief, almost a too simplistic outline of the movements of the nations at the end of the age. I am not setting out a timetable. There is danger in dogmatism, but the events that are developing rapidly before our eyes suggest that the end of the age is near.

It is at this point in history that the King emerges from heaven, accompanied by His angelic hosts. He comes to planet earth to destroy the enemies and establish His Millennial Kingdom.

Carefully examine the details of the painting (Plate 23) and compare it with the text of Revelation 19:11-21

Plate No. 23

Then I saw heaven opened, and behold, a white horse! He who sat upon it is called Faithful and True, and in righteousness he judges and makes war. His eyes are like a flame of fire, and on his head are many diadems; and he has a name inscribed which no one knows but himself. He is clad in a robe dipped in blood, and the name by which he is called is The Word of God. And the armies of heaven, arrayed in fine linen, white and pure, followed him on white horses. From his mouth issues a sharp sword with which to smite the nations, and he will rule them with a rod of iron; he will tread the wine press of the fury of the wrath of God the Almighty. On his robe and on his thigh he has a name inscribed, King of kings and Lord of lords. Then I saw an angel standing in the sun, and with a loud voice he called to all the birds that fly in midheaven, 'Come, gather for the great supper of God, to eat the flesh of kings, the flesh of captains, the flesh of mighty men, the flesh of horses and their riders, and the flesh of all men, both free and slave, both small and great.' And I saw the beast and the kings of the earth with their armies gathered to make war against him who sits upon the horse and against his army. And the beast was captured, and with it the false prophet who in its presence had worked the signs by which he deceived those who had received the mark of the beast and those who worshipped its image. These two were thrown alive into the lake of fire that burns with brimstone. And the rest were slain by the sword of him who sits upon the horse, the sword that issues from his mouth; and all the birds were gorged with their flesh.

John saw heaven opened. What an experience! But we must not forget the eschatological situation. All the peoples of the earth are at war. All is black, as our painting suggests. Then the scene is changed. The heavens are opened and the Conqueror comes to stab the darkness. The Light of the World has the ability to disperse the gloom of despair.

THE ROYAL PERSON
He rides upon a white horse. There is a touch of dramatic intensity as John, the Seer, exclaims, 'Behold, a white horse!' In a Roman triumphal procession, the victorious general rode at the head of his legions on a white horse. A greater than the emperor is here! Compare the white horse of the first seal in Revelation 6 with this horse that carries the Commander of the heavenly hosts. In the first seal we have the Antichrist, the impersonator, the one who attempts to replace the true Christ. Now all shams are removed. The government of the world will be under new management. Christ's white horse is seen as a symbol of His judicial righteousness.

The rider has a special name — 'Faithful and True'. There is no doubt about His identification. In Revelation 1:5 Christ is called the Faithful: Chapter 3:7 reminds us that He is True. When our Lord speaks to the church at Laodicea, He describes Himself as the 'Faithful and True Witness', and in the concluding chapter of the Apocalypse, we are reminded that His sayings are 'faithful and true'. Our Lord's teaching has a double strength; it is consistent, so we can depend upon the author; in its content there is authenticity so we can declare the substance. Some men who have a poor character can preach a good content, and others who have good character may preach a poor content. The Lord is 'Faithful *and* True'; content and character are perfectly balanced.

He judges in righteousness. God's righteousness is an attribute and an activity. Righteousness is not a mere abstraction that is static in heaven. It is energised by the holiness of God. The activity of God's righteousness is described in two ways in our passage. It judges and it makes war. Man is made accountable and all opposition is destroyed.

Eyes like a flame of fire are obvious in the painting. These blazing eyes possess a profound penetrating power. Complacency and hypocrisy are exposed by the burning intensity of His spiritual scrutiny.

On His head are many diadems. We have noticed that the Greek word *diadema* means the ruler's crown. This multiplicity of crowns has great significance. He is *the* King over kings; He is *the* Lord over lords. Many sovereignties belong to Him; thus He has many diadems.

There is a secret name (v12). No one knows what it is except the Lord. Many of us would like to know this name, but the secret is locked in the Godhead. It is dangerous to tamper with hidden truth. 'He has a glory and a character of His own, incommunicable and incomprehensible'.

He is clothed in a robe dipped in blood. Our painting gives the impression that the robe is sprinkled with blood, rather than dipped in blood. The footnote in the Revised Standard Version reminds us that there is a strong basis in some ancient manuscripts for favouring the translation 'sprinkled'. In this context we are considering not the blood of 'the Lord Jesus, but the blood of His enemies. His robe is sprinkled with their blood'. An Old Testament passage will help us to understand the significance of the context here in Revelation.

'Who is this that comes from Edom, in crimsoned garments from Bozrah, he that is glorious in his apparel, marching in the greatness of his strength? 'It is I, announcing vindication, mighty to save'. Why is thy apparel red, and thy garments like his that treads in the wine press? 'I have trodden the wine press alone, and from the peoples no one was with me; I trod them in my anger and trampled them in my wrath; their lifeblood is sprinkled upon my garments, and I have stained all my raiment. For the day of vengeance was in my heart, and my year of redemption has come . . .'

Isaiah 63:1-4

There is a geographical factor in this text. He comes from Edom. Why Edom? It has been suggested that as the remnant of Israel escaped to the wilderness in Edom (Revelation 12) so the Lord has dealt with the enemies of the Lord's people in Edom, which is a wilderness area. Notice that the garments are crimsoned, sprinkled with the blood of His enemies. The Lord is glorious in His apparel. He marches in the greatness of His strength. One of the important features of the passage reminds us that He is announcing vindication. Some have thought that Isaiah 63 is speaking about Calvary, but it is obvious that the context is dealing with the coming of Christ in power, vindicating the righteousness of God. That is why He is called 'The Word of God'.

In Plate 23 the armies, arrayed in fine linen and riding on white horses, form part of the King's flowing head-dress. Jude 14-16 assists us to identify the large retinue.

It was of these also that Enoch in the seventh generation from Adam prophesied, saying, 'Behold, the Lord came with his holy myriads, to execute judgment on all, and to convict all the ungodly of all their deeds of ungodliness which they have committed in such an ungodly way, and of all the harsh things which ungodly sinners have spoken against him. These are grumblers, malcontents, following their own passions, loudmouthed boasters, flattering people to gain advantage.

'Holy myriads' suggests the saints. The Lord is accompanied by His Church, and many angels. Remember that the Lord comes *for* His Church before the Great Tribulation and at the end of that terrible phase comes *with* His Church to vindicate the rule of God. 2 Thessalonians 1:7-10 complements Revelation 19.

. . . and to grant rest with us to you who are afflicted, when the Lord Jesus is revealed from heaven with his mighty angels in flaming fire, inflicting vengeance upon those who do not know God and upon those who do not obey the gospel of our Lord Jesus. They shall suffer the punishment of eternal destruction and exclusion from the presence of the Lord and from the glory of his might, when he comes on that day to be glorified in his saints, and to be marvelled at in all who have believed, because our testimony to you was believed'.

At the time of Christ's coming three weapons are mentioned (v15).

A sharp sword. This issues from His mouth. The solemnity of this is obvious from the painting. The sword envisaged is the long Thracian sword. It represents the effective thrust and incisiveness of the word of the Lord. With this weapon He will smite the nations.

A rod of iron. Here is an iron control, demanding obedience. Compulsion comes to the nations and there is no way that they can escape. The warrior Christ shall break them with a rod of iron, and shall dash them in pieces like a potter's vessel.

The fury of the wrath of God the Almighty. We have already seen the devastation caused by that wrath in the seven bowls of judgment. Who can stand before the wrath of God? Who can resist the One who is King of kings and Lord of lords?

The imagery of verse 15 is important here — 'He will tread the wine press'. Two stone troughs formed the wine press. They were positioned at different heights and were connected by a channel. Grapes were placed in the top trough and were trampled with the feet. As the juice was squeezed out it flowed down into the bottom trough where it was collected. Christ treads the grapes, that is, His enemies who are crushed and reduced to nothingness.

Verse 16 tells us how the name King of kings and Lord of lords was written on His robe and that part of the robe rested on His thigh. Christ is the King and the Ruler of the universe!

THE REPULSIVE CARNAGE

The painting represents the angel standing in the sun. With a loud voice he issues an invitation to the birds of prey to gorge themselves with the flesh of God's enemies. The army of the beast has become carrion-flesh. This strange supper is a banquet of flesh! The word flesh occurs five times in this passage. Romans 8:5-7 is appropriate here:

For those who live according to the flesh set their minds on the things of the flesh, but those who live according to the Spirit set their minds on the things of the Spirit. To set the mind on the flesh is death, but to set the mind on the Spirit is life and peace. For the mind that is set on the flesh is hostile to God; it does not submit to God's law, indeed it cannot;

Death, hostility and displeasure are associated with the flesh.

It is during this crisis that our Lord descends to the earth. Zechariah 14:3-4:

Then the Lord will go forth and fight against those nations as when he fights on a day of battle. On that day his feet shall stand on the Mount of Olives which lies before Jerusalem on the east; and the Mount of Olives shall be split in two from east to west by a very wide valley; so that one half of the Mount shall withdraw northward, and the other half southward.

This text from Zechariah provides the explanation. Our Lord who ascended from the Mount of Olives to heaven, will return to the Mount of Olives at the end of the Great Tribulation and before the Millennium. According to the prophecy of Zechariah, the Mount of Olives will fall apart and become a great valley stretching toward the east from Jerusalem and extending down to Jericho at the river Jordan. Geologists have made it clear that it is dangerous to build on the Mount of Olives because it is the centre of a geological fault. A severe earth tremor or an earthquake could divide the mountain in two, but this will not take place until the King's feet touch the mountain.

Returning to our painting, we see the lake of fire symbolised in the left corner of the visual. Verse 20 reminds us that the beast and the false prophet (we examined their ministry in Chapter 13), were thrown into the lake of fire. Human language cannot describe the severities of this judgment. Only God can know the depths of suffering and agony that overtake the lost.

No struggle is mentioned in this section of Scripture. In so far as the powers of evil are concerned, it is a non-event. Two members of the unholy trinity are judged, that is, the Antichrist and the false prophet, but the first member of the unholy trinity is destined for the same fate.

Matthew 25:31-46 provides the details that bridge the Great Tribulation and the Millennium. There are three classes of people: sheep, goats and My brethren. Who are His brethren? They are the Jews. During seven years of Tribulation they have known his special treatment. Remember how the Lord raised 144,000 dedicated ambassadors who preached the message regarding the King's arrival? Many accepted their message and refused to accept the mark of the beast. Others rejected the message and persecuted those who accepted the truth.

When the Lord sets up His throne upon the earth, He shall gather all the nations of the earth and He shall come before them as the King of the Jews. The division of the nations is based upon their treatment of the Jews. The 'goats' are those who ill-treated the Jews and the 'sheep' are those who 'as you did it to one of the least of these my brethren, you did it to me'. Christians who have insight and spiritual apprehension can divide the nations today because of their attitude towards Israel.

The Millennial Kingdom

Chapter XXIII

The word millennium is derived from two latin words, *mille* meaning thousand and *annum* meaning year. So the literal meaning of the term is a thousand years. This expression is found six times in the New Testament and all of these references are found in Revelation 20:1-7. Eschatological terminology uses three prefixes 'post', 'a' and 'pre' to indicate the particular view held relating to the thousand years.

Post-millennialism is advocated by some excellent Christian scholars. One bible teacher, who holds to the general principle of the post-millennial position, but is not happy with its limitations, describes himself as a 'royal redemptionist' or an 'optimistic soteriologist'. He prefers these titles because he believes that labels are dangerous, but 'optimistic soteriologist' could be interpreted by some as a 'universalist'! The post-millennialist believes that eventually the world will be Christianised. As the world is improved through the propagation of the Gospel, we shall enter into a reign of righteousness and peace and at the end of this long reign, Christ will come to take His Church to heaven and judge those who denied Him.

A-millennialism is the view that the Bible does not predict a Millennium. Once again we have to acknowledge that some outstanding Christian teachers have taught this theory. It is necessary to remind ourselves that the basis of our Christian fellowship is not Eschatology but Christology. In a general way a-millennialism teaches that there will be a parallel and contemporaneous development of good and evil, that is to say, God's kingdom and Satan's kingdom will continue until the Second Coming of Christ, when the resurrection and judgment will take place; this will be followed by the eternal order, the absolute perfect Kingdom of God. Those who hold to this view tend to allegorise all the prophecies about the promised Kingdom. They also believe that the Church is the fulfilment of the millennial kingdom.

Pre-millennialism is the view of the last things which holds that the Second Coming of Christ will be followed by a period of world-wide peace and righteousness before the end of the world. During the Millennium Christ will reign as King upon the earth. There are reputable Christian scholars who hold to this view.

From these three principal views we may generalise that post-millennialism holds that Christ will return after the Millennium; the a-millennialist holds that there is to be no Millennium at all in the accepted sense of the term: and the pre-millennialist holds that Christ's return precedes the Millennium.

It is my personal view that the pre-millennial approach to prophecy is the best one for the understanding of God's theocratic programme. Dr. J. Dwight Pentecost in his book *Things to Come* reminds us that 'The Millennium will be the period of the full manifestation of the glory of the Lord Jesus Christ. There will be the manifestation of glory associated with the humanity of Christ. There will be the glory of a glorious dominion, in which Christ, by virtue of his obedience unto death, is given universal dominion to replace that dominion which Adam lost. There will be the glory of a glorious government, in which Christ, as David's Son, is given absolute power to govern . . . '

THE MILLENNIUM

During the Millennium what will be the relationship of the Church to the planet earth? Different answers have been given. Some have believed that the Church will be forever removed from the earth at which time the inhabitants and the planet will be destroyed by fire. Others have maintained that the earth will be purified and renewed and will become the eternal and exclusive home of the saints. Both views are extreme. It is taught in Revelation that the saints shall 'reign over the earth', but this does not mean that they will be earthbound.

Consider the teaching of the Lord Jesus in Luke 20:35-36

But those who are accounted worthy to attain to that age and the resurrection from the dead neither marry nor are given in marriage, for they cannot die any more because they *are equal to angels* and are sons of God, being sons of the resurrection.

From the Bible we learn that the angels are ministering spirits. It is obvious that they visit this earth and fulfil the will of God. As the servants of the Lord they intervene in the affairs of the earth, but their residence is in the heavenly realm. The Church, then, comprised of those who take part in the first Resurrection, are like the angels – in continual contact with the earth, but not inhabitants of it.

A New Atmosphere

It may be difficult to grasp the significance of this situation – that during the Millennium the Church will hold a close relationship with earth, and a relation to heaven similar to that which the angels enjoy. There will be a new atmosphere associated with the Millennium. The explanation is provided in Revelation 20:1-3

Then I saw an angel coming down from heaven, holding in his hand the key of the bottomless pit and a great chain. And he seized the dragon, that ancient serpent, who is the Devil and Satan, and bound him for a thousand years, and threw him into the pit, and shut it and sealed it over him, that he should deceive the nations no more, till the thousand years were ended. After that he must be loosed for a little while.

Compare the Scripture with the painting (Plate 24). The angel is the divine gaoler. He has the key in one hand and the chain in the other, symbolising the imprisonment of the Evil One. Dragon, Serpent, Devil and Satan are the descriptive titles used of the Prince of this World. Dr G. R. Beasley-Murray commenting on the binding of Satan writes, 'The incarceration of the Devil is trebly circumscribed. He is bound up, locked in, and sealed over. The writer could hardly have expressed more emphatically the inability of Satan to harm the race of man'. The malignant activity of Satan is crippled. With the source of evil paralysed, civilisation is free from satanic influence. The painting indicates the abyss, that is, the bottomless pit, at the bottom right-hand corner. Satan and his emissaries are rendered inoperative. What kind of planet will it be when the Prince of Darkness is expelled?

Many Old Testament passages predict what will take place during the Millennium. According to Isaiah 30:26 there will be a seven-fold increase of light.

Moreover the light of the moon shall be as the sun and the light of the sun shall be seven-fold as the light of seven days, in the day that the Lord binds up the breach of His people, and heals the stroke of their wound.

Another amazing feature of the Millennium will be the prolongation of life. Isaiah 65:20 provides the information:

No more shall there be in it an infant that lives but a few days, or an old man who does not fill out his days, for the child shall die an hundred years old . . .

Climatic conditions and atmospheric changes, plus God's power counteracting all kinds of pollution that will affect man's life expectancy assist man to live longer. Who can visualise the changes that will take place in a decontaminated planet!

In Isaiah 11:6-9 we have the teaching that the ferocity of brute creation will be altered. Consider the amazing disclosure.

The wolf shall dwell with the lamb, and the leopard shall lie down with the kid, and the calf and the lion and the fatling together, and a little child shall lead them. The cow and the bear shall feed; their young shall lie down together; and the lion shall eat straw like the ox. The sucking child shall play over the hole of the asp, and the weaned child shall put his hand on the adder's den. They shall not hurt or destroy in all my holy mountain; for the earth shall be full of the knowledge of the Lord as the waters cover the sea.

This prophetic statement will be fulfilled during the Millennium. Changes will take place in the animal kingdom.

The Bible speaks about creation groaning. During the Millennium the groan will be taken out of creation. Joel 3:18 reminds us that

. . . in that day the mountains shall drip sweet wine, and the hills shall flow with milk, and all the stream beds of Judah shall flow with water; and a fountain shall come forth from the house of the Lord and water the valley of Shittim.

Mountainsides are covered with vineyards and pasture, lands sustain vast herds of milk cattle.

Ponder on the statement in verse 3 — 'he should deceive the nations no more'. Think of it — politics without deception! Here is a change of atmosphere and attitude that will have an effect upon all the nations.

A New Administration

The Millennium will be characterised by a new administration. In Revelation 20:4 John states,

Then I saw thrones, and seated on them were those to whom judgment was committed.

Nations will not be sinless during the Millennium. Men and women will not be free from their sinful natures. But Satan is imprisoned and the pressure of temptation has lost its effectiveness; administrative justice is necessary.

Two Scriptures will assist us to understand more clearly what is

involved in the administrative offices of the Millennium. Our Lord taught in Matthew 19:28

> Truly, I say to you, in the new world when the Son of man shall sit on his glorious throne, you who have followed me will also sit on twelve thrones, judging the twelve tribes of Israel.

This teaching is amplified in Jude 15

> Behold the Lord comes with His holy myriads, to execute judgment on all, and to convict all the ungodly of all their deeds of ungodliness which they have committed in such an ungodly way, and of all the harsh things which ungodly sinners have spoken against him.

The government shall be upon the shoulder of the true Messiah, and theocratic rule will be recognised by all the nations. The saints live and reign with the Lord for a thousand years. This is the real golden age of which the weary nations have so long dreamed.

THE TWO RESURRECTIONS

Revelation 20 contains important teaching about two resurrections. Some Christians believe in a general resurrection but that is not the teaching of verses 4-6 in this chapter.

> Then I saw thrones, and seated on them were those to whom judgment was committed. Also I saw the souls of those who had been beheaded for their testimony to Jesus and for the word of God, and who had not worshipped the beast or its image and had not received its mark on their foreheads or their hands. They came to life, and reigned with Christ a thousand years. The rest of the dead did not come to life until the thousand years were ended. This is the first resurrection. Blessed and holy is he who shares in the first resurrection! Over such the second death has no power, but they shall be priests of God and of Christ, and they shall reign with him a thousand years.

The Christian may be surprised that he does not meet this important doctrine of two distinct resurrections with a Millennium between, until the last book of the Bible. But is this so? Consider John 5:28-29

> Do not marvel at this; for the hour is coming when all who are in the tombs will hear his voice and come forth, those who have done good, to the resurrection of life, and those who have done evil to the resurrection of judgment.

Some would have us believe that we have in this teaching the doctrine of a general resurrection. Such a doctrine does not harmonise with other Scriptures in the New Testament. Our Lord mentions 'the hour' and this is interpreted in the Apocalypse as covering the Millennium.

Attention is given to certain passages of the New Testament that represent the resurrection of believers as electic and special. How can we interpret the words of our Lord in Luke 20:35 in the context of a general resurrection when He said,

. . . those who are counted worthy to attain to that age and to the resurrection from the dead.

The word 'from' in the Greek could be translated 'out from' so that we read 'out from the dead'. Obviously, it accords with the resurrection at the opening of the Millennium, in which only the righteous share. The apostle Paul uses startling words in Philippians 3:11

that if possible, I may attain the resurrection from the dead.

The Greek would allow this strong translation 'the out-resurrection from the dead'. This can only refer to an electic resurrection, a separation and quickening to life out from among the dead. Those who hold to the doctrine of a general resurrection must face the difficult question, 'Why should one strive to attain what is inevitable, as Paul's resurrection must have certainly appeared to be, had he held that all men will be raised together?'

It is important that we ponder on the phrase, 'this is the first resurrection'. Donald Grey Barnhouse suggests an appropriate analogy. A man may say with great satisfaction, 'All of the harvest is gathered in . The harvest may have included a few handfuls gathered on the first day, then after a long interruption due to a rain storm, for example, the major part of the harvest may have been gathered, and then after another momentary interruption, the final sheaves are gathered.'

Let us examine this analogy in the light of the Scriptures. Christ is the first-fruit of the resurrection, but in Matthew 27:52-53 we find this startling revelation.

the tombs also were opened, and many bodies of the saints who had fallen asleep were raised, and coming out of the tombs after His resurrection they went into the holy city and appeared to many.

Here we have the first sheaf of the harvest. The believing dead were given resurrection bodies. Ephesians 4:8 throws light on this subject —

When he ascended on high he led a host of captives,

That is to say, the spirits of the Old Testament saints were taken from Hades to Heaven.

The second phase of the resurrection occurs at the *Parousia*, that is, when Christ comes for His Church. 1 Thessalonians 4:13-18 is of importance here. There is a phrase in this passage which refutes the teaching of a general resurrection –

And the dead in Christ will rise first.

The Church is taken to heaven before the Great Tribulation, but at the end of this period the saints who have been martyred will be raised and will reign with Him a thousand years. The harvest is completed in three stages.

In Luke 14:14 the Lord made this comprehensive statement

You will be repaid at the resurrection of the just

An electic resurrection? Certainly! And the just include Old Testament saints, Church saints, and Tribulation saints, that is, those who have been hated, persecuted and put to death by the Antichrist.

GOD'S FINAL INTERVENTION
The final conflict between good and evil takes place at the end of the Millennium. Revelation 20:7-10 provides the necessary insights.

And when the thousand years are ended, Satan will be loosed from his prison and will come out to deceive the nations which are at the four corners of the earth, that is, Gog and Magog, to gather them for battle; their number is like the sand of the sea. And they marched up over the broad earth and surrounded the camp of the saints and the beloved city; but fire came down from heaven and consumed them, and the devil who had deceived them was thrown into the lake of fire and brimstone where the beast and the false prophet were, and they will be tormented day and night for ever and ever.

By the sovereign act of God, Satan is loosed from his prison, the abyss. Once again he deceives the nations. The manner of the deception is not described. Two names are mentioned – Gog and Magog. Who are these personalities? We have noticed that the Antichrist, that is, the beast, and the false prophet have been consigned to the lake of fire. Satan cannot use these two members of the unholy trinity. So, he controls Gog and Magog. We have met these names before in Ezekiel 38 and 39. They played an important part in the events that led up to the battle of Armageddon. These leaders were destroyed by the direct intervention of the Lord Christ. Now we have two personalities with the same names, and as Satan entered into Judas, (John 13:27), so Satan controls these two personalities. Large armies under the leadership of Gog and Magog 'surrounded the camp of the saints and the beloved city'. God's cataclysmic intervention destroys the armies of the enemy and the devil is thrown into the lake of fire. Satan, the beast and the false prophet will be tormented day and night for ever and ever. This is a frightening statement, but the words of another will help us in our understanding — 'At all events the doctrine of conscious, eternal torment for impenitent men is clearly revealed in the Word of God. Whether we can defend it or not on philosophic grounds, it is our business to believe it, and leave it to the clearer light of eternity to explain what we cannot now understand, realising that God has infinitely wise reasons for doing things for which we in our ignorance can see no sufficient reason at all.' (Dr D. Grey Barnhouse)

The Great White Throne

Chapter XXIV

In the New Testament there are three important thrones. Chapter 4 of the Apocalypse introduced us to the throne in heaven. From this place of authority the universe is governed. Matthew 25:31 reminds us that during the Millennium God will set up a throne upon earth. Before this throne the nations will be judged. The Lord does not relinquish His grasp of the planet earth. He is intensely interested in what goes on in Parliament, Congress and the Kremlin. When the United Nations meet to discuss international affairs, He is the silent observer. He shall judge the nations on earth from His throne, located at Jerusalem. The great white throne cannot be identified with the throne in heaven or the throne on earth. Intriguing information is found in verse 11.

Then I saw a great white throne and Him who sat on it; from His presence earth and sky fled away, and no place was found for them.

This throne is represented in the painting by the circle effect at the top centre of the picture (Plate 24). God's holy power holds the throne in space. The material earth and heaven have passed away. Our Lord taught,

Heaven and earth will pass away, but my words will not pass away.

This teaching is related to what we have in Revelation 20:11. It is most significant that no place was found for the earth and the material heaven. This disintegration of the material world is represented by the broken pillar suggesting that the supportive and cohesive power of Christ has been withdrawn from the system. We believe that God can create something out of nothing. The scientist may argue that matter is eternal, that is, it cannot be made and it cannot be destroyed, but God is greater than the scientist and He makes something into nothing. Consider the words of 2 Peter 3:11-13

Since all these things are thus to be dissolved, what sort of persons ought you to be in lives of holiness and godliness, waiting for and hasting the coming of the day of God, because of which the heavens will be kindled and dissolved, and the elements will melt with fire. But according to His promise, we wait for new heavens and a new earth in which righteousness dwells.

Everything will be new in God's fabulous future!

The greatness of God's throne is overpowering. From the symbolism of the painting we observe the white light flowing down. This adjective 'white' is worthy of deep consideration. White is the victor's colour; it is the priest's colour speaking of purity; it is worn by the bride and the small child. Think of the white light of day, the white summit of the Alps, the white brilliance of the diamond, the white flakes of untrodden snow and the white radiance of eternity — all of these are eclipsed by the whiteness of the holiness of God. The One who sits upon the throne is august — He is the Judge.

Unbelievers appear before this great white throne.

And I saw the dead, great and small, standing before the throne, and books were opened. Also another book was opened, which is the book of life. And the dead were judged by what was written in the books by what they had done.

Revelation 20:12

They are not called to God's throne to contest the case, or to make an appeal, but to receive a sentence. Those who argue that God is love and maintain that 'Christ died for our sins' and therefore all sinners will escape the judgment, ought to remember that the Cross is simultaneously a judgment and a grace; a condemnation and a mercy. It is the most searching judgment known on earth, the parallel of which can only be that of the great white throne. It is true that the Cross is a shining revelation of the love of God, but let us not forget that the Cross is a disclosure of the immanent hell of our human nature. If we refuse to stand before the Cross with repentance and penitence, then we shall stand before the great white throne for judgment and our souls will be filled with torturing remorse.

The great and small stand before God. In the painting we see the crown that represents those who are considered important by the standards of the world. We see also the ordinary people who, with consternation, look towards the throne. They are held before the throne by the omnipotent power of God.

Books are opened by the authority of God. Men and women are examined and judged according to these books. Can the books be identified? We are given a description of one book, namely The Book of Life. In our study of the church in Sardis we discovered that the

Book of Life is like a census record, each person who is born into the world has his name inscribed upon this book. Revelation 3:5 assists us to understand the importance of this book.

He who conquers shall be clad thus in white garments; and I will not blot his name out of the book of life; I will confess his name before my father and before his angels.

This suggests that some names are blotted out, but only the names of those who reject Jesus Christ. The names of those who have accepted Christ and know the regenerative power of the Holy Spirit remain in the Book of Life. To avoid confusion we must differentiate between the Book of Life and the Lamb's Book of Life. Revelation 13:8 reminds us that names are written in the Lamb's Book of Life 'before the foundation of the world'. A categorical statement occurs in Chapter 21:27

Only those who are written in the Lamb's book of life shall enter into the new Jerusalem.

It seems that the Lamb's Book of Life contains the names of the elect, written before the foundation of the world, but the Book of Life is the census record from which the names of unbelievers are removed. There are no erasures from the Lamb's Book of Life. We could express the difference between the books in another way: the Lamb's Book of Life represents the doctrine of the sovereignty of God and the Book of Life reminds us that man is a responsible agent. This does not help us to resolve the mystery of the sovereignty of God and man's responsibility, but it enables us to recognise the eternal security of the believer and what takes place when a person's name is removed from the Book of Life.

It is obvious that God's book – the Bible – will be at the great white throne. Men and women will be reminded about its authority, especially the Law of God in the Ten Commandments. God's standards will be maintained. The Bible that men considered irrelevant in time, is most relevant in eternity.

Another book is mentioned. It contains the records of the deeds of the people who are being sentenced at the great white throne.

The dead were judged by what was written in the books, by what they had done.
Revelation 20:12

If a man-made computer can store informative facts and recall the same on request, so the eternal God can recall in a flash the lifestyle of each individual who did not trust Christ as Saviour. The books are represented in the painting. Ponder on the visual carefully. Make sure that Jesus Christ is your Saviour and Lord and thank Him that you will not stand before the great white throne.

The remaining verses of Revelation 20 are full of drama.

And the sea gave up the dead in it, Death and Hades gave up the dead in them, and all were judged by what they had done. Then Death and Hades were thrown into the lake of fire. This is the second death, the lake of fire; and if any one's name was not found written in the book of life, he was thrown into the lake of fire.

Revelation 20:13-15

It is said frequently that those who die without Christ as their Saviour are consigned to a 'lost eternity'. That expression is misleading and un-biblical. Eternity cannot be lost. But people who are 'lost' will exist in eternity separated from God. The awfulness of that lostness is accentuated by the concept of the lake of fire. No one can fully understand this judgment, but the agony of what is represented by it ought to burn into our hearts and minds.

The New Jerusalem

Chapter XXV

People who take the Bible seriously believe in heaven. D.L. Moody, the famous evangelist, faced death with these assuring words, 'Earth is receding, Heaven is opening, God is calling me!' 'Into Thy hands I commend my spirit', said the dying Martin Luther, 'God of truth, Thou hast redeemed me.' Paul, the Apostle, said with a bracing conviction,

Henceforth there is laid up for me the crown of righteousness, which the Lord, the righteous judge will award to me on that Day, and not only to me but also to all who have loved his appearing.

2 Timothy 4:8

Men and women of faith believe in the after-life. Their Lord and the teaching of the Bible encourage them to have a firm conviction regarding the place that we call heaven.

In the Old Testament the most frequently used word for heaven conveys the meaning of 'heaped up things' or 'the heights'. The Greek word for heaven in the New Testament is *ouranos*. This word is used of the aerial and siderial heavens, but most important, it is used of God's dwelling place; for example

Let your light so shine before men, that they may see your good works and give glory to your Father who is in heaven.

Matthew 5:16

We are reminded in 1 Peter 3:22 that the Lord Jesus Christ

has gone into heaven and is at the right hand of God, with angels, authorities and powers subject to him.

The New Testament uses word pictures to convey to us some aspects of the after-life which Christians shall enjoy in the presence of God. Our Lord in a parable, compares Himself to a nobleman who went into a far country (Luke 19:12). This analogy is taken up by the writer to the Hebrews when he reminds us that the Old Testament saints desired 'a better country . . . a heavenly one' (Hebrews 11:16). The analogy suggests the idea of the *vastness* of heaven.

Heaven is described as a kingdom in 2 Peter 1:11

. . . so there will be richly provided for you an entrance into the eternal kingdom of our Lord and Saviour Jesus Christ.

From this figure we recognise that there is an *orderliness* associated with the heavenly place.

One of the best known pictures of heaven is found in the Lord's teaching in John 14:1-2

Let not your hearts be troubled; believe in God, believe also in me. In my Father's house are many rooms; if it were not so, would I have told you that I go to prepare a place for you?

This well-known expression reminds us of heaven's *permanency*.

Heaven is called a city. We are reminded in Hebrews 11:10 that Abraham

looked forward to the city which has foundations, whose builder and maker is God.

It is this concept that is used in the Apocalypse. Associated with the city there is the announcement regarding the innumerable company of the inhabitants.

It has been predicted that two-thirds of the world's population will be living in an urban setting by AD 2000. There will be 3500 cities with a population of over 1 million, whereas at present there are only a few hundred cities with over 1 million population. Dr. J. S. Stewart has pointed out that there are different ways of seeing the city. The country lad from the remote village sees the city as the gateway of adventure. An ambitious businessman sees the city as a place for establishing a successful career. Some see the city as a prison, a place to be escaped from. Others, like the statistician, see the city as a social unit involving so many parliamentary voters, whilst the moralist sees the city as a microcosm of humanity.

What happened when John, the Seer, saw the holy city, the New Jerusalem? Revelation 21:1-4 explains.

Then I saw a new heaven and a new earth; for the first heaven and the first earth had passed away, and the sea was no more. And I saw the holy city, new Jerusalem, coming down out of heaven from God, prepared as a bride adorned for her husband; and I heard a great voice from the throne saying, 'Behold the dwelling of God is with men. He will dwell with them, and they shall be his

people, and God himself will be with them; he will wipe away every tear from their eyes, and death shall be no more, neither shall there be mourning nor crying nor pain any more, for the former things have passed away.

The artist has captured the supreme majesty of the New Jerusalem's descent (Plate 25). Out of the black velvet background there emerges God's priceless jewel. The golden splendour is overpowering. The city's dignity is that of a bride, beautifully adorned to meet her husband. We are given a new concept of city life. God himself becomes a city dweller! 'The dwelling of God is with men'.

Two immense themes surge through this passage — the conspicuous changes and the conspicuous absences.

THE CONSPICUOUS CHANGES

John saw a new heaven, a new earth and a new city. No information is supplied, describing the remarkable changes associated with God's new heaven and new earth. Isaiah, speaking for God predicted,

For behold, I create new heavens and a new earth; and the former things shall not be remembered or come into mind.

Isaiah 65:17

The Lord Jesus instructed His disciples that He had gone to prepare a place for them. Some students of prophecy believe that the New Jerusalem is the prepared place. Others suggest that during the Millennium the New Jerusalem will be a satellite city orbiting the earth, but when the new earth appears, then the new city will descend in all its splendour. This suggestion is made feasible by the achievements of space technology. Behind the suggestion there is the reasoning, if man can build a satellite and place it in orbit around the earth, so can God! Who can tell?

THE CONSPICUOUS ABSENCES

There is no more sea. We hear the dashing of the waves as we read through the Apocalypse. We saw a star called Wormwood fall upon the sea; a strange beast arose out of the sea; the great angel who announced the doom of Babylon took up a stone like a great millstone and threw it into the sea; and the song of the redeemed resembles the voice of many waters.

Some scholars take this statement about the sea as literal truth. The sea as we now know it will not exist. Before God's throne there is a sea of glass. No movement ruffles that sea! It is a permanent testimony to the peace of God. But the sea of glass does not have any relationship to the turbulent sea on earth. Other expository preachers, such as Alexander Maclaren, maintain that this is the language of symbolism with the sea as 'the symbol of mystery, of rebellious power, of perpetual unrest'.

There are no more tears. Apart from a few biological exceptions, none can claim exemption from tears. Mourning and tears are constant companions. In heaven they are conspicuous by their absence.

Death shall be no more. What a profound statement! Death itself shall die! 'The wedding-peal which welcomes the Bride of Christ will ring the funeral knell of death and all his sable company'. Perhaps the redeemed will sing with sheer inspiration the God-breathed song of 1 Corinthians 15:54-57:

Death is swallowed up in victory. O death, where is thy victory? O death, where is thy sting?' The sting of death is sin, and the power of sin is the law. But thanks be to God, who gives us the victory through our Lord Jesus Christ.

Pain is made redundant. Its work is done. Pain was a faithful companion on earth. If there had been no pain, countless people would have been 'painlessly' destroyed without being aware of the destruction. When the building is completed, the scaffolding may be removed. When the patient is in good health, drugs are unnecessary. Pain is an accompaniment of sin. The Christians have a sinless status in heaven. Due to the absence of sin no one will ever say 'I am ill!'

A triple statement occurs in verses 5-7

And he who sat upon the throne said, 'Behold, I make all things new'. Also he said, 'Write this, for these words are trustworthy and true'. And he said to me, 'It is done! I am the Alpha and the Omega, the beginning and the end. To the thirsty I will give water without price from the fountain of the water of life. He who conquers shall have this heritage, and I will be his God and he shall be my son.

These three exciting highlights ought to be written on the heart of all Christians. 'Behold, I make all things new'. 'It is done!' and 'I will be his God and he shall be my son'. We have the statement that is creative, an exclamation which is conclusive and a relationship that is personal and intimate, based on the redemptive act of Christ.

No one receives a passport for heaven with a retouched photograph. People cannot achieve a place in heaven on a do-it-yourself basis. New spiritual life, the gift God through Christ has given us, is the only authentic passport to heaven. There is a dark patch in this heavenly chapter

But as for the cowardly, the faithless, the polluted, as for murderers, fornicators, sorcerers, idolators, and all liars, their lot shall be in the lake that burns with fire and brimstone, which is the second death.

Revelation 21:8

Here we have eight categories of people not allowed into heaven.

'Cowards', wrote Dr William Barclay, 'are those who loved ease and comfort more than they loved Christ, and who in the day of trial were ashamed to show whose they were and whom they served.'

The *faithless* are those who refuse to accept the authority of the Bible. Individuals who prefer to walk by sight and become obsessed with the temporal.

Polluted is a word that bludgeons our respectability. It throws up a picture of the people who cannot enjoy pleasure unless they are saturated with smut. To them, man is only meaningful when he has fellowship with filth. They teach the youth of society that maturity cannot be reached unless they have a first-class honours degree in dirt and 'sexploitation'.

Hatred is *murder* in its embryonic form. Few people escape the disorientating emotion of hate. Sometimes hatred is expressed in murder. Heaven is barred to the murderers who have not known the grace of God in Jesus Christ.

Fornicators are kept out of heaven, that is, those who commit voluntary sexual intercourse between unmarried man and woman. Permissiveness is not acceptable to the standards of heaven.

Sorcerers have no part in the heavenly order. 'Magic, astrology and spells were the stock-in-trade of the ancient world'. Those who dabble in the occult having fellowship with demonic darkness cannot enjoy the glorious light of God's new world.

Idolators have formed a part of every culture. The form or shape of the idols change, but the principle is the same. An idol is someone or something that replaces God and His Son, Jesus Christ.

Liars are strangers to truth so it is impossible for the hypocritical and insincere to live in the place of eternal truth.

Having considered this black catalogue, let us register the words of 1 Corinthians 6:11

And such were some of you. But you were washed, you were sanctified, you were justified in the name of the Lord Jesus Christ and in the Spirit of our God.

Our painting of the New Jerusalem descending (Plate 25) relates to

Revelation 21:2, but it is obvious from verse 10 that John has a second view, or a closer observation, of the holy city,

And in the Spirit he carried me away to a great, high mountain, and showed me the holy city Jerusalem coming down out of heaven from God.

The second painting of the New Jerusalem (Plate 26) is abstract and detailed. Both paintings are complementary. The general and the particular combine. Study both paintings with adventurous faith and bring the narratives and the paintings together. Enter into the excitement of John's vision.

The City's Illuminations
These are described in verse 11

having the glory of God, its radiance like a most rare jewel, like a jasper, clear as crystal.

Verse 23 assists us in our understanding of the lighting system of the New Jerusalem

And the city has no need of sun or moon to shine upon it, for the glory of God is its light, and its light is the Lamb.

It is true that our Lord claimed 'I am the Light', and it is also true that He said to Christians, 'You are the light'. The picture is most significant. Christ is the glory of the New Jerusalem, and innumerable Christians reflect that radiance. Christians are luminaries in the eternal world.

THE PERIMETER OF THE CITY
After the overall impression of the New Jerusalem, the narrative gives information about the city's perimeter.

It had a great, high wall, with twelve gates, and at the gates twelve angels, and on the gates the names of the twelve tribes of the sons of Israel were inscribed; on the east three gates, on the north three gates, on the south three gates, and on the west three gates. And the wall of the city had twelve foundations, and on them the twelve names of the twelve apostles of the Lamb.

Revelation 21:12-14

Expositors have differed as to the degree in which the description should be taken literally. The one extreme suggests that the New Jerusalem is an actual satellite city in space that will descend upon the new earth; the other extreme suggests that the city is non-existent and is representing only symbolically the blessings of the saints in the

eternal state. There can be no doubt that John saw an actual city. He describes in detail what he saw. It is best that we accept the disclosed information and relate it to our understanding of the revelation of God.

Round the city there is an exceptionally high wall. This suggests exclusiveness. But in the wall there are twelve gates and these gates are never shut. Here we have the principle of open access. In this setting these two concepts are complementary, not contradictory. The high wall is a permanent testimony that many people were excluded from the eternal state; the open gates are an everlasting witness that an innumerable company have been redeemed and are eternally secure. Another interesting feature is the inscription of the names. The names of the twelve tribes of Israel are on the gates, that is, the Jewish representation, and the names of the twelve apostles are written on the twelve foundations of the wall, that is, the Church representatives, they are all one in the Lord. East, north, west and south each have three gates reminding us of Mark 1:45.

. . . and people came to him from every quarter.

In Acts 13:1 we have the arresting information,

Now in the church at Antioch there were prophets and teachers, Barnabas, Symeon who was called Niger, Lucius of Cyrene, Manaen a member of the court of Herod the tetrarch, and Saul.

There is no racism here. Two Jews, one Negro, one Gentile and a Roman aristocrat. Jews and Gentiles — one! Blacks and whites — one! Commonplace and exceptional — one! That is the genius of the New Jerusalem. They are all one in the Lord.

The two paintings remind us that the passage teaches that each gate has an angelic sentinel. An angelic guard of honour watches over the city. Safety is assured. Purity is guaranteed. It has been suggested that the angelic guardians are porters with a welcoming message to those who enter the city.

The City's Measurements
Having examined the city's perimeter, we are exhorted to study the city's measurements.

And he who talked to me had a measuring rod of gold to measure the city and its gates and walls. The city lies foursquare, its length the same as its breadth; and he measured the city with his rod, twelve thousand stadia; its length and breadth and height are equal. He also measured its wall, a hundred and forty-four cubits by a man's measure, that is, an angel's.

Revelation 21:15-17

A golden reed is used to measure the city. The angel on the right-hand side of the second painting has the golden reed in his hand. The length of the reed is 9 feet. The city is tetragonal and is in the shape of a perfect cube. Twelve thousand stadia are approximately 1500 miles, and that was the Greek standard of measurement.

The walls are measured in cubits which was the Jewish standard of measurement, 144 cubits approximating to 260 feet. A literal calculation of the area of the city is astounding; it covers 2¼ million square miles – 'a city of that area would very nearly stretch from London to New York'.

Most scholars assume that the New Jerusalem is in the shape of a cube, but a few Bible teachers such as William Hoste, propound the theory that the city is in the form of a pyramid, with the sides sloping to a peak at the height indicated. This theory is related to Revelation 22:1-2

Then he showed me the river of the water of life, bright as crystal, flowing from the throne of God and of the Lamb through the middle of the street of the city; also on either side of the river, the tree of life with its twelve kinds of fruit, yielding its fruit each month; and the leaves of the tree were for the healing of the nations.

If we accept that the city is literal, then there is a strong reason for recognising that the shape of the city is like a pyramid.

The City's Wealth

Now consider the city's wealth. This is revealed in verses 18-21

The wall was built of jasper, while the city was pure gold, clear as glass. The foundations of the wall of the city were adorned with every jewel; the first was jasper, the second sapphire, the third agate, the fourth emerald, the fifth onyx, the sixth carnelian, the seventh chrysolite, the eighth beryl, the ninth topaz, the tenth chrysoprase, the eleventh jacinth, the twelfth amethyst. And the twelve gates were twelve pearls, each of the gates made of a single pearl, and the street of the city was pure gold, transparent as glass.

Here is a passage that dazzles our eyes, strains our imagination, overwhelms our minds and defies descriptive language. Visualise the magnificence of the glory of God reflected and refracted by the brilliance of a multiplicity of jewels.

Jasper formed the super-structure of the wall, but the foundations were adorned and constructed with other precious jewels. Twelve different stones adorned the foundation. It is significant that the stones were similar in nature with those which were set in the breast-plate of the high priest. (Exodus 28:17-20). The shape of the breast-plate, like the city, was foursquare, having four rows of three precious stones. These stones symbolised Israel's relationship with God; each jewel had the inscription of one of the twelve tribes. Now the jewels are the foundations of the New Jerusalem having the inscription of the twelve apostles. The colour scheme of these jewels is represented in the painting, each layer extending around all four sides of the city. These precious stones symbolise the variety and durability of the relationship that exists between the Lord God and His people.

G.R.Beasley-Murray highlights the interesting observation drawn up by Kircher regarding the signs of the zodiac, which was noted by R.H. Charles. The stones associated with the signs of the zodiac are exactly those that relate to the jewels of the New Jerusalem. The signs of the zodiac were connected with the city of the gods — somewhere among the stars. Man's quest for the eternal city has its fulfilment in the New Jerusalem. It is not an accident that John enumerates the precious stones in precisely the reverse order of the signs of the zodiac. He seems to be saying that God's city is the complete reversal of what human nature desires.

The description of the twelve gates is breathtaking. Each of them consists of one gigantic pearl. These massive pearls remind us of the beauty which is born out of suffering. All the people who inhabit the New Jerusalem are there because of the suffering of the Lamb of God.

The Character of the City
The character of the city is revealed in verses 22-27

And I saw no temple in the city, for its temple is the Lord God the Almighty and the Lamb. And the city has no need of sun or moon to shine upon it, for the glory of God is its light, and its lamp is the Lamb. By its light shall the nations walk; and the kings of the earth shall bring their glory into it, and its gates shall never be shut by day — and there shall be no night there; they shall bring into it the glory and the honour of the nations. But nothing unclean shall enter it, nor any one who practises abomination or falsehood, but only those who are written in the Lamb's book of life.

Adoration is characteristic in the New Jerusalem. There is no temple in the city, that is to say, there is no need for a place of worship for the whole of the city is full of worship. Once again the artist has captured the meaningfulness of this important aspect by including all types of religious architecture in the abstract painting. No one can say, 'I am going to church'. They live in church. There is no temple — it is all temple.

Another amazing characteristic is that of access. The gates are never shut. Why? In ancient cities the gates were closed at night. There is no night in God's city, so the gates remain open. The way is open into God's presence.

There is the thrilling revelation of acceptance in this passage. 'And the kings of the earth shall bring their glory into it.' Ephesians 1:5-6 reminds us of the privilege of being accepted.

He destined us in love to be his sons through Jesus Christ, according to the purpose of his will, to the praise of his glorious grace which he freely bestowed on us in the Beloved.

Acceptance brings us into the blessing of access and that experience inspires our adoration. We shall sing with inspired adoration in the New Jerusalem, the city of God!

The Incomparable Christ
and the Fabulous Future

Chapter XXVI

God's guiding hand is apparent in the Apocalypse. Sometimes He leads us beside the still waters; other times He leads us in the paths of righteousness. These two concepts are the inescapable experiences of life. In this part of the Apocalypse the ways of righteousness merge into the waters of rest. 'The Lord of the restful valley is also King of the flood and Sovereign of the terrible heights.'

The approach to this chapter highlights couplets and contrasts.

THE RIVER AND THE ORCHARD

Then he showed me the river of the water of life, bright as crystal, flowing from the throne of God and of the Lamb through the middle of the street of the city; also, on either side of the river, the tree of life with its twelve kinds of fruit, yielding its fruit each month; and the leaves of the tree were for the healing of the nations.
Revelation 22:1-2

In Chapter 21 we have a description of the exterior of the city of God. We are informed about the walls, foundations and gates; we are given the external dimensions. In these verses we have the explanation about the interior of the city. God's city is an exquisite place. Flowing through it there is the life-giving river. Ezekiel 47 teaches that the river flows from the temple of God. The prophet Joel asserted, 'A fountain shall come forth from the house of the Lord' (Joel 3:18). Zechariah predicted, 'Living waters shall go out from Jerusalem'. (Zech. 14:8) In the Apocalypse the river streams from the throne of God. This throne is depicted at the top of the painting. Issuing from the throne is the semi-abstract representation of the river of life. Rivers have been great devastators, but they have also been great benefactors. The Bible reminds us of these benefits that culminate in the river which flows from the throne of God.

Psalm 1 reminds us that rivers *fructify*. The spiritually integrated man is symbolised in the tree that is planted beside the rivers of water. Isaiah proclaimed,

Oh that you had listened to my commandments! Then had your peace been as a river.

Isaiah 48:18

Rivers *pacify*. Many lives remind us of the babbling brook, restless and noisy! God's river is deep and silent.

Another amazing analogy was given by Isaiah,

A man shall be as rivers of water in a dry place.   Isaiah 32:2

These rivers *vivify*. They symbolise the renewing ministry of the Holy Spirit.

A song from the Psalms swells with volume.

. . . and you shall make them drink of the river of your pleasure.   Psalm 36:8

These rivers *satisfy*. The fulfilled life is found in God.

Ezekiel, the mystic, declared

The waters made him great, the deep set him on high with her rivers running about his plants,and set out her little rivers unto all the trees of the field and his boughs were multiplied.

Ezekiel 31:4-9

Here are rivers that *multiply*. Many a city and country have been enriched by noble rivers; in God's city there is the river of life, pellucid, beautifully bright. Abundant life surges from the throne of God to fructify, pacify, vivify, satisfy and multiply.

An orchard is associated with the river of water of life. The tree of life yields twelve kinds of fruit. We are informed that the river flows down through the middle of the city. It has been suggested that the word 'tree' is a collective reference, representing twelve trees with six on either side of the river. The alternative to that is a mammoth tree spanning the river like a bridge with the water flowing underneath.

Examine the artistic presentation (Plate 27). Incorporated in the tree of life there is the Cross. Surrounding the Cross there is the foliage which gives a two-fold symbolism. First of all there is the shape of the crown reminding us of God's sovereign reign, and second, there is the outline of the heart, typifying the love of God. In Chapter 5 of the Apocalypse we observed the throne and the Lamb. Again we have the symbolism of sovereignty and sacrifice – the crown and the heart. Our redemption and the tree of life are based upon the sovereign love of God.

Plate No. 27

The leaves of the tree are for the healing of the nations. *Therapeia* is the Greek word. From this derives the words therapy and therapeutic. The leaves are used to sustain health not to cure illness; they have the ability to promote the enjoyment of life in the New Jerusalem. Great results emerge from such a glorious prospect.

There shall no more be anything accursed, but the throne of God and of the Lamb shall be in it, and his servants shall worship him; they shall see his face, and his name shall be on their foreheads. And night shall be no more; they need no light of lamp or sun, for the Lord God will be their light, and they shall reign for ever and ever.

Revelation 22:3-5

Heaven is free from the curse. Frustrations and irritations will be no more. This is followed by the wonderful disclosure — 'his servants shall worship him'. The word used here for worship is *latreuo* in Greek meaning religious service and homage, and relates to the idea of 'servants'. The next disclosure defies analysis — 'they shall see his face'.

His face, His joy supreme!
Our souls find rapture only at His feet,
Blameless! Without a spot!
We enter into heaven's joy complete.

'His name shall be upon their foreheads'. Who can tell what that name will be? The saints will reign with Him in that eternal day.

STABILITY AND INSTABILITY

And he said to me, 'These words are trustworthy and true. And the Lord, the God of the spirits of the prophets, has sent his angel to show his servants what must soon take place. And behold, I am coming soon.' Blessed is he who keeps the words of the prophecy of this book. I John am he who heard and saw these things. And when I heard and saw them, I fell down to worship at the feet of the angel who showed them to me; but he said to me, 'You must not do that! I am a fellow servant with you and your brethren the prophets, and with those who keep the words of this book. Worship God'.

Revelation 22:6-9

God's words are trustworthy and true. This is the basis of our stability. Only those who have faith in the trustworthiness of God have heaven in their soul. We can depend upon God. We must trust Him when we cannot see the purpose that lies behind the agonised circumstance. We can depend upon the Lord Christ.

Now we consider man's instability. John falls down to worship at the feet of the angel. Idolatry is wrong. Angelic idols may be pleasant, but they too become sinful if they are permitted to take the place of the Lord. The angel rebuked John and told him to worship God. We need the preaching that will direct our hearts and minds to God alone.

One of the weaknesses of the visible church on earth is the instability of professing Christians. They make high-sounding promises, but never fulfil them; they inaugurate new projects, but never complete them; they criticise the activities of the genuine spiritually alive church, but they do not participate in the services of that church. Heaven is the place of eternal stability. We ought to prepare ourselves now for the future.

THE SAVED AND THE LOST

And he said to me, 'Do not seal up the words of the prophecy of this book, for the time is near. Let the evildoer still do evil, and the filthy still be filthy, and the righteous still do right, and the holy still be holy. Behold, I am coming soon, bringing my recompense, to repay everyone for what he has done. I am the Alpha and the Omega, the first and the last, the beginning and the end.' Blessed are those who wash their robes, that they may have the right to the tree of life and that they may enter the city by the gates. Outside are the dogs and sorcerers and fornicators and murderers and idolaters, and everyone who loves and practises falsehood.

Revelation 22:10-15

Strong language is used to describe those who are lost. Walter Scott reminds us in his commentary, 'Habits fix character, and character fixes destiny'. Dogs are outside the new city, that is, they are eternally separated from God. This statement may grieve dog-lovers, but it should be understood that the dog envisaged is not the household pet, but 'the pariah dog, the street scavenger, homeless and savage and mangy and thieving'. The Jews insulted the Gentiles by calling them 'dogs'. This term was used as a symbol for all that is disgusting and unclean. It was also applied to the priest, or male prostitute in the pagan temples. 'Dog' was a descriptive title for a thoroughly bad character.

Consider the language used to describe the saved (verse 14):

. . . and the righteous still do right, and the holy still be holy . . . Blessed are those who wash their robes that they may have the right to the tree of life and that they may enter the city by the gates. . .

There is a solid permanency about the salvation we have in Jesus Christ. In the Authorised Version we have the translation - 'Blessed are they who do his commandments.' This is in harmony with the teaching of the New Testament, but the best manuscripts support the translation we have in the Revised Standard Version, namely, 'Blessed are those who wash their robes'. Man cannot earn his salvation, yet we are exhorted in Philippians 2:12

Work out your own salvation with fear and trembling.

But we cannot work out our salvation unless God has put his salvation within. Indeed, Philippians 2:13 states

God is at work in you, both to will and to work for his good pleasure.

This same principle may be applied to Revelation 22:14; those who wash their robes are not working for their salvation but they are working at their salvation.

THE ROOT AND THE OFFSPRING OF DAVID AND THE BRIGHT MORNING STAR

I Jesus have sent my angel to you with this testimony for the churches. I am the root and the offspring of David, the bright morning star.

Revelation 22:16

Here is a strange combination; the earthly root and the heavenly orb! A part of a tree and a glowing orb are complementary. There is a profound meaning in this analogy. The root and the offspring take up the idea of the Davidic lineage. Here we have the Messianic background. Our Lord is the root of David, that is, the Lord in deity is before David; but our Lord is the offspring of David, which means that in His humanity He is after David. Jesus Christ is the pledge of a new race — the Church. We should never lose sight of this great fact — the Lord came to us as a descendant of David. He came to us as God manifest in the flesh.

The hope of every Christian is Christ Himself. In this context He presents Himself as 'the bright morning star'. Why? Most people can grasp the significance of the symbolism. The morning star is not daylight. It is not normal for a man to be awakened by the morning star. If one wishes to see the morning star, one must make a disciplined effort to see it. Starlight does not wake people, but sunlight does, that is daylight. The bright morning star is Christ for the watching Christian. Whilst the world is buried in slumber, the Lord will come for His watching Church.

The expression 'the morning star' occurs three times in the New Testament. 2 Peter 1:19 reminds us

And we have the prophetic word made more sure. You will do well to pay attention to this as to a lamp shining in a dark place, until the day dawns and the morning star rises in your heart.

We have already noticed what the Lord said to the church at Thyatira:

And I will give him the morning star.

Revelation 2:28

Before the Lord arises as the sun of righteousness of Malachi's prophecy (Mal 4:2), he appears as the morning star. He is the morning star to the Church. He is the sun of righteousness to Israel.

We ought to believe whole-heartedly in the personal return of Jesus Christ as the bright morning star. He shall come for His Church, quickly but not unexpectedly. In the year 1930 a certain sect sent a slogan around the world – 'Millions now living will never die'. It was a daring assertion which many considered as the faith of fanatics. Events disproved it. It is not surprising that a famous laundry, which had more humour than reverence adopted the revised slogan as its own in this way – 'We do the dyeing for the millions now living!' Christians dare not treat the paramount truth of the Second Coming of Christ as a kind of heavenly humour. The Second Advent is a Biblical fact. We ought to have faith in that fact and look forward to the fabulous future.

AN INVITATION AND WARNING;
A PROMISE AND BENEDICTION
The inspirational invitation is in verse 17

The Spirit and the Bride say, 'Come'. And let him who hears say, 'Come'. And let him who is thirsty come, let him who desires take the water of life without price.

Christ and the Church issue a joint invitation. This emphasises the evangelical witness of Christ's Spirit and Christ's servants. All who hear and accept the invitation are exhorted to join the ranks of those who issue the invitation. It is the responsibility of every Christian to witness for Christ. The third part of the invitation offers complete satisfaction to the thirsty.

A lesson regarding addition and subtraction is found in the strong warning of verses 18-19.

I warn every one who hears the words of the prophecy of this book: if any one adds to them, God will add to him the plagues described in this book, and if any one takes away from the words of the book of this prophecy, God will take away his share in the tree of life and in the holy city, which are described in this book.

Any person who considers that the book of the Revelation is irrelevant ought to ponder on these two warnings. Tampering with the Word of

God is a serious sin. To 'write off' the Apocalypse is to forfeit great blessing, but to add words and notions to the content of the book is to invoke judgment.

The glorious promise is found in verse 20

He who testifies to these things says, 'Surely I am coming soon'. Amen. Come, Lord Jesus!

This promise evokes a prayer. These words should be on the lips of all Christians. The prayer itself is a fitting climax to the amazing book which we call the Apocalypse. It is an appropriate culmination to the marvellous library that we call the Bible.

Benedictions can be profound. In verse 21 we have an economy in words.

The grace of the Lord Jesus be with all the saints. Amen.

We need the grace to sustain us until we reach the glory of God's heaven!

MARANATHA!

BIBLIOGRAPHY

Barclay, Dr William, *Revelation of John, Daily Bible Readings,* St. Andrews Press, 1959

Barnhouse, Donald Grey, *Revelation,* Zondervan Publishing House, Grand Rapids, 1971

Beasley-Murray, G.R., *Jesus and the Future.*

Boettner, Loraine, *The Millennium,* The Presbyterian & Reformed Publishing Co.

Brown, Charles, *Heavenly Visions,* James Clarke & Co.

Chappell, Clovis G., *Sermons from Revelation,* Abingdon-Cokesbury Press.

Collins, Larry and Lapierre, Dominique, *O Jerusalem!* Weidenfield & Nicolson, 1972.

Cullman, Oscar, *The Return of Christ in the Early Church,* Student Christian Movement.

De Haan, Richard N., *Israel and the Nations in Prophecy,* Zondervan Publishing House, Grand Rapids.

Dodd, C.H., *The Coming of Christ,* Cambridge University Press.

Gordon, A.J., *Ecce Venit,* Hodder & Stoughton.

Gowen, Herbert H., *The Revelation of St. John the Divine, An Analytical Transcription,* Skeffingtons.

Graham, Billy, *Angels: God's Secret Agents,* Doubleday & Company Inc.

Guinness, I. Oswald, *The Dust of Death,* Inter Varsity Press, 1973.

Hendriksen, William, *More Than Conquerors: Revelation,* Tyndale Press, 1973.

Hulse, Errol, *The Restoration of Israel,* Henry E. Walter Ltd., 1968.

Kelly, William, *Lectures on the Revelation,* W.M. Broom, 1874.

Lang, G.H., *The Revelation of Jesus Christ,* Oliphants, 1945.

Lahaye, Tim, *Revelation,* Zondervan Publishing House, Grand Rapids.

Lindsay, Hal, *The Late Great Planet Earth,* Lakeland, 1971.

Lindsay, Hal, *There's a New World Coming,* Vision House.

MacArthur, Jack, *Revelation,* Certain Sound.

McCall, Thomas S. & Levitt Zola, *Satan in the Sanctuary,* Moody Press

Maclaren, Alexander, *Exposition of Scripture,* W. B. Eerdmans.

Milligan, William, *The Book of Revelation, The Expositors Bible,* Hodder & Stoughton.

Morris, Leon, *Apocalyptic,* Inter Varsity Press, 1973.

Morris, Leon, *The Biblical Doctrine of Judgment,* Tyndale Press, 1960.

Newell, W.R., *The Book of the Revelation,* Moody Press, 1935.

Pentecost, Dwight J., *Prophecy for Today,* Zondervan Publishing House, Grand Rapids, 1961.

Pentecost, Dwight J., *Will Man Survive?* Moody Press.

Pentecost, Dwight J., *Things to Come* Zondervan Publishing House, Grand Rapids, 1974.

Powell, Ivor, *The Rising of the Son,* M. & N. Printing, Oxnard, California.

Robertson, A.T., *Word Pictures in the New Testament,* Volume 6, Broadman.

Robinson, J.A.T., *In the End, God . . .*, Clarke.

Rogers, Edward, *The Christian Approach to the Communist,* Lutterworth Press, 1958.

Scott, Walter, *An Exposition of the Revelation of Jesus Christ,* Pickering & Inglis.

Scroggie, W. Graham, *The Unfolding Drama of Redemption,* Volume 3, Pickering & Inglis, 1970.

Smith, Oswald J., *Prophecy, What Lies Ahead?* Marshall, Morgan & Scott, 1973.

Smith, Wilbur M., *Israeli/Arab Conflict,* Regal Books.

Tatford, Frederick A., *Prophecy's Last Word,* Pickering & Inglis.

Tenny, Merrill C., *Interpreting Revelation,* Pickering & Inglis.

Travis, Stephen, *The Jesus Hope,* Word.

Unger, Merrill F., *Biblical Demonology,*

Vaughan, Dr C.H., *Lectures on the Revelation of St. John,* Macmillan & Co.

Vincent, Mervyn R., *Word Studies in the New Testament,* Volume 2, W. B. Eerdmans.

Walvoord, John F., *The Revelation of Jesus Christ,* Marshall, Morgan & Scott.

Walvoord, John F., *The Church in Prophecy,* Marshall, Morgan & Scott.

Walvoord, John F., *Israel in Prophecy,* Marshall, Morgan & Scott.

Walvoord, John F., *The Nations in Prophecy,* Marshall, Morgan & Scott.

White, Wesley John, *Re-Entry*, World Wide Publications.

Wilcock, Michael, *I Saw Heaven Opened*, Inter Varsity Press.

Wolston, W.T.P., *Behold, The Bridegroom*, J. K. Souter & Co.

Wood, Skevington A., *Prophecy in the Space Age*, Marshall, Morgan & Scott.

Zoller, Dr John E., *Heaven*.